Well Aware

Developing **Resilient**, **Active**, and **Flourishing** Students

Patrick Carney, Ph.D.

Feedback on this publication can be sent to editorialfeedback@pearsoned.com.

Pearson Canada Inc.
26 Prince Andrew Place
Don Mills, ON M3C 2T8
Customer Service: 1-800-361-6128

7   17

Printed and bound in USA

Publisher: Elynor Kagan
Research and Communications Manager: Mark Cressman
Managing Editor: Joanne Close
Developmental Editors: Chelsea Donaldson, Monica Schwalbe
Project Managers, Editorial: Lisa Dimson, Deborah Lonergan
Copy Editor: Kate Revington
Proofreader: Karin Fediw
Indexer: Noeline Bridge
Permissions: Lumina Datamatics
Manager, Project Management K–12: Alison Dale
Art Director: Alex Li
Cover Design: David Cheung
Interior Design and Composition: Aptara, Inc.
Vice-President, Publishing: Mark Cobham

ISBN: 978-0-13-376056-9

Dedication

Every little breeze surely whispers *Anne Louise*.

Acknowledgments

In memory of my parents, Fred and Frances, and their zest for life, through thick and through thin. In appreciation also for the encouragement of my adult children, Erin, Bryan, and Shannon.

With thanks to the many teachers who have opened their doors and shared their experiences about encouraging children to be resilient, active, and flourishing. Thank you likewise to my mental health colleagues for their ideas and feedback.

Through all of you, my journey to understand positive mental health has been greatly enriched.

Author's Note: All characters and situations in this book, unless referenced outright, are fictitious. They are based on an amalgamation of experiences and stories over several years and multiple settings with variation in points of reference such as age, place, sex, and circumstance. Any resemblance to persons living or dead is purely coincidental.

Table of Contents

Chapter 3

A Social–Emotional Learning Approach 53

Chapter 4

A Strengths-Based Approach 93

Chapter 5

Resilient, Active, and Flourishing 130

Chapter 6

What About Me? Educator Well-Being   **178**

Reviewers

Dr. Sue Ball
Chief Psychologist, York Region District School Board
Newmarket, ON

Dr. Jennifer Batycky
Principal, Rosscarrock School
Calgary Board of Education
Calgary, AB

Steve Charbonneau
Superintendent of Elementary Schools, Simcoe Muskoka Catholic District School Board
Barrie, ON

Dr. Bruce Ferguson
Senior Consultant, Community Health Systems Resource Group
The Hospital for Sick Children
Toronto, ON

Paula Jurczak
Child and Family Therapist
Richmond, BC

Joyleen Podgursky
Learning Support Team Co-ordinator
Prairie South Schools
Moose Jaw, SK

Taunya Shaw
School Psychologist, School District #36
Surrey, BC

Dr. Suzanne L. Stewart
Associate Professor, OISE/University of Toronto
Toronto, ON

A Culture of Positive Mental Health

"The role of the school has been regarded both nationally and internationally as an important environment for promoting the psychological wellness and resilience of children and youth."

—PAN-CANADIAN JOINT CONSORTIUM FOR SCHOOL

HEALTH, 2013, p. 20

There is no doubt that mental health has become a vital concern in our schools and communities. Research has shown that about one in five children and youth in Canada has a mental health problem. Understanding disorders, recognizing symptoms, and providing effective treatment are all critical to addressing this issue.

But beyond the focus on symptoms and disorders, we are seeing a shift toward understanding that developing *positive* mental health is foundational to student academic achievement, effective life skills, and overall well-being. Positive mental health encompasses *all* students and supports the goals of prevention, inclusion, compassionate support, and healthy development.

As educators, we have always been concerned with students' well-being and healthy development. What is new is a recognition that we need to be

- more informed about mental health promotion
- more tactical about promoting healthy habits and addressing problems early
- more focused when using evidence-based strategies at the classroom, school, and community levels

Ideally, promoting mental health in the classroom will be part of a coordinated approach involving the whole school community, local community resources, and government initiatives and supports. The aim is to create a culture of mental health in all our schools.

The goal of this resource is to provide you with the research-based evidence, tools, and strategies to help create that culture and support students' healthy development in practical and effective ways. It is difficult to overstate the difference that a teacher or a school can make in the mental health of a child or youth not through expensive or sophisticated interventions, but through compassion, inclusion, encouragement, and effective instruction.

Helpful Resources for Tiers 2 and 3

The focus in this resource, therefore, is on what has been called Tier 1, in the three-tier model shown in Figure 1.1. At Tier 1, the emphasis is on mental health promotion and universal support for *all* students through teaching, modelling, and supporting the development of key skills and healthy behaviours. Targeted support and intervention for mental health problems fall into Tiers 2 and 3, largely beyond the scope of this resource. (You can find more information on the three-tier model in the Spotlight feature on pages 4–5 and some helpful resources for Tiers 2 and 3 on pages 16–17 and on the companion website.)

This chapter introduces a framework for understanding and supporting the development of positive mental health for all students. It provides a brief overview of the essential elements that constitute positive mental health and introduces the foundations that we as educators can cultivate to help students achieve that goal. Each chapter in this resource then explores an aspect of that framework in more depth.

What Is Positive Mental Health?

First, let's look at what we mean by *positive mental health*. Positive mental health has been defined by the Public Health Agency of Canada as "the capacity of each and all of us to feel, think, and act in ways that enhance our ability to enjoy life and deal with the challenges we face. It is a positive sense of emotional and spiritual well-being that respects the importance of culture, equity, social justice, interconnections, and personal dignity" (Public Health Agency of Canada [PHAC], 2006, p. 2).

A key phrase in this definition is "a positive sense of emotional and spiritual well-being." Positive mental health *is* well-being, and we will use the two terms interchangeably in this resource. The idea of well-being means that positive mental health goes beyond the more clinical definition of mental health as the absence of illness or disorder. A state of well-being encompasses a sense of enjoyment in life, of realizing our potential, meeting challenges, being productive, respecting ourselves and others, and making a positive contribution to our communities.

In this sense, mental well-being is possible regardless of mental illness. We can all work toward fulfilling our potential and achieving enjoyment in life. Positive mental health is based on the values of equity and personal dignity.

Respect for "culture, equity, social justice, interconnections, and personal dignity"—none of that is new to you as an educator. Many of the values and attitudes you are already fostering are directly linked to positive mental health. Helping students understand these links and take charge of them to foster their own well-being is the ultimate goal.

We can help students learn to recognize feelings and regulate their emotions so that they are less likely to get caught in emotional distress. We can help them develop social and emotional skills to build positive relationships and community connections to support well-being. When students come to understand that positive mental health is a goal for which to strive and that all of us will experience stress and challenge throughout our lives, they can become better able to manage their emotions and deal with issues. They can become more resilient and focused on achieving their potential.

Mental health literacy and the focused use of effective mental health strategies in the school environment will help us create the conditions for student success and well-being. In the chapters that follow, we will explore some of these strategies and conditions in more detail.

> Mental health is more than the absence of mental illness, just as physical health is more than the absence of disease.

The Three Tiers

The three-tier model of supporting students socially, behaviourally, and emotionally is backed by research that demonstrates improvements in academic performance, resolution of discipline problems, and attitudes toward school, in addition to the mental health benefits of symptom reduction and improved well-being (Cowan, Vaillancourt, Rossen, & Pollitt, 2013; National Association of School Psychologists, 2009). In this resource, we focus on Tier 1 through strategies and approaches that benefit all students.

Figure 1.1: Three Tiers of Help for Students

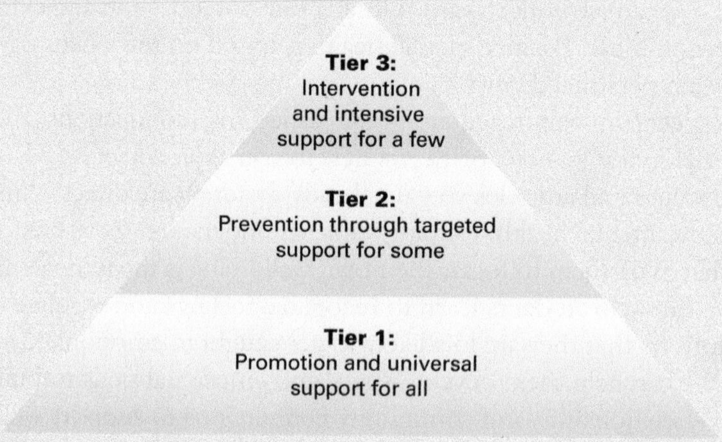

Tier 3:
Intervention
and intensive
support for a few

Tier 2:
Prevention through targeted
support for some

Tier 1:
Promotion and universal
support for all

Tier 1

At this level, schools promote mental health for all students. Consider this example. We know that all students experience nervousness to some degree, and all students have anxiety-provoking experiences at some point in their lives. Schools can help students recognize anxiety and acquire the resiliency skills to navigate through these challenges. When we do a good job at Tier 1, using a whole-school and whole-community approach, there is much less work to do at Tiers 2 and 3.

- In the classroom, we can teach students a wide range of healthy behaviours and provide them with opportunities and encouragement for practising them.

- School boards can anticipate areas of need for teaching healthy behaviours based on the known prevalence of common mental illnesses in youth.

Here is a second example. Social anxiety is a common disorder among youth. We know that experiences of situational anxiety are common to some degree in all of us, and most students will benefit from learning concepts of physiological arousal, relaxation skills, and even skills for public speaking. All of these can be considered Tier 1 mental health promotional activities.

Tier 2

At this level, school staff partner with professional staff at the school board to catch common behavioural, emotional, and social problems. Together, using a small-group format, they provide programs that teach specific social and emotional skills to those at risk before these students acquire more significant problems or diagnosable conditions. For example, school and mental health professionals commonly conduct small-group sessions that teach skills for self-regulation, such as simple breathing exercises, mental imagery, and positive self-talk.

Tier 3

At Tier 3, students experience difficulties to such a degree that their normal functioning is seriously hampered, and learning is compromised. These students require more intensive intervention involving mental health professionals. Teachers and other school staff work with mental health professionals to provide a system of wraparound support, accommodation, and welcome for students as they practise their self-regulation and other coping skills in the school environment. The term *wraparound* refers to the support that an interdisciplinary team of teachers, parents, and professionals provide to support a student with complex needs.

Promoting Positive Mental Health

Effecting this change in understanding of mental health requires active promotion. Mental health promotion requires a different mindset from mental health intervention (Institute of Medicine and National Research Council, 2009). Mental health intervention is important for students who have mental health disorders or who may be at high risk of developing mental health disorders. These students need specific support and referral to mental health professionals.

With mental health promotion, the focus is on opportunities for *all* students to celebrate and develop their gifts, be physically active, achieve a true sense of belonging, experience joy, and learn social and emotional resiliency skills for their lives ahead. *A mental health promotion mindset helps to reduce the number of individuals who will develop mental health disorders and to provide optimal environments for all to flourish, including those with challenged mental health.*

Mental health promotion requires work at all levels of education—national, regional, local, and classroom. The Canadian Joint Consortium for School Health, for example, has created an internationally recognized framework to support the promotion of comprehensive school health (Joint Consortium for School Health [JCSH], 2009). The framework includes four integrated pillars that work to support positive mental health outcomes: social and physical environment, teaching and learning, partnerships and services, and healthy school policy.

As you will see in subsequent pages, this book follows a model similar in its integration of factors that contribute to positive mental health. In our model, which is designed for school-based implementation, we outline three key foundational structures that support our goal for all our learners—to be resilient, active, and flourishing students.

The Well Aware Model

Our model comprises two main sections: foundational blocks and key elements of positive mental health.

The model for well-being that Figure 1.2 illustrates provides a framework for our understanding of well-being and for implementing the evidence-based strategies and approaches in our schools and classrooms that give all students the opportunity to achieve well-being. We will return to this model in each chapter, focusing first on the foundations for supporting well-being: a healthy caring environment, social emotional learning, and a strengths-based approach. In Chapter 5,

Figure 1.2: A Model for Well-Being

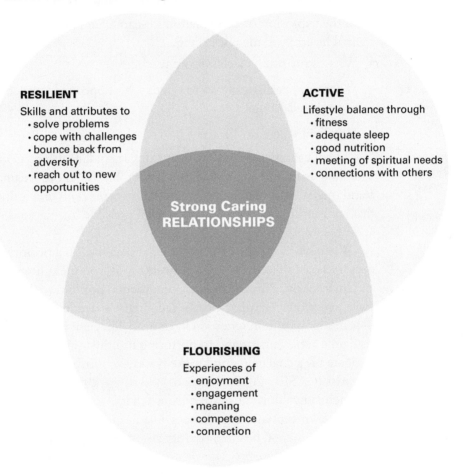

RESILIENT
Skills and attributes to
- solve problems
- cope with challenges
- bounce back from adversity
- reach out to new opportunities

ACTIVE
Lifestyle balance through
- fitness
- adequate sleep
- good nutrition
- meeting of spiritual needs
- connections with others

Strong Caring RELATIONSHIPS

FLOURISHING
Experiences of
- enjoyment
- engagement
- meaning
- competence
- connection

School-Based Approaches for Promoting and Supporting Well-Being

A whole-school, whole-community approach
- actively promoting positive mental health and creating a healthy, caring, inclusive class and school environment

A social emotional learning approach
- developing self-awareness, self-management, social awareness, relationship skills, and responsible decision-making

A strengths-based approach
- recognizing and cultivating the inner strengths, capabilities, and resources we all have for well-being

we examine the essential elements of optimal well-being in more depth. We explore what it means to be resilient, active, and flourishing.

For the purposes of this introduction, let's look at each element of the model briefly to set the context.

A Whole-School Whole-Community Approach

With the explosion of information, research, and policies related to mental health, you may be asking:

- What is my role as a classroom teacher?

- What can I realistically do to effectively support my students' mental well-being?

- How and where do I start?

"Teachers' roles and relationships reach through and beyond the substance of the curriculum to impact students' feelings of self-worth, dignity, identity, and belonging. Through inter-actions with both students and their parents, teachers are in a unique position to strengthen these important elements of mental health."

—Hincks-Dellcrest Centre, 2014

As educators, we can start by making mental health a priority. That may seem like a simplistic statement, but the more we under-stand mental well-being and intentionally foster skills and attitudes that support it, the more we can make it possible for our students and ourselves.

When we make the promotion of mental health a priority, it becomes part of our everyday conversations, routines, interactions, and instruction. Research tells us that mental health development and social emotional learning are not secondary to academic achievement —something to fit in when we have time. They are foundational to academic achievement and to nurturing healthy individuals who can navigate life's challenges and make positive contributions to our com-munities (CASEL, 2013; Durlak & Weissberg, 2011). Fostering posi-tive mental health is most effective when it is integral to our students' and our own everyday experiences, inside and outside the classroom.

Making mental health a priority also starts with awareness and knowledge. *Problematic behaviour does not necessarily mean that a student has a mental health disorder, and only professionals can diagnose an illness,* but there is much you can do by developing the knowledge to support healthy development, identify potential problems, send students on the pathway to care, and ultimately help them develop autonomy over their own mental well-being. As a teacher, you can empower students to make the choices and find the strategies that work for them.

A Teacher's Role in Supporting Mental Health

1. Recognize how your relationship and interactions with students affect their positive mental health.

2. Develop awareness and knowledge, using the resources available through schools, boards, and professional development opportunities.

3. Know what school resources and community services are available, so that you can turn to them when you and your students need support.

4. Implement curriculum-based practices and expectations related to mental health development, and provide direct instruction in key concepts and skills.

5. Create a healthy, caring classroom environment for positive mental health for all.

Promoting mental health requires focus and intentionality, but it does not need to be an extra burden. Healthy practices and instruction can be woven into daily routines, and with a whole-school and community-wide approach, you are not alone. We will look in detail at classroom and wider school practices to promote mental health in Chapter 2.

A Social Emotional Learning Approach

So, how can you effectively promote positive mental health? Social emotional learning, or SEL, is one evidence-based approach. According to the Pan-Canadian Joint Consortium for School Health (2013), social emotional learning is the process through which children and youth develop the knowledge, attitudes, and skills to

- identify and manage their emotions

- set and pursue positive goals

- communicate caring and concern for others

- initiate and sustain positive relationships

- make decisions that demonstrate respect for self and others

- deal with interpersonal concerns and challenges effectively

Pan-Canadian Joint Consortium for School Health

About the Icons
You will notice icons in the page margins throughout this book. These icons indicate resources for further research and information provided on the book's companion website: www. pearsoncanada.ca/ wellawarepdbook

CASEL Guide

"Self-regulation is
the ability to man-
age your own *energy
states, emotions,
behaviours,* and *atten-
tion* in ways that are
socially acceptable
and help to achieve
positive goals, such
as maintaining good
relationships, learn-
ing, and maintaining
well-being."

—*Shanker, 2013*

Adults and youth alike need help to figure out why they feel trou-bled, how to deal with those emotions, and how to be more effective in relating to others. We all need to develop an effective vocabulary of emotions. When individuals feel troubled but cannot understand or express why and do not know how to deal with anxiety, they are at risk of developing poor habits to release tension, which can lead to mental health problems.

We can all benefit from better skills to identify and regulate our emotions, and understand how our emotions affect our social relationships. Social emotional learning can exist as an intentional, authentic process that is woven into the school culture with common understandings, competencies, and language. All members of the school community, including teachers, education assistants, parents, administrators, consultants, custodians, and bus drivers, can learn to apply SEL language in all their interactions. The Collaborative for Academic, Social, and Emotional Learning has published research-based evidence of the effectiveness of SEL programs in schools across North America; its evidence of success includes the role of social emotional learning in promoting student academic success and mental well-being (Collaborative for Academic, Social, and Emotional Learning [CASEL], 2013).

Related to social emotional learning is the research into self-regulation. Stuart Shanker (2013) describes self-regulation as having five domains: (1) biological, (2) emotional, (3) cognitive, (4) social, and (5) prosocial. In this sense, self-regulation moves from a biological basis—the ability to self-regulate physiologically—through a prosocial basis—the ability to empathize and place the needs of others ahead of personal needs.

Across the country, ministries or departments of education and school boards are applying the principles of SEL evidence-based programs in their learning practices and curriculum materials. Life in the classroom is a rich environment for social emotional function and learning. With daily routines and activities, there are many opportuni-ties for direct instruction in and practice of social emotional skills.

A classroom in which all members have SEL skills creates an envi-ronment that allows both teachers and students to flourish socially, emotionally, and academically. You will find more in-depth informa-tion on social emotional learning and self-regulation in Chapter 3.

A Strengths-Based Approach

Another key approach for positive mental health is a focus on identifying and developing students' *strengths* rather than fixing their *deficits*. This approach recognizes that when children and youth are withdrawn or acting out and experiencing difficulties in succeeding at school, we need to understand their circumstances and recognize that they are doing the best they can. When we look closely, we may see that they are demonstrating innate strengths and terrific resilience at getting their developmental needs met. A strengths-based approach acknowledges that we all have inner strengths, capabilities, and resources that can be cultivated to support our well-being.

Chapter 4 explores how a strengths-based approach supports students' healthy development. To explain what we mean by this approach, let's consider a brief example. You have probably noticed the student who seems alert and focused in a lively group activity, but then quickly becomes withdrawn and cannot easily transition to the next task. Susan Cain's research has shown that introverted individuals often feel drained after lively group activities, even though they are involved and enjoy them. These individuals need time to withdraw and recharge before they are ready to take on another activity (Cain, 2012).

When we can recognize this behaviour as a strength and a way for these students to promote their own mental health, we can provide practical supports that benefit the whole class. Providing a quiet place in the classroom where these students can go to read or perform another independent task before they move on to another group activity is one practical strategy. Cain points out that the quiet strength, caution, and deep thinking introverted individuals demonstrate are highly prized qualities in financial advisors and diplomats, for example. When we focus on strengths, challenges become learning opportunities rather than deficits or disruptions.

There are many students whose strengths or "gifts" can lead to elevated levels of stress and sometimes inappropriate behaviour without understanding, support, and encouragement. Chapter 4 explores ways to recognize and understand these gifts, and provides some specific classroom strategies that support healthy development.

Resilient, Active, and Flourishing Students

Chapter 5 focuses on the key elements that constitute positive mental health or well-being. If we ask ourselves what positive mental health looks like, perhaps the best description we can give is an individual who is resilient, active, and flourishing. My experience as a psychologist, parent, and educator has led me to conclude that *resilience*, commitment to an *active* lifestyle, and the experience of *flourishing* through joy in self-realized talents are the essential elements of well-being. As Figure 1.2 shows, at the centre of these overlapping elements is relationships. Strong, caring relationships can be seen as the most reliable factor in, and indicator of, positive well-being. Social emotional learning, a strengths-based approach, healthy, caring environments, and a whole-community approach to healthy development are all foundations for promoting and supporting children and youth on the pathway to well-being.

Resilient

To be resilient, we need to believe in our own strengths, abilities, and worth. Resilience can be defined as the ability to cope with life's disappointments, challenges, and pain. Developing resilience is a particular challenge for adolescents who are dealing with so many physical and emotional changes.

In *Duct Tape Isn't Enough: Survival Skills for the 21st Century,* Ron Breazeale (2009) provides an evidence-informed list of skills and attitudes that constitute resilience in children and youth. The five skills are as follows:

- developing effective relationships
- showing flexibility
- doing realistic action planning
- listening and problem solving
- managing emotions

The attitudes Breazeale identifies are these:

- having self-confidence
- seeing meaning and purpose
- holding an optimistic perspective
- keeping a sense of (appropriate) humour
- keeping balance and fitness
- nurturing empathy and making a social contribution

If we think about it, it quickly becomes clear that these skills and attitudes work together. Developing good relationships, communicating effectively, and being flexible and able to plan help to produce a positive self-image and the confidence to tackle a problem with success in mind. These skills also help us to maintain an optimistic perspective and even to find humour in a situation. Likewise, when we feel confident and competent, we enjoy good relationships and we are more likely to take care of ourselves with exercise and a reasonable diet. When we reach out to others in our communities, we feel empowered and optimistic about ourselves and our relationships.

Recent research also supports the importance of the environment in developing resilience (Ungar, 2013). Individuals do develop skills for resilience when they are successfully engaged in school activities, have opportunities to develop positive relationship skills, and strengthen confidence at problem solving. Research further supports the pivotal role an adult can play in helping a student engage in the school environment and access resources needed for success and well-being: see *Supporting Minds*, authored by the Ontario Ministry of Education (2013). Resilience is possible for all children, providing the resources are available.

Active

The importance of regular exercise in helping to maintain mental and physical health is supported by a robust base of evidence (Otto & Smits, 2011; Ratey, 2008). Research also supports the use of physical exercise to help manage a wide range of mild to severe psychological difficulties among adolescents and adults (Richardson et al., 2005).

In healthy individuals, regular physical activity has been associated with improved interpersonal relationships, social skills, self-image, self-worth, cognitive functioning, and brain composition changes.

At a time when Canadian children and youth spend approximately 62 percent of their waking hours engaged in sedentary activities, including sitting in front of a computer screen (Canadian Society for Exercise Physiology, 2011), a conscious focus on physical education and activity in the classroom seems ever so important. Physical education can play a key role in shaping students' attitudes to a healthy lifestyle—both for now and for their futures.

In our model for well-being, an active lifestyle encompasses regular physical activity for fitness, adequate sleep, good nutrition, and attention to spiritual needs, which may include participation in family, cultural, community, faith-based, or personally enriching activities. The key is to achieve a vital balance in these interconnected aspects of our lives.

Flourishing

The term *flourishing* describes an optimal level of mental health, regardless of mental illness. In his book *Flourish*, psychologist Martin Seligman bases optimal well-being, or the experience of flourishing, on five elements (Seligman, 2011):

- positive emotion (fun and enjoyment)
- engagement (passionately absorbed; in the flow)
- meaning (sense of purpose)
- accomplishment (competence)
- positive relationships (connection; valued; belonging)

Ultimately, we can look at mental health promotion in a school setting as an endeavour to promote lifestyle experiences for all students where there are regular opportunities for positive emotion, engagement, meaning, accomplishment, and positive relationships.

The explosion of research, as well as school and government initiatives, is providing us with new tools and supports to successfully reach that goal.

What About You? Educator Well-Being

While we focus primarily on students, we cannot overlook the critical importance of your well-being as an educator. In many ways, it all starts with you. If we do not take care—individually, within our school and board communities, and through provincial strategies—to support educator well-being, we are all at a disadvantage. Research shows that teacher well-being supports student well-being (Roffey, 2012). Mental health promotion needs to be a whole-school and whole-community approach, encompassing all of us.

In Chapter 6, we will look at how you, as an educator, can enhance your experiences of positive emotion and engagement, a sense of meaning and accomplishment, and positive relationships to support your well-being. In fact, it could be argued that this chapter should be the first in the book—and it certainly could be. It is helpful to note, however, that all of the skills and strategies we consider for students throughout the book can be applied to you as an educator—only the lens is different. That is what we do in Chapter 6: apply the strategies to educators and view them through a slightly different perspective. Throughout the book, however, it is worthwhile thinking about how the concepts and strategies discussed for students can enhance your own well-being.

References

Breazeale, R. (2009). *Duct tape isn't enough: Survival skills for the 21st century.* Portland, ME: Bounce Back USA.

Cain, S. (2012). *Quiet: The power of introverts in a world that can't stop talking.* New York, NY: Crown.

Canadian Society for Exercise Physiology. (2011). *Canadian physical activity guidelines and Canadian sedentary behaviour guidelines.* Retrieved from http://www.csep.ca/guidelines

Collaborative for Academic, Social, and Emotional Learning (CASEL). (2013). *Effective social and emotional learning programs: Preschool and elementary school edition.* Chicago, IL: Author. Retrieved from http://casel.org/

Cowan, K. C., Vaillancourt, K., Rossen, E., & Pollitt, K. (2013). *A framework for safe and successful schools* [Brief]. Bethesda, MD: National Association of School Psychologists.

Institute of Medicine and National Research Council. (2009) *Preventing mental, emotional, and behavioral disorders among young people: Progress and possibilities.* Washington, DC: The National Academies Press.

Joint Consortium for School Health (JCSH). (2009). *What is comprehensive school health?* Retrieved from http://www.jcsh-cces.ca/upload/ JCSH%20CSH%20Framework%20FINAL%20Nov%2008.pdf

National Association of School Psychologists. (2009). *Appropriate behavioral, social, and emotional supports to meet the needs of all students* [Position statement]. Bethesda, MD: Author.

Ontario Ministry of Education. (2013). *Supporting minds: An educator's guide to promoting students' mental health and well-being* [Draft version 2013]. Toronto: Queen's Printer for Ontario. Retrieved from www.ontario.ca/edu

Otto, M., & Smits, J. (2011). *Exercise for mood and anxiety: Proven strategies for overcoming depression and enhancing well-being.* New York, NY: Oxford University Press.

Pan-Canadian Joint Consortium for School Health (JCSH). (2013). *Schools as a setting for promoting positive mental health: better practices and perspectives.* Second edition. Retrieved at http://www.jcsh-cces.ca/upload/ JCSH%20Best%20Practice_Eng_Jan21.pdf

Public Health Agency of Canada (PHAC). (2006). *The human face of mental health and mental illness in Canada.* Ottawa, ON: Author.

Ratey, J. J., with E. Hagerman. (2008). *Spark: The revolutionary new science of exercise and the brain.* New York, NY: Little, Brown.

Richardson, C., Faulkner, G., McDevitt, J., Skrinar, G., Hutchinson, D., & Piette, J. (2005). Integrating physical activity mental health services for persons with serious mental illness. *Psychiatric Services, 56*(3), 324–331.

Roffey, S. (2012). Pupil well-being—Teacher well-being: Two sides of the same coin? *Educational & Child Psychology, 29*(4), 8–17.

Shanker, S. (2013). *Calm, alert, and learning: Classroom strategies for self-regulation.* Toronto, ON: Pearson Canada.

Seligman, M. E. P. (2011). *Flourish: A visionary new understanding of happiness and well-being.* New York, NY: Free Press.

Ungar, M. (2013). The impact of youth–adult relationships on resilience. *International Journal of Child, Youth and Family Studies, 4*(3), 328–336.

A Whole-School Whole-Community Approach

"An essential advantage of school programming is the opportunity to promote positive mental health of all students rather than focusing solely on those identified as having mental health problems."

—SCHOOL-BASED MENTAL HEALTH AND SUBSTANCE
ABUSE CONSORTIUM, 2013, p. 5

Key Roles of the Teacher as Core Member of the Wider Mental Health Community

- making mental health promotion a priority
- improving mental health literacy and reducing stigma
- working with parents, the school, and the broader community to support student mental health
- creating a healthy, caring environment
- using effective strategies in the classroom

A whole-school, whole-community approach
Actively promoting positive mental health and creating a healthy, caring, inclusive class and school environment.

It is helpful to view the teacher's role in positive mental health as falling under four main overlapping areas, as shown in Figure 2.1: (1) the teacher–student relationship, (2) mental health literacy, (3) teaching and learning, and (4) the school and classroom environment. Let's look at these areas more closely.

Figure 2.1: The Role of the Teacher

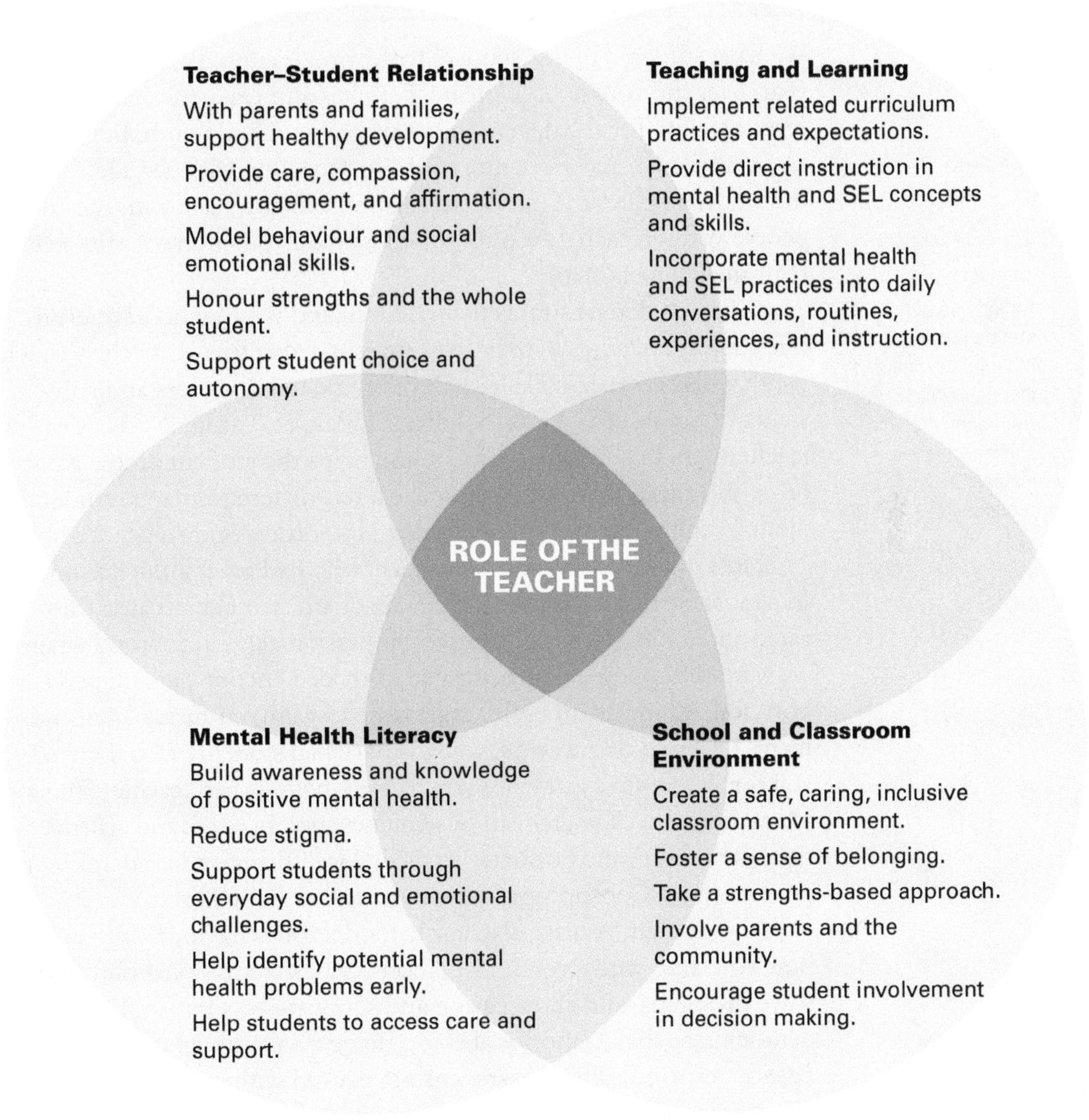

ROLE OF THE TEACHER

Teacher–Student Relationship

With parents and families, support healthy development.

Provide care, compassion, encouragement, and affirmation.

Model behaviour and social emotional skills.

Honour strengths and the whole student.

Support student choice and autonomy.

Teaching and Learning

Implement related curriculum practices and expectations.

Provide direct instruction in mental health and SEL concepts and skills.

Incorporate mental health and SEL practices into daily conversations, routines, experiences, and instruction.

Mental Health Literacy

Build awareness and knowledge of positive mental health.

Reduce stigma.

Support students through everyday social and emotional challenges.

Help identify potential mental health problems early.

Help students to access care and support.

School and Classroom Environment

Create a safe, caring, inclusive classroom environment.

Foster a sense of belonging.

Take a strengths-based approach.

Involve parents and the community.

Encourage student involvement in decision making.

The Teacher–Student Relationship

We have students in our schools for approximately 1000 hours per year, over the course of 14 years. Families and teachers share the responsibility for the development of children and youth, but in some cases, a teacher may have more face-to-face time with a student than the student's parent. The special relationship you have with the young people you see each year puts you in a unique position to influence their mental well-being.

Research demonstrates that children and youth who have even one supportive adult in their lives (parent, close friend, teacher, coach, youth worker) are less likely to develop mental disorders and substance abuse issues (Weisz, Sandler, Durlak, & Anton, 2005). A caring teacher who believes in a student and helps the student access what he or she needs to do well can make a real difference to the student's mental health and even prevent mental disorders and substance abuse.

Most of us can remember teachers who had great influence on us. In almost every case, those teachers made a difference because they cared about our interests, listened compassionately, understood when we were struggling or truly engaged, provided encouragement and support, found hidden strengths, and created a calm, nurturing environment. Likewise, as a teacher, you will have had students who thanked you for the positive influence you had on them. When teacher–student interactions are characterized by genuine empathy, care, and affirmation, they contribute positively to mental well-being and academic competence (Joint Consortium for School Health [JCSH], 2010).

As a teacher, you are also a role model for behaviour. Students see how you cope with stressful situations, react to emotional outbursts, solve problems, and show caring and support—essentially, how you demonstrate social emotional skills. Being a role model is not always an easy responsibility. Classrooms are packed with students who have diverse strengths and needs, and who go through a range of positive and negative emotions each day. Regulating your own emotions and the myriad of positive and negative student emotions in the classroom, navigating stressful situations, and staying calm and focused to create a healthy learning environment—these are all challenges teachers face. Social emotional skills are as important for teachers as they are for students.

In Chapter 6, we will focus on teacher well-being and ways to maximize resilience, competence, and balance. Your abilities to read emotional information and to regulate your own and your students' emotions are significant factors in learning and mental well-being. It is encouraging to know that SEL skills can be learned and that there are practical and realistic things you can implement in your classroom.

Ultimately, helping students to flourish involves valuing the dignity and worth of each individual, regardless of scores on report cards or achievement tests. Traditionally, academic achievement trumped all else, and final marks meant more than effort and improvement. We now know that when we join with parents, families, and the school and broader communities to help each child be the best person he or she can be—socially, emotionally, physically, intellectually, spiritually, culturally, and academically—we remember to value the whole child. We acknowledge that these aspects of development are interdependent and that they all contribute to the well-being of the child and the well-being of our communities.

In Loco Parentis: The Unique Relationship Between Teachers and Students

Teachers and administrators assume a special relationship with students who are entrusted to their care each day. This relationship is recognized by common law in the concept of *in loco parentis*—"in the place of a parent." *In loco parentis* could be described as a standard of care in the school environment whereby teachers and principals provide what a reasonable and prudent parent would provide in a given circumstance. Teachers are expected to provide a higher standard of care than a patron in a restaurant or a friend invited onto your property would receive, for example. In effect, school authorities stand in place of the parent in the school environment, and teachers accept legal responsibility for acting on parents' behalf to keep children safe. In addition to teachers providing safety, the teacher–student bond is a significant care-giving relationship.

Mental Health Literacy

Mental Health Commission of Canada and the Mental Health Strategy for Canada

Improving mental health literacy is a concern across all sectors of society. We have all heard about situations where mental health problems are not recognized and where people are afraid or stigmatized. People often do not know that they need help or where to get it, and when they do seek help, find that services are fragmented and uncoordinated. There has been little focus on developmental understanding of a person, on the positive aspects of recovery, or on positive mental health development.

Fortunately, we are seeing initiatives for change. Nationally and provincially, programs have been developed to bring schools, community services, and health-care sectors together for a broad and more coordinated approach to addressing mental health literacy and mental health concerns. For the first time, Canada has a national strategy on mental health, created by the Mental Health Commission of Canada (MHCC). A large part of this strategy is to bring mental health "out of the shadows" and to promote positive mental health. Even corporations are contributing to the cause with programs such as the Bell "Let's Talk" campaign to reduce the stigma associated with mental issues.

Schools have been recognized as a critical environment for fostering mental health and mental health literacy. The School-Based Mental Health and Substance Abuse Consortium has provided a useful definition of mental health literacy for schools:

> Mental Health Literacy includes the knowledge, skills, and beliefs school staff bring to:
>
> - promoting positive mental health in the classroom,
> - reducing stigma,
> - identifying risk factors and signs/symptoms,
> - preventing mental health and substance use problems,
> - helping students to access support,
> - recognizing the connection between positive mental health and student success.
>
> —*SBMHSA Consortium, 2012*

As educators, it is helpful to start by honestly assessing our own and our students' understanding and beliefs about mental health and well-being. To begin, consider answering the following questions as a short self-assessment.

1. What do I know about mental well-being?

   _____

   _____

   _____

2. What questions do I have?

   _____

   _____

   _____

3. How can I improve my knowledge and understanding?

   _____

   _____

   _____

4. What attitudes toward mental health and mental illness do I notice in people and media around me?

   _____

   _____

   _____

5. How can I promote healthy values, attitudes, and understanding?

   _____

   _____

   _____

If you can, keep your answers to these questions at hand. Refer to them after you have read all of this book and at points in the coming year as you monitor your class environment.

What we know about mental health and how we perceive it has a significant influence on our students' attitudes and perceptions. Answering these questions can help you be an effective role model, provide compassionate support, and help students on the pathway to care. You can also work together with your students to address these questions. Ministries and departments of education and school boards are providing quality targeted resources for mental health literacy.

Mental Health First Aid Canada

Reducing Stigma

The Canadian Mental Health Association, Ontario, (n.d.) offers this insight into stigma: "Stigma is the negative stereotype, and discrimination is the behaviour that results from this negative stereotype."

The stigma associated with mental health problems has been identified as a key issue. Stigma undermines the caring, inclusion, and compassion critical to positive mental health; it is also one of the most significant barriers to seeking support. The Mental Health Commission of Canada (2008, p. 9) describes stigma in this way: "Stigma is a mark of disgrace or discredit that sets a person apart from others. It involves negative stereotypes and prejudice. Stigma results from fear and mistrust of differences. It builds on repeated exposure to misinformation reinforcing negative perceptions and false beliefs that are intensely held and enduring. Stigma leads to social exclusion and discrimination."

In other words, many people with mental health issues face distrust, fear, and avoidance. These attitudes can lead people to disregard or hide their struggles and avoid seeking the care and support they need. It is not difficult to see how young people especially can be affected by stigma since they are at a stage in their development when trust, acceptance, and peer-image are critical. If they encounter fear, mistrust, or discrimination, it will negatively affect their sense of self-worth, as well as that of their friends and family, which makes care and support that much more difficult to obtain.

Stigma depicts only a negative image of mental illness—it ignores the positive aspects of strength, resilience, recovery, and good quality of life. People with mental challenges can recover and do live satisfying and contributing lives even when there are ongoing concerns. Stigma undermines the fact that we all have the capacity for positive mental health and well-being.

The promotion of mental health will be most effective when it is seen as a positive goal for *all* students rather than something that should be applied only to those with "disorders" or those "at risk." While early intervention systems are needed for those with a diagnosable mental illness or for those at risk, universal programs and strategies that teachers can use to promote positive mental health with all students may have the biggest impact on reducing mental illness and the stigma associated with it.

Mental Health Stigma: Facts and Misconceptions

The Facts

Sixty percent of people with a mental health problem or illness will not seek help for fear of being labelled.

Only one in three people who experience a mental health problem or illness—and as few as one in four children or youth—reports having sought and received services and treatment.

Twenty-seven percent of Canadians are fearful of being around people who suffer from serious mental illness.

Only 49 percent of Canadians said they would socialize with a friend who has a serious mental illness.

Canadians surveyed said they were less comfortable being around people with depression than around people with physical disabilities.

Many people living with mental illness say the stigma they face is often worse than the illness itself.

Stigma is often internalized by people with mental illness. They may self-stigmatize, which can be an obstacle to accessing care and achieving good quality of life.

Stigma is a significant barrier to seeking help, especially for youth.

Sources: The Bell Let's Talk Initiative (2014), Centre for Addiction and Mental Health (n.d.), Mental Health Commission of Canada (2012).

Common Myths and Misconceptions

Mentally ill people are violent and dangerous.

In reality, individuals with mental illness are more likely to be the target of violence than the catalyst for it.

People who are poor and unintelligent are more apt to be mentally ill.

In fact, everyone faces mental challenges, and anyone can develop mental health problems.

Mental illness is a sign of personal weakness and lack of self-control.

Mental illness has no relation to weakness or lack of will. People with disorders have little control over the onset of their symptoms.

There is also a tendency to view mental illness as a single disorder.

Mental illness is an umbrella term for a broad range of conditions.

Source: Canadian Mental Health Association (n.d.).

Teachers can help by fostering open and honest conversations about mental health issues in class and providing students and parents with information to challenge stereotypes and misconceptions. There is widespread evidence that "contact-based education"—meeting and talking with people who can share their experiences of mental illness and recovery—is an effective way to break down stigma. Sharing videos of people talking about their experiences and reading stories can be equally effective (Mental Health Commission of Canada, *Opening Minds*). Beyond changing attitudes, there is also a need to change behaviours.

Later in the chapter, we will look at the characteristics of safe and caring school and classroom environments, and some practical strategies for supporting open conversations.

The Mental Health Continuum

It is important for students to recognize that everyone deals with emotional, social, and mental health problems at some point in their lives. Loss of friends or loved ones, trauma from accidents, family break-ups, a move to a new school or community, loss of a job—we all know these are not uncommon occurrences in life. In fact, we deal with stressful situations and even crises daily. Being late, not being able to finish an assignment, having a conflict with a parent, sibling, or friend—all of these are not unusual stresses in a student's everyday routine.

Children and youth need to know that we can all develop knowledge, skills, and attitudes to help navigate these issues successfully. Even when a crisis such as the loss of a loved one leads to depression or prolonged grief—the marked long-term distress that signals mental illness—what we need most is support and care to recover. We can recover, just as we can recover from a physical illness when we receive appropriate care and treatment. But too often, people dealing with mental issues are instead hurt and harmed by being shunned, feared, misunderstood, and pushed away just when help and compassion are most needed.

The mental health continuum (Figure 2.2) is a useful tool for recognizing that even in a state of mental well-being, we deal with mild distress. Problems and concerns that cause us moderate distress and disrupt our lives are also not uncommon. We can recognize the signs of illness when the distress becomes intense, prolonged, and disabling.

It is also important to recognize that mental health and mental problems are complex. Several factors can affect mental health, and these need to be considered when we encounter a problem. Factors include the following:

- individual factors—temperament, learning ability, and social skills

- family factors—attachment, parenting style, communication, parental and sibling relations, family structure and circumstances

- environmental factors—physical conditions and social conditions, such as sense of belonging in school and community

Mental health is a complex interaction of biological, genetic, economic, social, and psychological factors.

"There is no single cause of any mental health problem or illness, and no one is immune, no matter where they live, how old or young they are or their social standing."

—Mental Health Commission of Canada, 2012, p. 12

Figure 2.2: The Mental Health Continuum

Mental Health Problems		
Health		**Illness**
Well-Being	**Emotional Problems or Concerns**	**Mental Illness**
Occasional to mild distress	Mild to moderate distress	Marked distress
No impairment	Mild to temporary impairment	Moderate to disabling or chronic impairment

Source: MHealthy–University of Michigan Health & Well-Being Services (2012).

For teachers, these factors underline the importance of getting to know your students, dialoguing with parents and families to understand a child's or youth's circumstances, and creating a caring and inclusive school and classroom environment. As already noted, problematic behaviour does not necessarily indicate a mental health issue, and only professionals can diagnose an illness; however, you are often well attuned to changes in your students' behaviour. You have an important role to play in observing signs of potential problems; recording observations; dialoguing with the students, their families, and school support services; and helping students access the care they need.

Figure 2.3 shows a continuum of knowledge. Ideally, you want to move from awareness to literacy, and tap into the people who have expertise when it is needed. This continuum aligns with the three-tiered approach outlined in Chapter 1 (pages 4–5). Gaining the deeper understanding at the literacy level is important for teachers who have daily close contact with students. It means that you can actively promote positive mental health and support students who may be struggling. For us as educators, key goals are to promote, prevent, and support.

Figure 2.3: Mental Health Literacy—Continuum of Knowledge

The ABCs of Mental Health

Awareness	Literacy	Expertise
a basic level of understanding of mental health and common problems that might be observed at school among students, and how to help	a deeper level of knowledge and skill to actively promote mental well-being at school, and to identify and effectively support students who struggle with their emotions and behaviour	a fluency with evidence-based mental health promotion, prevention, and **intervention** strategies and programs

Sourced from: School Mental Health ASSIST (2013, pp. 40–41).

Observing and Recording Behaviour

As a teacher, you are often well attuned to signs when something may not be right with your students. Observing and recording behaviour is an important first step in helping to identify a potential issue, preventing a more serious problem, and helping students navigate everyday issues or find the pathway to care.

When to Be Concerned

Consider three factors when you notice that one of your students may be struggling:

1. Frequency: How often does the student exhibit the behaviours of concern?

2. Duration: How long does the behaviour last?

3. Intensity: To what extent do the behaviours interfere with the activities of the child or youth?

Your school or board may have tools to help you document your observations. Recording your observations over time gives you a basis for discussion with the student, parents, and families. It also provides you with data if you need to discuss the situation with a counsellor, principal, or mental health professional. Often, you may see behaviour that parents do not see at home or that professionals will not see in their offices. The list below includes behaviour that might be seen at school, at home, or in the community.

Some Signs for Concern

Significant changes in behaviours, appearance, or mood

Behaviours that affect school performance (concentration, motivation)

Highly negative, angry, or aggressive interactions with friends and/or family

Extreme mood swings and/or emotional outbursts

Disruptions with eating and/or sleeping

Problems dealing with authority

Risk-taking behaviour

Not doing the things he or she used to enjoy

Damaging others' property

Worrying constantly

Children's Mental Health Ontario

Child and Youth Mental Health Information Network

Obsessing about weight or appearance

Showing aggression to others or self

Lacking energy or motivation for a prolonged period

Sources: Children's Mental Health Ontario; Ontario Centre of Excellence for Child and Youth Mental Health [Presentation slides]; Student Support Leadership Initiative, Hamilton District Team (2011).

S P O T L I G H T

Supporting Students Who May Be Suicidal

Sometimes, students may feel trapped or helpless in situations that they believe are beyond their control. When this occurs, some students may begin to view self-destructive behaviour as a possible solution to escape their emotional pain and perceptions of difficulty.

School staff members have a unique opportunity to spend dedicated time with students and to establish positive relationships with them. Thus, staff may become aware of a student's challenging life circumstances or may notice warning signs of a student's distress. It is useful for teachers to be aware of potential warning signs and for school staff to have a protocol to follow when concerned about a student's potential risk for suicide.

Potential Warning Signs

The student may demonstrate any of the following:

- a desire or specific intent to die by suicide (Such thoughts that come to a student may be scary and unwanted, but real.)

- feelings of hopelessness or helplessness expressed through comments or writings about death and dying

- behaviour that is out of character for the individual or characterized by marked mood changes, including a sudden, unexpected change to cheerfulness after a depressed mood

- social withdrawal, loss of appetite, loss of interest in usual activities, sleep problems, or a marked change in academic performance

- giving away of prized possessions or saying goodbye to loved ones and friends
- a marked reaction to a bereavement, a specific loss, or a significant triggering event, such as the end of a romantic relationship or a disciplinary crisis
- destructive or risky behaviour related to drug or alcohol use

Note: One sign alone may indicate high risk.

Practical Protocols

When concerned about a student's risk for possible suicide, a typical staff protocol to follow could go something like this:

- If the student (or student's friend) approaches you, stay calm and listen without judgment.
- Do not minimize the concerns or impose your own beliefs. Be supportive. Do not make promises to keep the information confidential. Safety takes precedence over confidentiality.
- Share the information with administration, guidance, or special services staff as soon as possible (not end of day).
- Ensure that a staff person supervises the student while you consult (including lunch, class changes, washroom breaks, and recess).
- It is often best to escort the student to the guidance or administration office directly, or request a staff escort.

Ideally, each school will have identified trained staff who will be responsible for interviewing the student and arranging for the appropriate action, which is likely to include parental contact and involvement of board staff or other services. It is often best when the staff member who received a communication about suicidal ideation is able to become part of the school support team for that student in the days ahead.

The school support team will work with parents/guardians and health professionals to formulate a safety support plan with the student. The safety support plan would include monitoring and an action plan for the student if he or she feels "at-risk" at some future time. There would be predetermined people to contact and places to go for support.

Schools may also have protocols in place for situations in which students share other serious concerns or sensitive information with teachers. These concerns may include bullying, noticing symptoms of an eating disorder in themselves or others, drug use, family difficulties or illness, and abuse. Listening without judgment, avoiding leading questions, maintaining appropriate confidentiality but never promising not to share the information, consulting for appropriate help, documenting the circumstance and what the student reports in a confidential record, and re-engaging the relationship with the student at the first available opportunity are all important considerations.

Sourced from a brochure produced by the Simcoe Muskoka Catholic District School Board.

Teaching and Learning

Across the country, curricula are being revised to incorporate positive mental health and social emotional learning (SEL) concepts, skills, and attitudes. Mental health may be part of the physical and health education, English/language arts, drama, social studies or social sciences, and arts curricula among others. These changes reflect the understanding that mental health is integral to all areas of student development across all disciplines.

Teaching and learning involves a multi-faceted approach:

- explicit teaching of positive mental health and social emotional skills and concepts across the curriculum through formal lessons and structured activities with specific learning goals

- modelling, learning, and practice of skills and attitudes by embedding them in classroom routines and informal instruction practices

- modelling and practice of skills and attitudes in all school and classroom interactions, including recess, extracurricular activities, sports, and hallway interactions

Clearly, developing positive mental health cannot be just an academic pursuit. It is part of our everyday interactions in all facets of our lives—social, emotional, intellectual, cultural, spiritual, physical, and academic. Later in the chapter, we will see how incorporating circles into classroom routines accomplishes several goals at once: practising SEL skills and attitudes, supporting a caring environment, fostering positive mental health, and deepening the teacher–student relationship.

The Goal of Positive Mental Health

We have defined positive mental health as "the capacity of each and all of us to feel, think, and act in ways that enhance our ability to enjoy life and deal with the challenges we face. It is a positive sense of emotional and spiritual well-being that respects the importance of culture, equity, social justice, interconnections and personal dignity" (Public Health Agency of Canada [PHAC], 2006). We can help our students recognize that mental well-being is a goal they can actively work toward and achieve.

When students understand mental well-being as a goal, they

- understand the skills and attitudes that underlie mental well-being

- develop the vocabulary to talk about mental health issues and well-being

- have opportunities to practise the skills that support their mental health

- create their own personal toolkit of techniques and strategies that help them navigate their challenges and stresses

- feel confident they can make decisions that enhance their mental well-being

- anticipate feelings of joy, healthy relationships, active lifestyles, and freedom to develop their talents and interests

The chapters that follow aim to provide you with the understandings and tools to support your students in these areas.

Figure 2.4: Positive Mental Health

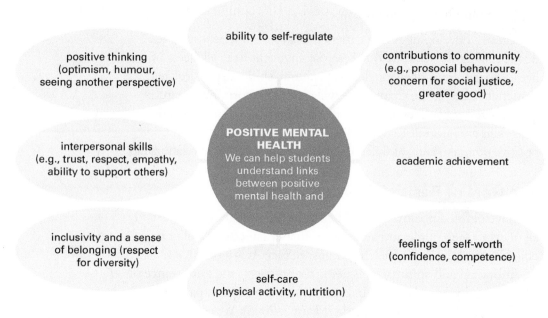

Social Emotional Learning Outcomes

Social emotional learning (SEL) is a key pillar in supporting the development of positive mental health. In Chapter 3, we will look at social emotional learning in more depth. Here, it is useful to note that research supports the link between social emotional learning and positive outcomes for student well-being and academic achievement (Payton et al., 2008).

Social emotional learning focuses on five key competencies:

- Self-awareness
- Self-management
- Social awareness
- Relationship skills
- Responsible decision-making

©P

According to extensive literature reviews conducted by the Collaborative for Academic, Social, and Emotional Learning (2013), the main outcomes associated with the five SEL competencies are positive social behaviour, fewer conduct problems, less emotional distress, and academic success.

CASEL Guide

Creating a Healthy, Caring Environment

When I talk to parents about what is important to them in their child's educational setting, oftentimes a caring environment where their child is engaged in school activities and "fits in" trumps concerns about academic outcomes. Many parents know the importance of a sense of belonging to their children's development—and the importance of school as a place where their children feel safe, secure, supported, and able to be the best they can be.

Schools and classrooms are hubs of physical, social, and emotional interactions. Student interactions with peers, teachers, and other educators can be either rich opportunities to develop positive skills and relationships, or primarily random and negative situations focused on coping. Students often have underdeveloped skills for understanding and managing their emotions, resolving conflicts, and creating sustainable friendships. As a teacher, you know that these skills do not necessarily develop when students are put together in schools and classrooms. Without modelling, direction, encouragement, and support, corralling students together into classrooms could just create havoc. Likewise, we have all seen situations where stress, negativity, and a culture of complaint and gossip can easily spread throughout an entire school.

A Whole-Community Approach

Increased mental health literacy can help to create conditions for healthy caring environments. We mentioned in Chapter 1 that a key goal is to create a culture of mental health in all our schools. Creating a "culture" means that values, attitudes, and practices are followed by the whole community consistently, everywhere and every day. What goes on in the classroom cannot be different from what goes on in the hallways, at recess, or on the bus home. Clear and consistent expectations for behaviour, a common language, and common practices are keys to building and sustaining a positive culture.

Positive mental health promotion in the classroom can be part of an integrated whole-school approach involving all staff and students, the parent community, and the broader community. Figure 2.5 shows the elements of a whole-community approach.

Figure 2.5: The Community

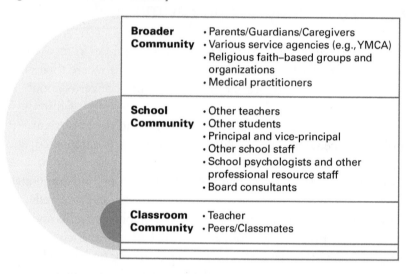

Broader Community	• Parents/Guardians/Caregivers • Various service agencies (e.g., YMCA) • Religious faith–based groups and organizations • Medical practitioners
School Community	• Other teachers • Other students • Principal and vice-principal • Other school staff • School psychologists and other professional resource staff • Board consultants
Classroom Community	• Teacher • Peers/Classmates

Community Connection

Partnerships for Mental Health

Schools and school boards are fostering partnerships with community organizations and agencies to support mental health awareness and well-being. Parent and student voices are actively encouraged in these partnerships and programs.

Find out what programs and partnerships are available at your school. These may include mentorship and leadership programs, access to community mental health professionals and youth services, and substance abuse educational programs. Many schools also have a healthy school policy with leadership, resources, and protocols in place to support teachers and other staff with promoting mental health literacy and care.

Characteristics of a Healthy, Caring Environment

So, how can you create a healthy, caring classroom environment that promotes mental well-being? Obviously, physical safety is a fundamental priority. School safety protocols and procedures help to ensure that students are safe from physical harm on school grounds. Social and emotional safety are equally fundamental. Codes of conduct and progressive discipline programs set out clear expectations for behaviour in schools. Most schools also have programs to eliminate bullying. These programs teach children empathy for others and the need to speak up when they are witness to aggressive acts.

But in the classroom, at a deeper level, feeling safe has to do with relationship trust. There needs to be a sense of personal dignity, or "whole-hearted worthiness," to use a term coined by Brené Brown in her research on emotional connection. Brown (2012) suggests that feeling worthy of love and belonging is integral to our willingness to be vulnerable, take risks, and make mistakes.

A healthy environment needs to help students develop self-esteem, learn about and develop their strengths, and feel confident. When students are confident in their self-worth and feel a true sense of belonging and trust, their relationships are positive ones and they show **prosocial behaviours**—caring for others, for social justice, and about making connections and contributions to the wider community.

We know that students build self-esteem and confidence when their voices are heard and they have opportunities to make decisions and deal with the natural and logical consequences of their decisions.

> "Because true belonging only happens when we present our authentic, imperfect selves to the world, our sense of belonging can never be greater than our level of self-acceptance."
> —Brown, 2012, pp. 145–146

> "Students love to have choice...it gives them a sense of personal power...a sense that their decision-making counts, and that they can make a difference."
> —JCSH, 2010, p. 51

Characteristics of a Healthy, Caring Environment

Physical safety

Emotional safety

Clear expectations for behaviour

Inclusivity; respect for diversity, personal dignity, and other perspectives

Sense of belonging

Sense of self-worth and confidence

Open, trusting relationships

Strengths-based approach—honouring strengths over deficits

Student decision-making and autonomy as appropriate

Students having a voice and being encouraged to take leadership roles

Caring and concern for others

Prosocial behaviours (e.g., concern for social justices, contributions to the wider community)

Diversity and Inclusivity

Respecting diversity and actively promoting inclusivity are also vital to creating a healthy, caring environment. The goal is to help ensure that all students have an equal opportunity for healthy development and positive mental health.

Diversity encompasses differences in
- racial and ethnocultural background
- sexual orientation
- special physical, emotional, or behavioural needs
- learning needs and strengths
- personal preferences or strengths

Recognizing specific issues some groups and individuals face, understanding their needs, and taking positive actions to break down barriers can help to promote sensitivity, inclusion, and caring. LGBTQ (lesbian, gay, bisexual, transgender, queer), FNIM (First Nations, Inuit, and Métis), refugee and newcomer, and various ethno-cultural and racial groups, for example, face particular issues that we need to be aware of as educators, while at the same time recognizing and honouring individual differences and differences within larger cultural and social groups.

It is equally important not to identify these groups or individuals with deficit-only or crisis-only characteristics. There is a place for crisis management and intervention, as noted earlier, but health promotion focuses on creating an environment in which all of these students can feel they belong and have equitable opportunities to learn and achieve well-being.

Refugee, Newcomer, and ELL Children and Youth

A study by the Canadian Centre for Addiction and Mental Health (CAMH, 2012) highlighted the following key issues that *some* refugee, recent immigrant, and ELL (English Language Learner) children and youth may face:

- in some cases, issues of pre-migration trauma, exposure to violence, and prolonged separation from family members

- economic disadvantages (such as parental unemployment and poverty), social exclusion, isolation, racism, discrimination, and cultural pressures

- barriers to accessing health care, which include language and cultural factors, discrimination, stigma, and mistrust of mainstream service providers

Of course, not all new immigrant children and youth face these issues, but many will experience the stresses of adjusting to a new culture and environment (Kobus-Matthews, Agic, & Tate, M., 2012).

In addition, some parents or guardians may be too busy with day-to-day challenges, such as getting employment and housing, to think about mental health. All of these issues require sensitivity, understanding, compassion, and sometimes referrals for specific and appropriate professional or social support. While a school or classroom environment alone cannot resolve these issues, one that fosters sensitivity and inclusion can help ease the stresses, including the **acculturative stress** that many of these students face, and offer them positive opportunities for healthy development.

It is also important to recognize that different cultures have different understandings of mental health and wellness—and this applies not only to recent immigrant or refugee groups, but also to FNIM and ethnocultural groups that have had roots in Canada for

"Equity means fairness. It means that people's needs, rather than social privileges, guide the distribution of opportunities for well-being."
—World Health Organization, 1996

Centre for Addiction and Mental Health

Acculturative stress often occurs when an individual is trying to adjust to a new culture. This stress can manifest through the feelings of marginality, depression, anxiety, and identity confusion (Leach, 2006, p. 169).

Sound knowledge of the community agencies that help to support refugees, newcomers, and various cultural groups, as well as appropriate referrals or partnerships with these agencies, is fundamental.

generations. Cultural and spiritual beliefs and practices are often deeply interwoven with health and well-being in many cultures. Culture may also affect how children and youth show signs of mental difficulties, how they communicate with others about these difficulties, and how they label them (Ontario Ministry of Education, 2013).

Acknowledging and respecting different cultural perspectives is important to the cultural needs, health, and identities of all children and youth. Sharing and promoting understanding of these various perspectives supports students' sense of self-esteem, confidence, identity, and well-being. For us as educators, it means being non-judgmental, modelling respect, expanding **cultural competence** as much as possible, and finding what is most likely to achieve health promotion goals in a given situation.

First Nations, Inuit, and Métis Children and Youth

For First Nations, Inuit, and Métis children and youth, the effects of colonization and governmental policies of forced assimilation continue to cause acculturative stress and marginalization. When effects such as these are passed on from one generation to the next, it is referred to as **intergenerational trauma** (Centre for Suicide Prevention, 2013).

Forced adoptions and foster care, forced relocation from one community to another, denial of existence as a people (as in the case of the Métis Nation) (Kirmayer, 2007), and residential school experiences are some of the lasting effects of colonization on First Nations, Inuit, and Métis people. Many have experienced the loss or erosion of traditional values and culture, and a disruption of traditional family stability (Elias, 2012).

Currently, about 54 percent of FNIM people live in cities and towns. Some move between First Nations communities and cities. A loss of connection to the land and cultural community can heighten feelings of isolation and marginalization, and further disrupt family stability. While some individuals adapt well to urban life, many face racism, discrimination, and social exclusion.

Research has shown that legitimizing FNIM cultural history, practices, ways of knowing, and understandings of health and wellness all play a critical role in the well-being of FNIM children, youth, and adults. Suzanne Stewart (2008) has posited a model for

"Cultural competence is acceptance of and respect for difference developed through continuous self-assessment regarding culture, an attention to the dynamics of difference, the ongoing enlargement of cultural knowledge, and the willingness to adapt resources and procedures within service models to meet the needs of minority populations (Saldana, 2001)," as cited in Ontario Ministry of Education (2013, p. 15).

"...Cultural identity impacts mental health, in terms of self-esteem and the ability to cope with life."

—Stewart, 2008, p. 52

©P

Indigenous wellness and healing that focuses on moving forward from problems rather than following a crisis perspective, and that emphasizes the importance of community, cultural identity, interdependence, and a holistic approach for Indigenous mental health. Many boards and districts across the country are working on policies and approaches for FNIM students which include overall health. In the school and classroom, respect, understanding, and inclusion of culturally specific beliefs and practices are positive steps toward supporting student well-being.

Best Start Resources – Open Hearts, Open Minds: Services That Are Inclusive of First Nations, Métis, and Inuit Families

LGBTQ Children and Youth

Lesbian, gay, bisexual, transgendered, and queer (LGBTQ) children and youth face issues of isolation, discrimination, and harassment. In 2011, the Egale Canada Human Rights Trust released a national study, *Every Class in Every School: The First National Climate Survey on Homophobia, Biphobia, and Transphobia in Canadian Schools*, led by researchers Catherine Taylor and Tracey Peter. Both LGBTQ and non-LGBTQ students participated in the survey. Results showed the following:

- Sixty-four percent of LGBTQ students and 61 percent of students with LGBTQ parents reported that they felt unsafe at school.

- More than one in five LGBTQ students reported being physically harassed or assaulted due to sexual orientation.

- More than a third of youth with LGBTQ parents reported being verbally harassed about the sexual orientation of their parents, and over a quarter reported being physically harassed.

- LGBTQ youth are three to six times more likely to commit suicide than their straight counterparts.
  (Pike, 2014; Taylor & Peter, 2011)

The study also found that policies for safer schools can have an impact on reducing harassment and that groups such as Gay-Straight Alliances (GSAs), Positive Space Groups (PSGs), and other student groups focused on supporting diversity have contributed to decreases in homophobic remarks and harassment. Students were also less likely to feel unsafe because of their sexual orientation or gender

Egale Canada Human Rights Trust—provides resources for educators and parents and identifies 220 Positive Space groups across Canada

expression, were less likely to miss school because of safety concerns, and reported a greater sense of belonging to their school community (Pike, 2014).

Promoting Diversity and Inclusivity

A safe, caring, and healthy school and classroom environment

- allows all students to feel included and welcomed so they can focus on academic objectives and take an active part in school social life and co-curricular activities

- encourages inclusion of diverse peoples' lives, politics, cultures, families, and histories in curricula, course offerings, and research opportunities

- presents multiple perspectives on topics and encourages perspectives from individuals with varied backgrounds and experiences

- invites students, as well as their family and community members, to act as resources of knowledge for sharing culturally relevant traditions and practices, and various lifestyles and experiences

- makes the classroom an inviting space through regular opportunities for dialogue among students, family members, and members of the wider community

- encourages prosocial behaviours, including empathy, compassion, and a concern for social justice

Comprehensive Strategies and Approaches for the Classroom

In addition to strategies for inclusivity noted above, there are other comprehensive strategies and approaches to support a sense of belonging vital for all students.

Dreikurs and Encouragement

One approach that focuses on developing all students' self-worth and sense of belonging is what Rudolf Dreikurs called **encouragement** (Dreikurs, Cassel, & Dreikurs Ferguson, 2004). According to Dreikurs, all children have a positive desire to solve problems and to belong. All misbehaviour can be seen in terms of a child's discouragement. Discouraged students respond in one of four ways: by seeking attention, power, revenge, or by giving up (depression). Through use of encouragement strategies, Dreikurs believed teachers could help students get attention and power in positive ways.

Encouragement is based on improvement rather than only on achievement so that students consistently feel worthwhile and appreciated. Dreikurs asserted that the more encouraged students feel, the more they experience a sense of belonging, take an interest in others, and have the courage to face challenges and take them in stride.

Timothy Evans (2004) has written extensively on the topic of encouragement. He makes the distinction that where encouragement is aimed at highlighting a student's effort and behaviour, praise focuses on a finished product. The statements below model encouragement versus discouragement and encouragement versus praise:

- "You can do this." versus "That's hard. Let me help."

- "That assignment was hard. You put a great effort into completing it." versus "Your assignment was great."

A climate of encouragement also supports shared decision-making. Students participate in class planning, make choices about their own learning, solve problems and resolve conflicts through class meetings, and give encouragement to others.

Evans notes that classrooms based on an attitude of encouragement exhibit six traits:

- make relationships a priority
- conduct respectful dialogue
- practise encouragement daily
- make decisions through shared involvement (classroom meetings)

> Encouragement is different from praise. Encouragement motivates students to keep trying. Praise focuses on the level of achievement.

- resolve conflicts

- have fun on a regular basis

What is interesting in this example is that the six traits were originally developed in an article by Carlson, Sperry, and Dinkmeyer (1992). The topic: how to maintain a marriage.

The Power of a Circle

Many teachers have also found that circles are an effective way of fostering healthy classroom environments and achieving social emotional learning. Good teachers know that self-knowledge and self-management come from self-reflection and the sharing of authentic experiences. Students will not excel at social emotional learning that is too didactic or relies too heavily on concept explanations; they need chances to reflect on real-life experiences and opportunities to express themselves and receive feedback within a safe and interested environment.

First Nations, Inuit, and Métis Circles and Ways of Knowing

Circles are, and continue to be, a vital part of many First Nations, Inuit, and Métis cultures. The circle is used and interpreted in different ways in various cultures, but it most commonly denotes wholeness, inclusion, connection, and continuity. In the circle, everyone is equal and all are connected. Indigenous cultures use many types of circles, including trust circles, healing circles, and justice circles. Students can be encouraged to explore the Indigenous cultural roots of the circle, and ask FNIM students and community members to share their knowledge to enhance the understanding and experiences in the classroom.

In the classroom, the circle can be used for students to share observations or feelings at the start of the day, to provide support and encouragement or share inspirations, to solve problems or resolve conflicts, to make decisions about what goes on in their classroom, or to discuss world news. The circle provides a respectful and supportive forum where students can learn about one another, develop an increased sense of community and respect, show empathy and caring, and engage in problem solving. Students build skills in recognizing and managing emotions, addressing challenging situations constructively, and formulating responsible decisions. Skills learned in the circle can be promoted throughout the school day by teaching staff and parents.

Facilitating a Circle

Teachers and students can work together to create a contract or agreement that will govern interactions in their circle. Agreements help create a safe atmosphere of trust and respect. They might include items such as these:

- One person has the floor at a time; the others listen thoughtfully.

- Out of respect, what is discussed in the circle stays in the circle. (The circle has to remain safe for everyone to share their voice and opinions.)

- All students are expected to make a contribution at check-in, but students have the option of passing when sharing ideas.

- Not everyone will have the same opinion, and that's okay.

- We all benefit when we respect, appreciate, and celebrate our differences.

- We respond to each other's ideas with a meaningful comment.

Circle Routines and Goals

Many elementary teachers choose to make the circle a weekly or even a daily routine. The circle format typically starts with the taking of attendance. This might be followed by an inspirational reflection. Students then take turns checking in. For example, the teacher might say: "Choose an animal [or colour, or object] that represents your state of mind this morning." After check-in, there might be a sharing of news (world, national, and local) from various sources and open discussion.

For the circle, there will be goals related to student well-being. Some of the goals may be as follows:

- to enhance the trusting, cohesive, and "comfortable" atmosphere for *all* students

---

- to emphasize that the everyone in the circle belongs
- to know that someone cares ("You are not alone!")
- to improve problem-solving skills
- to create common ground for everyone in the class
- to clarify our life purpose
- to commit (or recommit) to personal growth and to education
- to hear opposing views
- to discuss the world around us
- to reconcile and celebrate differences
- to find or offer solutions to situations
- to offer honest information on various topics
- to improve the ability to see our role in situations and the effect on others
- to practise the way we want to be
- to learn to collaborate ("How can we support each other?")
- to communicate with purpose (respond to ideas with a meaningful comment)
- to improve self-esteem and love
- to provide guidance

—*Source: Gabriella Bator*

The circle sharing exercise can also be a useful segue into specific aspects of mental health promotion related to any one of a number of curriculum areas, such as the health and physical education curriculum. The segue could be an activity with a mini-lesson on fitness, identification of emotions, or problem-solving strategies.

Guidelines for Initiating Classroom Circles

Process

1. Have the students help you safely and quietly organize the classroom so that everyone can sit in a circle.
    a. Try to ensure that there are no desks or other pieces of furniture between circle participants.
    b. Sit in an equal position in the circle.

2. Welcome the group. Introduce yourself as a circle facilitator (or guide).
    c. Let everyone know that while in the circle your voice is equal to theirs.
    d. Ask that when they are speaking, they address the circle as a whole, and not just you (the facilitator).

3. Outline the purpose of the circle and review the agreement before starting. If the circle as a whole wishes to add other components to the agreement, feel free to facilitate that. It may help to post the agreement somewhere visible in the classroom.
    e. Start with safe topics to encourage discussion and develop a forum where students feel comfortable talking about their thoughts and feelings.
    f. When a level of comfort and trust is established, more difficult topics can be brought to the circle.

4. Explain the circle process:
    g. This is a "structured" conversation.
    h. One person speaks at a time without interruption.
    i. There are no right or wrong comments or thoughts.
    j. We use a talking piece. Everyone will have a turn to speak, and we agree to share the time we have equally.
    k. It's okay to pass, and we will come back to you at the end.
    l. What is discussed in the circle is not to be shared outside the circle. We respect privacy.
    m. Bring your full attention and presence to the circle. Focus to stay on topic.

n. Listen and speak with respect for others. Please do not interrupt a speaker or have private conversations during the circle.

o. Address your comments to the whole group or to the centre of the circle.

p. Be as honest, open-minded, and non-judgmental as possible.

5. Ask questions and guide the conversation.

q. Use restorative reflective statements:

r. *What do you think about...?*

s. *What comes to mind or what resonates with you when...?*

t. *What happened?*

u. *How does _____ impact us/the classroom?*

v. After asking a question, allow a pause for silent reflection before passing the talking piece.

w. You may choose to pass the talking piece around the entire circle or have participants raise their hands to speak and receive the talking piece. For difficult conversations or brainstorming, you may choose to have everyone write down their thoughts (no names) and put them in a basket in the middle of the circle. One person can read the responses.

x. Listen to what is said and pose thoughtful questions to encourage deeper conversation and problem solving.

y. *I heard the word "judged" being used. When you hear that word, what does it mean to you?*

z. Take your turn to speak. As facilitator, do not otherwise interject to teach or respond unless directly asked.

6. End the circle by thanking the group for their honesty and courage.

Reflection

If necessary, review the agreement terms at any time. Discuss the skills students have practised that can be applied throughout their day in other situations.

—*Source: Ashley Oliver*

Checklist for a Mentally Healthy Classroom

√ The teacher systematically promotes positive mental health.

√ Positive mental health promotion in the classroom is part of an integrated, whole-school approach involving all staff and students, the parent community, and external partners.

√ Each student has a good connection with the teacher, or perhaps one other teacher or teaching assistant.

√ Each student has at least one good friend at school.

√ Diversity in the classroom is recognized and celebrated, and positive actions are taken to ensure inclusivity, empathy, and caring so that all students have an equal opportunity for healthy development and well-being.

√ All students have a strong sense of belonging.

√ Students in need are noticed and supported along a pathway to care.

√ Students understand and appreciate the value of positive mental health, for feeling good and being resilient for the road ahead.

√ Students understand the connection between positive mental health and academic achievement.

√ Students understand links between positive mental health and positive thinking, including such things as optimism versus pessimism, and being able to step back and take another perspective when discouraged.

√ Evidenced-based practices and strategies related to curriculum expectations are implemented.

Bell Let's Talk Initiative. (2014). Retrieved from http://letstalk.bell.ca/en/end-the-stigma/facts/

Brown, B. (2012). *Daring greatly: How the courage to be vulnerable transforms the way we live, love, parent, and lead.* New York, NY: Gotham.

Canadian Mental Health Association [CMHA]. (n.d.). *Stigma and discrimination.* Retrieved from ontario.cmha.ca/mental-health/mental-health-conditions/stigma-and-discrimination/

Canadian Mental Health Association [CMHA]. (n.d.). *Understanding mental illness.* Retrieved from www.cmha.ca/mental-health/understanding-mental-illness/

Carlson, J., Sperry, L., & Dinkmeyer, D. (1992). Marriage maintenance: How to stay healthy. *Topics in Family Counseling & Psychology, 1,* 84–90.

Centre for Addiction and Mental Health [CAMH]. (n.d.). *Talking about mental illness community guide.* Retrieved from www.camh.ca/en/education/teachers_school_programs/resources_for_teachers_and_schools/talking_about_mental_illness_a_community_guide_for_developing_an_awareness_program_for_youth/Pages/tami_commguide_part1.aspx

Centre for Addiction and Mental Health [CAMH], Dalla Lana School of Public Health, University of Toronto, & Toronto Public Health. (2012). *Best practice guidelines for mental health promotion programs: Refugees.* Retrieved from https://knowledgex.camh.net/policy_health/mhpromotion/Documents/BPGRefugees.pdf

Centre for Suicide Prevention. (2013). FNMI [First Nations, Métis, and Inuit] suicide prevention resource toolkit. Calgary, AB: Author.

Collaborative for Academic, Social, and Emotional Learning [CASEL]. (2012). *2013 CASEL guide: Effective social and emotional learning programs—Preschool and elementary school edition.* Chicago, IL: Author. Retrieved from http://casel.org/

Dreikurs, R., Cassel, P., & Dreikurs Ferguson, E. (2004). *Discipline without tears: How to reduce conflict and establish cooperation in the classroom* (Rev. ed.). Toronto, ON: Wiley.

Durlak, J. A., & Weissberg, R. P. (2011). Promoting social and emotional development is an essential part of students' education. *Human Development, 54*(11), 1–3.

Elias, B., et al. (2012). Trauma and suicide behaviour histories among a Canadian indigenous population: An empirical exploration of the potential role of Canada's residential school system. *Social Science & Medicine, 74*(10), 1560–1569.

Evans, T. D. (2004). The tools of encouragement. *Cyc-Online, 65.* Retrieved from http://www.cyc-net.org/cyc-online/cycol-0604-evans.html

Hincks-Dellcrest Centre. (2014). *The ABCs of mental health.* Toronto, ON: Author. Retrieved from www.hincksdellcrest.org/ABC/Teacher-Resource/Mental-Health-for-All-Children-and-Youth.aspx

©P

Joint Consortium for School Health [JCSH]. (2010). *Schools as a setting for promoting positive mental health: Better practices and perspectives.* Retrieved from http://www.jcsh-cces.ca/upload/PMH%20July10%202011%20WebReady.pdf

Kirmayer, L., et al. (2007). *Suicide among Aboriginal people in Canada.* Ottawa, ON: Aboriginal Healing Foundation.

Kobus-Matthews, M., Agic, B., & Tate, M. (2012). *Culture counts: A roadmap to health promotion—A guide to best practices for developing health promotion initiatives in mental health and substance abuse with ethnocultural communities.* Toronto, ON: Centre for Addiction and Mental Health [CMHA].

Leach, Mark M. (2006). *Cultural diversity and suicide: Ethnic, religious, gender and sexual orientation perspectives.* New York, NY: Hawthorn Press.

Mental Health Commission of Canada. (n.d.). *Initiatives: Opening minds.* Retrieved from www.mentalhealthcommission.ca/English/initiatives-and-projects/opening-minds

Mental Health Commission of Canada. (n.d.). *The facts.* Retrieved from http://strategy.mentalhealthcommission.ca/the-facts/

Mental Health Commission of Canada. (2008). *Mental Health Commission of Canada Anti-Stigma/Anti-Discrimination Planning Session Summary of Discussions, December 1, 2008.* Retrieved from http://www.mentalhealthcommission.ca/sites/default/files/filefield_private_download/Stigma_Anti_Stigma_Planning_Session_ENG_0.pdf

Mental Health Commission of Canada. (2012a). *Changing directions, changing lives: The mental health strategy for Canada.* Retrieved from http://strategy.mentalhealthcommission.ca/pdf/strategy-text-en.pdf

Mental Health Commission of Canada. (2012b). *Together against stigma: Changing how we see mental illness. A report on the 5th International Stigma Conference.* Retrieved from www.mentalhealthcommission.ca/English/system/files/private/document/Stigma_Opening_Minds_Together_Against_Stigma_ENG.pdf

MHealthy—University of Michigan Health & Well-Being Services. (2012). *Understanding U: Managing the ups and downs of life—What is mental health?* Retrieved from http://hr.umich.edu/mhealthy/programs/mental_emotional/understandingu/learn/mental_health.html

Ontario Centre of Excellence for Child and Youth Mental Health. (n.d.). Mental health literacy by I. Manion, D. Papdopoulos, & K. Short [Presentation slides]. Retrieved from kidsmentalhealth.ca

Ontario Ministry of Education. (2013). *Supporting minds: An educator's guide to promoting students' mental health and well-being* [Draft version 2013]. Toronto, ON: Queen's Printer for Ontario.

Payton, J. et al. (2008). *The positive impact of social and emotional learning for kindergarten to eighth-grade students.* Chicago, IL: Collaborative for Academic, Social, and Emotional Learning [CASEL].

Pike, D. (2014). *The gift of positive space groups: A transformation for LGBTQ students.* Toronto, ON: Canadian Education Association.

Public Health Agency of Canada [PHAC]. (2006). *The human face of mental health and mental illness in Canada.* Ottawa, ON: Author.

School-Based Mental Health and Substance Abuse [SBMHSA] Consortium. (2012). School board decision support tool for mental health capacity building. Educator Mental Health Literacy Roundtable.

SBMHSA Consortium. (2013). *School-based mental health in Canada: A final report.* Retrieved from the Mental Health Commission of Canada: http://www.mentalhealthcommission.ca/English/system/files/private/document/ChildYouth_School_Based_Mental_Health_Canada_Final_Report_ENG.pdf

School Mental Health ASSIST. (2013). *Leading mentally healthy schools. A vision for student health and well-being in Ontario schools.* Toronto, ON: Author.

Stewart, S. L. (2008). Promoting indigenous mental health: Cultural perspectives on healing from Native counselors in Canada. *International Journal of Health Promotion and Education, 46*(2), 49–56. Retrieved from http://www.tandfonline.com/doi/abs/10.1080/14635240.2008.10708129#.U-jpg51zbcs

Student Support Leadership Initiative, Hamilton District Team. (2011). *Making a difference: An educators' guide to child and youth mental health problems* (4th ed.). [Developed for the Child and Youth Mental Health Information Network.]

Taylor, C., & Peter, T. (2011). *Every Class in Every School: Final Report on the First National Climate Survey on Homophobia, Biphobia, and Transphobia in Canadian Schools.* Toronto, ON: Egale Canada Human Rights Trust.

Weisz, J. R., Sandler, I. N., Durlak, J. A., & Anton, B. S. (2005). Promoting and protecting youth mental health through evidence-based prevention and treatment. [Review, 175 refs]. *American Psychologist, 60*(6), 628–648.

World Health Organization. (1996). Equity in health and health care: A WHO/SIDA initiative.

A Social–Emotional Learning Approach

"If children learn to express emotions constructively and engage in caring and respectful relationships before and while they are in the lower elementary grades, they are more likely to avoid depression, violence and other serious mental health problems as they grow older."

—LANTIERI, 2008, p. 16

Key Aspects of Social Emotional Learning

Children and youth can learn to

- identify and manage emotions
- set and pursue positive goals
- communicate caring and concern for others
- initiate and sustain positive relationships
- make decisions that demonstrate respect for self and others
- deal with interpersonal concerns and challenges effectively

Source: Joint Consortium for School Health (2010, p.8).

A social emotional learning approach developing self-awareness, self-management, social awareness, relationship skills, and responsible decision-making

Few of us could say that there was much focus on developing our social or emotional intelligence when we went to school. Traditionally, children were not always encouraged to reflect on their feelings and to pinpoint their source. More often, individuals were encouraged to put their feelings aside and focus on their work. "Being emotional" was seen as a weakness, clouding "objective" or rational thought. Unfortunately, many children learned to distrust their emotions. The focus on academic skill development, with minimal attention to social-emotional skill development, may have contributed to the increase in professional counsellors during the latter part of the 20th century as many adults struggled to recognize what they were feeling and to deal with their emotional and relationship issues.

Today, our fast-paced lives create stresses for children and youth that can negatively affect their well-being. We all catch ourselves going on automatic pilot and not reflecting on our feelings or on how our relationships are going. Childhood and adolescence are critical times for the development of social and emotional skills. Our emotions continue to develop through experience and reflection over the course of our lives. The ability to identify and understand what we are feeling, and share those feelings to create caring and eventually intimate relationships with others, is foundational to our well-being. Children and youth need rich opportunities at each grade level to learn more about emotions, to reflect on their own experiences, and to express emotions in oral communications, writing, art, and music.

"MOMMY, ARE YOU HAPPY OR SAD OR FWUSTWATED?"

"OH MY GOODNESS, WE DON'T EVEN KNOW WHAT WE ARE FEELING!"

Social Emotional Intelligence

Based on their work through the 1980s, Peter Salovey and John Mayer were the first researchers to put forward a definition of *emotional intelligence*. They stated that emotional intelligence

> involves the ability to monitor one's own and others' feelings and emotions, to discriminate among them, and to use this information to guide one's thinking and actions. (Salovey & Mayer, 1990, p. 189)

This definition did not deny cognitive thinking or intelligence; it integrated feeling, thinking, and behaviour and underlined the fundamental importance of emotions to thought and action. Our emotions and those of others need to be considered in our decisions, actions, and behaviour. In other words, we can use our emotions thoughtfully.

With the 1995 publication of his popular book *Emotional Intelligence*, Daniel Goleman played a key role in promoting emotional intelligence. Goleman (1998, p. 317) defined *emotional intelligence*, or EI, as "the capacity for recognizing our own feelings and those of others, for motivating ourselves, and for managing emotions well in ourselves and in our relationships." He emphasized awareness and management of emotions. He also recognized that, in addition to emotional self-awareness and self-management, there needed to be a level of social awareness and relationship management. He saw emotional intelligence and social intelligence as closely interwoven (Goleman, 2006).

Significantly, Goleman also believed that social emotional intelligence can and should be taught, and repeatedly practised. Recent research has supported the idea that students can learn how to use their emotions to make healthy decisions and to manage behaviour effectively (Durlak, Weissberg, Dymnicki, Taylor, & Schellinger, 2011; Durlak & Weissberg, 2011). The Collaborative for Academic, Social, and Emotional Learning, co-founded by Goleman, has become a major influence in advancing social emotional learning by promoting evidence-based approaches for children from the time they enter school to the end of high school. Recent research data has shown the effectiveness of systematic and comprehensive SEL programs in school communities in the United States (Collaborative for Academic, Social, and Emotional Learning [CASEL], 2012).

"The ingredients of social intelligence... can be organized into two broad categories: social awareness, what we sense about others—and social facility, what we then do with that awareness."

—Goleman, 2006, p. 84

Figure 3.1: Cognitive, Emotional, and Social Intelligence

Cognitive intelligence	Capacity to • reason • plan • solve problems • think abstractly • comprehend complex ideas • learn quickly • learn from experience Essentially, to make sense of things around us and figure out what to do.
Emotional intelligence	Capacity to • recognize our own emotions • recognize emotions in others • discriminate among emotions and their intensities • regulate emotions to motivate ourselves • manage emotions well in ourselves and in our relationships Essentially, to use understanding of emotions to guide thinking and behaviour for positive relationships and overall well-being.
Social intelligence	Capacity to • identify with what others are feeling and connect with them, that is, capacity for empathy • understand social and cultural norms (what emotions and behaviours are appropriate in particular social situations) • appreciate impact of emotions and behaviours on others • appreciate another person's perspective (how someone else views a situation) • cooperate with others • resolve conflicts Essentially, to effectively navigate and negotiate complex social relationships and environments.

The Core Competencies

The Collaborative for Academic, Social, and Emotional Learning describes five core social and emotional learning (SEL) competencies (CASEL, 2012). These competencies integrate cognitive, affective, social, cultural, behavioural, and **prosocial** aspects of development. They are based on the premise that children and youth can develop the skills that support positive mental well-being.

Prosocial behaviour is positive and intended to help others. It includes empathy and concern for the rights and welfare of others.

Collaborative for Academic, Social, and Emotional Learning (CASEL)

Self-awareness: The ability to accurately recognize one's emotions and thoughts and their influence on behaviour. This includes accurately assessing one's strengths and limitations and possessing a well-grounded sense of confidence and optimism.

Self-management: The ability to regulate one's emotions, thoughts, and behaviours effectively in different situations. This includes managing stress, controlling impulses, motivating oneself, and setting and working toward achieving personal and academic goals.

Social awareness: The ability to take the perspective of and empathize with others from diverse backgrounds and cultures, to understand social and ethical norms for behaviour, and to recognize family, school, and community resources and supports.

Relationship skills: The ability to establish and maintain healthy and rewarding relationships with diverse individuals and groups. This includes communicating clearly, listening actively, cooperating, resisting inappropriate social pressure, negotiating conflict constructively, and seeking and offering help when needed.

Responsible decision-making: The ability to make constructive and respectful choices about personal behaviour and social interactions based on consideration of ethical standards, safety concerns, social norms, the realistic evaluation of consequences of various actions, and the well-being of self and others.

Source: CASEL (2012, p. 9).

In this chapter, we will look at what underlies these SEL competencies and how they can be developed through focused strategies and approaches for the classroom. These strategies and approaches can complement what you are already doing in these areas and contribute to a more comprehensive and focused approach to social emotional learning and positive mental health.

It is important to note that the selection, training, and implementation of *particular* social emotional learning programs is best guided by a mental health professional and made at a school or district level to ensure alignment with the board direction.

SPOTLIGHT

SEL Resources for Elementary Schools

While social emotional learning refers to an overall approach to learning, there are also specific programs and curricula that have been developed to teach SEL skills and concepts. SEL programs have been developed primarily for elementary and middle school students. Programs such as MindUP, PATHS, Right from the Start, Second Step, Zippy's Friends, I'm Thumbody, and YODA are effective at helping students develop SEL skills while simultaneously teaching concepts related to positive mental health (Smith-Fowler & Lebel, 2013). The programs emphasize skills such as problem solving, identifying and communicating about emotions, managing stress, resolving conflict, enhancing self-esteem, and building self-confidence.

Other examples of SEL programs relevant to elementary students, with a specific focus on relationship skills, include the Fourth R program and Mary Gordon's Roots of Empathy (discussed later in the chapter). A positive youth development program focused on asset development is Lions Quest: Skills for Adolescence.

The Collaborative for Academic, Social, and Emotional Learning is an excellent source of information about the effectiveness of school-based SEL programs in the United States. In 2012, the Collaborative produced a comprehensive guide that provides a framework for evaluating the quality of SEL programs and rates a range of programs with potential for board implementation.

Social Emotional Learning in the Classroom

Let's look at how one teacher began to consider and integrate SEL strategies into his classroom.

A Classroom Scenario

Charley was really wound up from the first day she arrived in class. She crawled under desks, hid in the closet, said outrageous things, squealed with exaggerated delight, and literally jumped around. As Charley's new teacher, I wondered if Charley had eaten breakfast or had a good night's sleep. Her dad explained that the sleeping and eating routines were not a significant issue, and he was able to get Charley to eat some breakfast each morning before school. I was beginning to wonder whether we would need to make a referral for a psychological assessment to help us understand Charley's learning needs.

After talking further with Charley and her father, it became clear that Charley was really nervous about moving to a new school and that she was a high energy individual with a history of some frightening experiences. Charley's dad had provided information about Charley's allergies and medical conditions. I also learned that when Charley was younger, she had had several visits to hospital emergency wards and on more than one occasion, had experienced significant pain and trauma from the emergency procedures. Charley's dad warned me that it would be best to give Charley some space if she seemed scared or agitated. I could see that Charley was going to need our understanding and support. I felt she hadn't yet developed a vocabulary for expressing her feelings and probably wasn't completely aware of what she was feeling.

Charley also seemed determined to play the clown for the other students. On one occasion on the very first day, Charley showed everybody a surgical scar from years past and declared, "I am a freak." I knew that Charley wanted to be noticed, to fit in, and to belong, but she was going about it in a negative way and did not seem to know where to start to make friends.

Emotional Awareness

Charley's teacher saw how Charley could benefit from help in recognizing and understanding her emotions so that she could better manage her feelings and behaviour, and make more positive connections with others. In other words, Charley could start building self-awareness and social awareness.

As a first step, Charley could learn to become aware of her emotions and develop the vocabulary to talk about them. In *Calm, Alert, and Learning*, Stuart Shanker (2013) describes a wonderful story about a Grade 6 classroom teacher, Kyle, who was particularly interested in teaching his students about emotions. The strategies and activities Kyle used would be helpful not only for Charley, but for all students.

Kyle began by asking his students what they already knew about emotions and how they could read emotions in others. The responses were somewhat superficial. ("What is happiness?" he asked. "When you feel good" was a typical answer.) As a result, Kyle prompted further. He posed the question of whether animals have emotions. This question captured the students' curiosity, and they began searching through videos, blogs, and various websites.

Kyle then guided his students to think about where emotions come from, whether all humans have the same basic emotions, what they look like or how we express them, and why we sometimes try to hide emotions or think of them as negative. The students developed a list of common emotions and began to explore the facial expressions and body language associated with them. In one activity, Kyle asked the students to take pictures of their parents pretending to communicate various emotional states. In class, the students tried to identify the emotions in the pictures and noted the associated facial expressions and body language.

The class then drew a wheel of eight basic emotions—joy, trust, fear, surprise, sadness, disgust, anger, and anticipation—and arranged the emotion labels so that the emotions they felt were most closely connected appeared in close proximity. Students further developed their understanding and vocabulary of emotions by describing intensity gradations for each of the emotions (e.g., anger—annoyance, hostility, rage, fury). Kyle also introduced books and stories for students to read and review, allowing them to explore and discuss the emotions of the characters.

It is not difficult to see that activities like these could help Charley begin to identify and talk about her emotions. You can develop your own series of lessons for any particular grade level. I heard of one teacher experimenting with a game of charades involving the acting out of feelings, though always with sensitivity to the comfort level of the students and their vulnerabilities. Some strategies and ideas are summarized in the Strategy Focus box on page 64.

Understanding Emotions

Charley reacted to her feelings of stress and nervousness by acting out. Other children may freeze up or withdraw. As teachers we know that students can have quite different emotional reactions in any given situation. They also may not all feel anger or joy in the same way. A basic understanding of emotions can help us make sense of these differences.

Emotion can be defined as "a complex psychological state that involves three distinct components: a *subjective experience*, a *physiological response*, and a *behavioural* or *expressive response*" (Hockenbury & Hockenbury, 2007).

Researchers have developed a number of classification systems and lists for the various emotions. For example, Eckman (1999) concluded that there are 13 basic emotions common to human cultures:

fear	disgust	anger	surprise	happiness
sadness	amusement	excitement	contempt	
shame	satisfaction	embarrassment	pride	

If we think about it, all of these emotions involve a subjective experience, a physiological response, and a behavioural response.

Subjective Experiences

Our emotions are shaped over time through our unique experiences. We may all feel sadness, but our particular memories, past experiences, perceptions of the situation, and thoughts mean we may experience sadness differently. We also feel emotions at different levels, or gradations. I can be amused to the point of a gentle smile or to the point of rolling around on the floor in laughter. It is also true that we generally experience more than one emotion at a time. For example, you may feel both proud and excited to win a race.

The psychological experience of any one emotion can also be tricky for an individual to explain. It can take some time to reflect on the sensations of an emotional state and then find the right words to describe what you are feeling to someone else.

Physiological Responses

Having your face turn red with embarrassment, being teary-eyed with sadness, or experiencing your heart speed up with excitement are common examples of physiological responses involving emotions. These physiological responses are largely involuntary and are regulated by the autonomic nervous system along with the limbic system of the brain. They are also the physical cues that help us to recognize emotions in ourselves and others. Emotions can be brought to our mental awareness by the physiological and muscular sensations in our bodies.

In addition, particular events or situations may repeatedly bring up certain emotions for us, along with specific bodily responses. For example, Charley's repeated experiences in the emergency ward mean that she feels fear and tenses up every time she goes to the hospital. We "learn" or become **conditioned** to respond in particular ways emotionally and physiologically to certain events or situations. This is a key point because it means that once we recognize the **triggers** for our emotional responses, we can de-condition ourselves. We *can learn* to calm ourselves down when we feel too emotionally charged or motivate ourselves to be alert when needed, as we will see later in this chapter.

Behavioural Responses

Behavioural responses are what we do to communicate our emotions through our words or various forms of body language from facial expressions to the clenching of muscles. We laugh, cry, smile, clench our fists or jaws, say angry or joyous words. Behavioural responses are said to be under voluntary control, as opposed to physiological responses, which are more involuntary. (Nonetheless, the study of biofeedback has taught us that individuals can learn a fair degree of voluntary control over many physiological responses.)

Humans have a great capacity to observe behaviour patterns in others and to show **empathy** with the emotions being expressed. Sometimes, the communications of emotion are quite clear. But quite frequently we have to ask what another person is experiencing in order to understand. Cultural differences and social norms also play a role in how we express and interpret emotions. Sensitivity to, and understanding of, social and cultural diversity are part of the social awareness associated with social emotional learning.

The autonomic nervous system controls largely involuntary bodily responses such as blood flow and heart rate. Recent research using brain imaging has shown the role of the limbic system and amygdala in emotion as well.

Conditioning
a form of learning in which a given stimulus becomes increasingly effective at evoking a response

Trigger
a stimulus, such as a sight, sound, or smell, or other experience that sets off a psychological reaction, such as feelings of anxiety or reminders of trauma

Empathy
the capacity to share and understand the feelings of others, and to express concern for others

Body Maps of Emotions

"We often experience emotions directly in the body" (Nummenmaa, Glerean, Hari, & Hietanen, 2013, p. 646). Recent research published by Finnish scientists from Aalto University provides concrete evidence of how we experience emotions physiologically (Nummenmaa et al., 2013). These sensations are critical to our conscious emotional experiences.

In five experiments conducted online, the Finnish researchers had 700 participants colour-in silhouettes of bodies to depict sensations. The researchers induced various basic emotions, such as fear, happiness, and disgust, as well as non-basic emotions, such as shame, love, and contempt, using emotion-laden words, stories, movies, or facial expressions.

Participants coloured-in regions where they felt activity was increasing or decreasing in their own bodies, based on the materials they were viewing. Warm colours, such as red and yellow, indicated increased activity. Cool colours, such as blue and green, indicated decreasing activity. Scientists from biomedical engineering and computational science were able to compare the data from the 700 participants. Participants came from distinct cultures across Western Europe and Eastern Asia.

Results showed that sensations and their locations varied for the different emotions tested. The common emotions of anger, fear, disgust, happiness, sadness, anxiety, and love produced strong sensations. For example, love evoked a high density of warm sensations throughout most of the upper and mid-body regions, whereas surprise activated only a low density of warmth in the head and chest areas.

This research was especially significant in that the body maps of sensations were quite consistent across the different cultures. The results also clearly showed how emotions are registered in the body.

Body Map Research from Aalto University

Developing Emotional Awareness

There are several useful strategies and activities that can help students develop the skills to recognize, label, understand, and talk about emotions, as well as recognize emotions in others. These can be easily integrated with other aspects of the curriculum, such as language arts and physical and health education.

- **Build emotion-word vocabularies** by encouraging children to share how they label their feelings through using descriptive words found in stories and describing their feelings about art.

- **Construct emotion wheels** to explore relationships between, and gradations of, emotions.

- **Use pictures** to teach non-verbal cues and emotions in others.

- **Use stories/literature, movies, and films** that allow students to talk about the emotions of the characters.

- **Pose engaging questions** to pique students' curiosity. For example, ask: "Do animals have emotions? Do humans share common emotions?"

- **Personalize.** Allow students to explore personal emotional experiences by sharing stories, if they are comfortable, or keeping personal journals.

- **Engage in fun activities,** such as charades, drama, and role plays, that allow students to act out and explore emotional situations.

Self-Management, or Self-Regulation

Classroom Scenario

Let's return to Charley for a moment and consider how, with guidance and support, she can begin to manage or regulate her emotions.

One day in her first week, I found an inappropriate picture of me that Charley had hung up in the washroom. I took a deep breath and tried not to react angrily. Little Aisha whispered to me that she thought I was using good self-regulation skills to stay calm. Once they learn emotional self-regulation skills, children can become very astute at reading the teacher!

After a moment, I was able to reflect that Charley was a good artist, and if we were going to help her feel welcomed and develop a true sense of belonging, we might have to capitalize on Charley's talent for drawing. Blowing up at Charley would not have helped. Charley was able to apologize to me in private later. We had a respectful discussion on how I felt about the picture and the lack of respect it communicated. We also talked about the expectations for behaviour in the classroom to make sure that Charley understood what was appropriate and what was not.

My class at this point had jelled fairly well as a tight community of caring individuals. We started the day with a circle three times per week, and each child had the opportunity to share ideas and feelings with the others about current events, recent experiences, or stories about the lives of people from our books. We had a respectful atmosphere in these circles, where the students felt safe to share stories. We encouraged Charley to take part and share as she became more comfortable.

As it turned out, Charley was also an athletic child who could burn off a lot of energy during recesses. With minimal prompting, I was able to get some of the other students to engage Charley in noon-hour sports. Doing these eventually helped Charley calm down and focus better in the classroom. The structure of the games at noon hour also helped Charley to develop some social relationships with the other students and gain attention in more socially appropriate ways. The clowning antics gradually dissipated.

It took several weeks for Charley to learn how to down-regulate like the other students during quiet time right after recess. I was not surprised, as it had taken a number of other students several practice sessions earlier in the year to learn these transition skills. Our classroom has a video that models slower and deeper breathing routines to learn self-relaxation. The video also contains information about using imagery and mindfulness strategies. One of Charley's classmates offered to show Charley the video and work through it. Charley is fitting in quite well now. She even set a goal for herself to be able to "chill out" after recess and sit quietly for three minutes, using an egg timer to mark the time.

Developing Self-Regulation

Charley's teacher had come to understand that her hyperactivity and inappropriate behaviour were largely an expression of her anxiousness and confusion. But Charley was giving in to her nervousness—it was controlling her. She was just reacting. With an increased understanding of emotions, she was able to recognize that she was feeling nervous and that being nervous about attending a new school is natural and common.

With the teacher's guidance, Charley was also able to find appropriate outlets for her energy that took advantage of her strengths and that allowed her to relax, focus better in class, and develop more positive relationships. The caring classroom climate helped Charley realize that her classmates wanted to include her and support her. She didn't have to "be a freak" or act out to be noticed or included.

Charley had increased her self-awareness and her social awareness, and she had begun to learn to self-regulate, or manage, her emotions constructively. Stuart Shanker (2013) defines *self-regulation* in this way:

> the ability to manage your own energy states, emotions, behaviours and attention in ways that are socially acceptable and help to achieve positive goals, such as maintaining good relationships, learning and maintaining well-being.

Canadian Self-Regulation Initiative (CSRI)

Charley's ability to regulate her emotions led to stronger and more positive relationships. It was all a work-in-progress that would take time, practice, and reinforcement inside and outside the classroom, but the results were encouraging. If Charley had become stuck in her distress and not received positive encouragement, modelling, and support, the likelihood of her developing mental health issues would be greatly increased.

Models of Self-Regulation

Stuart Shanker (2013) and Leah Kuypers (2011) have developed models of self-regulation to support optimal classroom learning. Although their books focus primarily on strategies for classroom learning, they emphasize that self-regulation clearly applies beyond the classroom, includes social development, and ties directly to well-being. Research shows that engagement in meaningful learning is an important factor in positive mental health. Children and youth who can self-regulate for optimal learning are promoting their well-being.

The Five-Domain Model of Self-Regulation

Consistent with social emotional learning, Stuart Shanker has created **a five-domain model** for understanding and teaching optimal self-regulation. The five domains, which are essentially integrated, are listed below:

1. The biological domain

2. The emotional domain

3. The cognitive domain

4. The social domain

5. The prosocial domain

In Shanker's system, the ability to intentionally adjust emotional arousal states is a foundational skill. Shanker (2013) also notes that "emotion regulation is as much about up-regulating positive emotions, as it is about down-regulating negative ones." He outlines six critical elements for optimal self-regulation:

- when feeling calmly focused and alert, the ability to know that one is calm and alert
- when one is stressed, the ability to recognize what is causing that stress
- the ability to recognize stressors both within and outside the classroom
- the desire to deal with those stressors
- the ability to develop strategies for dealing with those stressors
- the ability to recover efficiently and effectively from dealing with stressors

—SHANKER, 2013, p. xiii

When students are able to apply these elements across all the domains, they enhance their physical, emotional, cognitive, and social well-being. Teaching students how to self-regulate is teaching them to understand that they can optimize their energy levels, emotions, and focus to make learning more meaningful and successful, to create more positive relationships, and to enrich their lives beyond the classroom.

In his book, *Calm, Alert, and Learning*, Shanker provides classroom strategies for self-regulation in each domain. The domains, self-regulation skills, and strategies are summarized in Figure 3.2.

Essentially, the steps for self-regulation involve reading the signs of stress or over-arousal, identifying the stressors, reducing those stressors, developing self-awareness of signs and stressors, and developing self-regulation strategies to avoid and lessen stress in future situations.

Figure 3.2: Shanker's Five Domains of Self-Regulation

Domain	What Regulation Looks Like in This Domain	What Teachers Can Do
Biological Energy activation levels in body which vary person to person based on temperament and situational factors	Ability to • maintain energy • stay calm • recoup energy • develop healthy routines and physical activity • adjust arousal states or energy levels to deal appropriately with tasks at hand	Reduce distractions and promote focus with adjustments to • the visual environment (e.g., natural light, reduced visual clutter) • the auditory environment (e.g., soothing sounds versus jarring bells) • classroom seating (e.g., disc cushions) • classroom activities (e.g., movement breaks)
Emotional Feelings and moods	Ability to • name emotional states in self and others • up-regulate positive emotions and down-regulate negative emotions as needed • bounce back from disappointments and other emotional challenges	• Encourage positive emotions such as curiosity, fun, and trust. • Develop students' self-awareness about emotions and emotional regulation. • Help students express emotions verbally so they are less likely to act out physically. • Model self-regulation in the classroom and throughout the day. • Build self-esteem based on awareness of personal efforts and achievements.

Domain	What Regulation Looks Like in This Domain	What Teachers Can Do
Cognitive Attention, information processing and retention, executive functioning, problem solving	Ability to • focus and switch focus as required • set goals and plan • execute steps in a logical sequence • understand personal strengths and challenges	• Encourage and practise metacognition. • Support cognitive self-regulation to help students find strategies to keep their focus (e.g., avoid distractions, go to a quiet place as needed). • Build executive functioning skills through problem solving, time management, realistic goal-setting, and so forth.
Social Connections and interactions with others	Ability to • understand their own and others' feelings and intentions • respond to others appropriately • monitor the effects of their behaviour on others • recover from and repair breakdowns in interactions with others	• Provide opportunities for collaborative learning. • Support co-regulation (students understanding one another and adjusting behaviour to help each other). • Allow students to select activities and set their own goals—autonomy promotes social self-regulation.
Prosocial Behaviour and actions to benefit others	Ability to • empathize with others • put needs and interests of others ahead of their own • want to do the right thing • be honest with themselves and others	• Promote understanding and development of empathy (e.g., Roots of Empathy program, literature, movies, anti-bullying programs). • Encourage seeing others' perspectives and engaging in altruistic behaviour, such as volunteer work and social activism.

The Zones of Regulation Model

Kuypers' Zones of Regulation model provides a practical approach to up-regulating and down-regulating that is based in cognitive behaviour theory and practices. The goal is to help students become more aware of and able to control their emotions and impulses, manage their sensory needs, and resolve conflicts.

In her book *Zones of Regulation*, Kuypers (2011) groups various emotional states into four categories along a continuum of arousal from blue (low arousal—sad, tired, laid-back, bored, sick), to green (optimal arousal for learning—happy, focused) to yellow (heightened arousal—excited, stressed, frustrated, anxious) to red (extreme arousal—furious, elated, devastated, terrified). There are no "bad" zones. Students come to understand that they will experience the emotions in each zone, but each zone is specifically suited for certain situations (e.g., yellow is fine for the soccer game but not in the library). The Zones of Regulation lessons teach students how they feel in each zone and how these zones influence their behaviour and that of others around them. Kuypers' model incorporates social thinking and awareness.

Students are encouraged to develop self-responsibility and do what works for them to get into the green zone for optimal learning. They learn about triggers—events that might bring on feelings such as worry, frustration, or anger—and how triggers can move them out of green and into yellow, or even red. Through experimentation and record keeping, students determine what alerting or calming strategies and tools are personally useful for moving up or down to green.

The approaches of both Shanker and Kuypers can easily be integrated throughout the curriculum. In mathematics, children might expand their facility with line and bar graphs, time, and pattern recognition by plotting their emotional regulation. In language arts, they can identify and increase feeling word vocabulary and develop their social thinking. For writing, they can apply their expanding knowledge of feelings and emotions to charting and journalling. Oral discussions about emotions and regulation can promote skill development in speaking and listening. Self-awareness and social awareness also contribute to character development and values education (e.g., truth, compassion, justice, hope, and love).

A Classroom Scenario

Now let's return to Charley's class once more and consider the self-regulation tools and strategies teachers could integrate into the classroom.

In our class, the students had done experiments to figure out what works for them to manage different feelings and different energy levels. For example, some students use fidget toys to up-regulate when they feel sleepy. Some use fidget toys to down-regulate when they feel antsy and unable to sit still. Students have agreed to be respectful of each other's space and try not to allow their tools to disrupt one another.

Each student has developed a personalized "toolkit" of strategies for up-regulating or down-regulating to maintain an optimal level of alertness during class time. The list of toolkit strategies is written on a card that is kept in a little box in each child's desk. The toolkit also contains such things as earplugs, doodle pads, and fidget toys. Basically, anything with texture, weight, and malleability that can be manipulated works. The students love bean bags, nuts and bolts from the hardware store, weighted balls, bowls of dry rice, Koosh balls, Theraputty, and twistable puzzles.

We keep an exercise mat at the back of the class for students to do stretching when they need an activity break. Some students are permitted to listen to background music through their earbuds while they do independent work, if this has proven useful. We have a rocking chair in a corner of the room, and we also have a desk carrel (set apart) where students can pull away and concentrate for independent work.

All of the students in my class keep a log of their activity levels, to ensure that they engage in aerobic activity at least 60 minutes per day. This initiative was developed with the participation of the parent community and the local health unit. The students have a long list of activity alternatives. Some students accomplish their activity goals after school. Some accomplish them during our recesses and noon hour.

In addition to instruction, encouragement, and modelling, Charley's teacher has provided his students with a wide variety of concrete tools and strategies to help them self-regulate. He has also arranged the classroom environment so that there are spaces for both activity and quiet independent work. With a wide range of choices and the freedom to experiment, the students are able to make their own decisions about what works best for them and keep personalized toolkits. Not every classroom can or needs to include all of these tools and strategies, but there are many ideas here from which to choose.

In a well-regulated classroom, students are mindful of their emotions, understand the emotion–learning connection and the importance of activity and self-care, and work together to create a climate of respect for each individual's space and differences. They develop the self-confidence to manage their own well-being and show caring for others. Parents and the local community are also involved in initiatives that support students' positive development.

Classroom management can seem a daunting task when we imagine our students as all having specific and conflicting needs or issues. When we recognize that students can learn to regulate themselves, consider student strengths rather than needs alone, begin with an attitude of flexibility, and work with students to make decisions about our classrooms, a caring, inclusive classroom is a more attainable goal. There will be bumps on the road, but a persistent approach has proven results.

Simple Ideas for Using the Senses to Up-Regulate or Down-Regulate

We all use our senses to up-regulate or down-regulate our arousal levels—even if we are not always aware of it. We may doodle, twiddle our hair, tap our pencil, or sip warm beverages. When students have difficulty regulating sensory input in their environments, they can easily become distracted. There are several concrete and non-disruptive strategies and sensory tools that can help them stimulate or calm their nervous systems.

Many of these strategies and tools are safe, quiet, and inexpensive, and fit easily into the classroom environment. Different students will have different sensory needs and challenges. Teachers can help students become aware of their needs and how their needs may vary based on how they are feeling and the situational demands. Needs may differ at different times of the day, for example, as a child fatigues over time. Students can experiment to learn what textures and sensations they prefer and work best for them.

	Strategies	Tools and Fidget Toys
Motor/ Tactile	deep breathing	stress ball
	gum chewing	smooth stones
	doodling	worry beads or worry dolls
	ribbon twiddling	playdough or Silly Putty
	inconspicuous stretching	rubber bands
	isometric pushing (e.g., pushing against a wall)	rice in bowl
	pantomime high grape-picking	bean bag
	sit-ups, push-ups, jumping jacks	floor mat
	muscle massage	Hacky Sacks or footbags
	washroom break	mini trampoline
	errand running	nuts and bolts
	wiggle dance	twistable puzzles
	hair combing	Koosh balls
	pencil sharpening	heat packs
	walking, running, reclining	bubble wrap

	Strategies	Tools
Auditory	music mnemonics self-talk or whispers info-songs (e.g., ABCs)	earbuds ear phones sound field system earplugs
Visual	reading relaxing imagery personally selected goldfish watching picture meditation or contemplation slow ocean-wave breathing doodling	flashlight sand timer soft light wide band lighting light stick

Self-Regulation and Patterns of Stress

Knowing how we feel, understanding the source, reasoning with these emotions, and being able to do something about problematic outcomes is especially important when we consider stress.

Children and youth face a wide variety of stressors every day. Some are common everyday stresses. Others stem from temperament, situational factors, family circumstances, crises, or trauma. Others are related to developmental factors. Research demonstrates that children and youth can learn to recognize the signs of stress in their bodies, identify the situations that trigger the stress, and learn strategies to help them relax and find balance. They will understand that it is not always possible to identify their feelings, but with strategies and tools they can develop the self-confidence to deal with their difficult feelings.

Developmental Stress Factors

- Children who are 8 to 11 years old are at a stage where they generally want to please so they may be more sensitive to criticism, more fearful of new situations and tasks, and more likely to have performance anxiety.

- Adolescents, 12 years and up, are on a roller coaster with their emotions and with change in many aspects of their lives. They generally have a strong need for physical release and need guidance to take time for self-reflection so that they can define their own sense of purpose or identity. They face pressures for conformity that can lead to risky behaviours at a time when they may not yet fully understand the consequences.

- At the same time, these children are at stages of life that offer opportunities, anticipation, and a sense of possibility not often seen again. These opportunities can also create a degree of stress and require self-regulation to take advantage of and fully realize them.

Essentially, stress is the body's alarm response to any situation that we perceive as overwhelming or threatening. Stress causes a specific set of physiological reactions in the body—our heart rate increases, blood is distributed to our large muscles, our pupils dilate, and digestion shuts down. As we know, stress is a double-edged sword: "good stress" allows us to be alert and ready to face challenges, but under "bad stress," we feel overwhelmed and shut down. Learning how to relax and regulating for balance is key.

My years of research and practice using biofeedback equipment taught me a great deal about the physiological stress patterns of children and adults, their varying states of body activation or arousal, and effective strategies for relaxation and balance.

The following checklist can be used with students to help them identify how they experience stress. To see the overlap of symptoms of stress experienced by both adults and children and youth, see Chapter 6, page 194.

Figure 3.3: Sample Stress Checklist

When I feel stressed,

Cognitive/Thinking Symptoms

- ❏ I have trouble remembering.
- ❏ I have trouble finishing homework.
- ❏ I worry a lot.
- ❏ I don't feel confident.
- ❏ It's hard for me to stay organized.

Physical Symptoms

- ❏ I get sick more easily.
- ❏ My heart beats fast.
- ❏ My hands sweat (or they get cold).
- ❏ My feet sweat (or they get cold).
- ❏ My stomach feels like I have butterflies.
- ❏ I feel sick to my stomach.
- ❏ I get headaches.
- ❏ My muscles feel tense.
- ❏ It's hard to sleep (or I sleep too much).

Emotional Symptoms

- ❏ I feel sad.
- ❏ I feel mad.
- ❏ I get silly.
- ❏ My mood changes quickly.
- ❏ Things bother me.

Behavioural Symptoms

- ❏ I bite my nails.
- ❏ I grind my teeth.
- ❏ I can't sit still.
- ❏ I don't like to be around people.

Sources: Centre for Addiction and Mental Health [CAMH] (2010), Lantieri (2008, p. 104), Smith, Segal, & Segal (2014).

Chronic Stress or Hyper-Arousal

Some individuals are hyper-aroused most, if not all, of the day—not unlike Charley. In some cases, they have fitful sleeping patterns, feel tension and fatigue when they wake up in the mornings, are jittery and shaky most of the time, experience indigestion, and feel cranky and humourless. When we are constantly alarmed, our nervous systems do not have time to recover and we can experience burnout from chronic stress. With the advent of cellphones and the internet, some children and adults never really wind down and are not aware of how constantly wound up they are.

The Stress Roller Coaster

Other individuals who become stressed are able to "blow it off" at the end of the school or work day. They get a good night's sleep, wake up fairly rested, and have things to look forward to in their days. But they may then struggle to keep up with the demands of their day and feel anxious and overwhelmed. They may skip breaks and take energy drinks to keep going. At the end of the day, they may be inclined to lie down or take alcohol to calm themselves. These individuals are at risk for poor health or burnout if they do not punctuate their days with relaxation, or get adequate rest, exercise, nutrition, and meaningful social contact.

There are many other stress patterns depending on the activities of the day and how people get tasks done while managing their energy levels. People who develop stress problems also often develop bracing habits, such as clenching their jaw or gripping hard on their pencil while sitting in class. Adults may grip the steering wheel tight while sitting at a red light. Bracing patterns can cause muscle fatigue pain associated with such afflictions as tension headaches and back pain. These bracing patterns under stress often start in childhood.

Achieving a Healthy Balance

Awareness and relaxation strategies can help individuals achieve balance. Studies show that it often takes four to six weeks of daily relaxation practice for people to develop deep relaxation skills. The goal is not to stay in a deeply relaxed mode throughout the day. It is to learn to produce deep relaxation efficiently and reliably, so that children and youth are in a better position to stay balanced. They need to be able to get excited, concerned, or upset as need be, but then get back to a desired level of relaxation or alertness again, for whatever the task at hand.

The Strategy Focus box on page 80 outlines some key strategies and tools shown to be effective in helping children and youth learn relaxation skills. Once they come to recognize the signs of stress in their bodies, they can apply the strategies that work best for them. Parents can play a key role by helping their children apply the strategies at home and by modelling techniques that work for them.

S P O T L I G H T

Stress, Biofeedback, and Behavioural Change

Biofeedback can be a useful tool for raising awareness of stress and prompting behavioural change. Studies I conducted with adult migraine sufferers provide evidence-based research relevant for children and youth.

Often, adult volunteers in the study initially lacked the skills to assess their levels of physiological stress accurately. Many recorded high levels of muscle tension in the forehead, and they could not let this go in order to relax. They had become used to a chronic state of muscle tension. We attached biofeedback sensors on their foreheads (to measure muscle tension in the head), fingers (to detect minute moisture changes), and hands (to measure hand temperature related to shunting of blood common with migraines). They were then given a stressor (subtracting 7s from 1000—very stressful!). Muscle tension spiked, and hands became clammy and cold to varying degrees.

At first, many subjects struggled to recover from the stress. We taught them to relax deeply, using techniques such as deep breathing exercises, tensing up and then releasing tension in various muscle groups, use of relaxation imagery, hypnotic self-talk, and mindfulness strategies. In between the treatment sessions, they continued to practise relaxation on their own and to monitor their headaches. The biofeedback allowed them to track their success in self-regulating their stress. They became acutely aware of stressors in their lives and more aware of their patterns of headache and various stress triggers. Many responded by making lifestyle changes, which included taking up exercise routines, practising meditation, confronting relationship issues, and even making career changes. They became more proactive in supporting their positive mental health.

Biodots with Children

Biofeedback research has been used as a basis for an inexpensive stress monitoring tool for children and youth, as well. **Biodots** are small biofeedback sensors that measure temperature changes in the hands. Blood flow to our hands and feet (our extremities) is reduced when we are stressed. The biodots are placed on the web of the hand between the thumb and forefinger and change colour according to skin temperature. A biodot colour chart helps children assess and monitor their stress levels. As they practise strategies to relax or calm down, the colour changes in the biodot give them immediate feedback on their success. Biodots may be a useful strategy to help children focus on body cues for stress and relaxation (Lantieri, 2008).

Strategies for Balance and Well-Being

There are several strategies and activities that support relaxation and stress relief with children and youth. The ideas here represent just a few.

- **Practise deep breathing exercises.** Have students focus on breathing from the abdomen rather than in the chest. Lying on the floor with a stuffed toy or other soft object on the abdomen can help children practise deep breathing by making the object go up and down as they breathe. They can then take a few deep breaths when they feel stressed to trigger relaxation and calm.

- **Take regular stretch breaks.** Students will be better able to release tension from their bodies and focus their minds. Classrooms can include mats or areas for stretch breaks.

- **Practise progressive muscle relaxation.** Actions encompass tensing up and then releasing tension in various muscle groups. For example, start by clenching each fist, holding, and then letting go; then move on to the neck and shoulders, head and face, chest, belly, legs and feet, and finally the whole body.

- **Practise body scans.** Doing so allows students to become aware of how they feel in each part of their bodies, noticing stress in any part of the body, picking up on bracing habits in jaws or hands, and releasing the tension. Start with the toes and move through the body—eyes closed to concentrate.

- **Use relaxation imagery or music.** What induces calm may be individual to each child. Encourage them to imagine the scene or listen to the music that helps them relax and refocus.

- **Establish "Peace Corners."** Students can go to these or other quiet places in the classroom for some moments of silence and stillness to get in touch with how they are feeling and self-regulate.

- **Encourage positive self-talk and journalling.** Doing so will help children name and express their feelings, recognize that these feelings are not permanent, and understand that they can work through difficult emotions and find calm.

- **Introduce body movement breaks.** Lead movements such as yoga or tai chi if appropriate in the classroom.

Community Connection

Engaging Parents in Social Emotional Learning

Engaging parents in their children's social emotional learning helps to ensure that learning is practised and reinforced in both the home and school environments. To help parents, teachers can share what they are doing in the classroom and suggest the following for at home.

Take time out for stillness and reflection. In our fast-paced lives, we often don't take time to stop, reflect, and share feelings to deepen relationships. Build quiet shared time into daily routines.

Be a co-learner and guide. Parents do not need to be the authority; they can learn along with their children as they share quiet reflective time together. Ask open-ended questions, such as "What stood out for you in today's time together?" Taking that approach rather than saying something like "Tell me all the things we did together in our quiet time" will support deeper sharing (Lantieri, 2008).

Give a time-in rather than a time-out. Provide the child with a quiet corner or space at home where he or she can go when feeling stressed, angry, or overwhelmed. The corner can include music, pictures, sounds, pillows—whatever helps the child to self-regulate and feel calm.

Help your child check into body cues. Before children can release stress, they need to recognize that they are stressed. Remind your child to check into body responses, and model body scanning for your own physiological signs of stress.

Teach, model, and share relaxation practices. There are many simple and effective relaxation practices from the classroom that parents and children can also do at home. These range from deep breathing to playing calming music, to doing yoga, nature hikes, or other physical activities together.

Sourced from: Lantieri (2008).

Social and Relationship Skills

As children grow older, they become more capable of cooperating with other children for mutual benefit, as opposed to depending on the egocentric approach we all start out with as infants: "I want and I get, or I cry." Children develop an increased capacity for self-regulation, which is based on executive function skills. *Executive function skills* may be described as the conscious control of what we think and do. These skills play an important part in successful social interaction. To be successful socially, a child needs to determine personal wants and needs, as well as appreciate the wants and needs of others. With this perspective, a child can size up a social situation, anticipate a mutually beneficial goal, create a plan, and then execute it. In other words, the child can self-regulate using executive function skills to plan and execute activities with others in a friendly fashion—for positive interactions and relationships. Philip Zelazo (2014) describes executive function skills as foundational for the development of empathy and empathetic behaviour toward others.

Communication and conflict resolution skills are equally critical for successful social interactions and relationships. Some disagreements that occur in the classroom require teacher intervention, but many can be resolved among the children themselves if they are encouraged to be responsible for working out their conflicts and develop the necessary skills. They can be encouraged to define what a positive and peaceful social environment or classroom community is, and participate in setting rules to maintain it. They can understand the value of communicating clearly, finding compromise, doing what is just or right, and the natural consequences of actions. Children and youth can become peacekeepers or peer mediators, helping each other to resolve social disputes and keep a harmonious classroom. The Strategy Focus box on pages 83–84 provides some practical suggestions for skill development in the classroom.

Social and Relationship Skill Development

Strategies for social and relationship skill development include the following:

Practise active and reflective listening. Students learn to validate feelings by reflecting back what others have expressed and by demonstrating empathy. Rather than saying "Don't be scared," they could say something like "It sounds like you're feeling scared. Is that right? I might feel the same way if that happened to me." Once clear understanding is established, they can move on to problem solving.

Encourage classroom meetings founded on student participation. Students can take an active role in establishing classroom rules, routines, and values. Meetings can also focus on problem solving and brainstorming, and collaborating for class projects or activities.

Use circles. Circles can encourage sharing, mutual support, respect of others' views and opinions, and problem solving (see Chapter 2, pages 47–48, for more on circles). Restorative justice circles can be especially effective for classroom conflict or discipline issues (see pages 87–89 in this chapter).

Try diversity panels. These are made up of students who make classroom presentations to trigger discussion of how the school can ensure respect for all.

Set up a "Peace Table." Children can go there to resolve a problem by talking to each other. The special place removes the children from the conflict situation and lets them work through the problem in a different environment.

Practise I-messages for conflict resolution. "I feel…I want…I will…." People involved each take ownership of a part in the conflict by stating their feelings under the circumstances. They then state what they want to happen and what they will do differently. Statements begin with *I* rather than *You* to reduce the likelihood of blaming and to focus instead on self-expression and problem solving. For example, a student might say: "I feel angry when I am told what to do. I want to have a choice. I will ask what my choices are to stay calm."

Practise win-win role plays. Students role-play and analyze conflict scenarios, and discuss as many win-win solutions as possible, taking into account the situation, the consequences, and all people involved.

Train peace helpers/peer mediators. Some schools participate in programs where selected students learn basic SEL skills and a step-by-step mediation process. The students then serve their schools by mediating disputes among their peers, working in teams of two, with adult support.

Use stories or literature to discuss and analyze conflicts and solutions. Most stories develop around a conflict, between characters or between parts of the self. Consider what started the conflict, who was involved, what happened, how it ended, and how each character felt in the end.

Responsible Decision-Making

Self-Regulating versus Self-Medicating

The importance of social emotional skills and positive mental health promotion becomes strikingly clear when we consider the issue of substance abuse among youth. Substance abuse often begins in adolescence. A report for the Centre for Addiction and Mental Health (Paglia-Boak, Adlaf, & Mann, 2011) found increasing drug use during the transition from Grade 7 to 8, and again from Grade 8 to 9. The intermediate years and the transition from elementary to secondary are important times for teaching about specific and common street drugs, and drugs accessible in family medicine cabinets. Many youth believe that prescribed medications are not harmful. After all, they are prescribed! Data collected by the Centre for Addiction and Mental Health suggest that students do benefit from straight facts about the harmful effects of substances as part of physical and mental health promotion (Paglia-Boak et al., 2011).

The CAMH study of Ontario students also showed a relationship between alcohol and drug abuse and mental health problems. Students with emotional difficulties are at greater risk of turning to alcohol or other drugs to relieve painful emotions. About 9 percent of the Grades 7 to 12 student sample reported both harmful drinking and elevated psychological distress (symptoms of anxiety and depression). This figure increased to 16 percent by Grade 12. The likelihood of drug use with mental distress increases as students go up the grades (Paglia-Boak et al., 2011).

High levels of stress are a clear factor in substance use. Teens who are feeling stressed and are unable to self-regulate their emotions are more likely to use a substance for relief from anxiety or low mood. They may also be more motivated to take the drug again for short-term relief. Social pressure and a desire to fit in are also factors.

Responsible decision-making about substances may take a combination of assertive skill, drug knowledge, positive life goals, and confidence to turn down drugs offered by a popular peer. A sizeable percentage of youth are propositioned with drugs. Youth will also be more vulnerable to continued substance use when they lack skills to effectively understand and regulate their emotions.

Self-Regulating versus Eating for Regulation

Promoting healthy eating aims to counter the issues of obesity, binge eating, poor nutrition, a reliance on junk food, obsession with body image or weight, and excessive exercise to keep slim. Children and youth need the knowledge, social awareness, and self-regulation skills to make responsible decisions.

Based on World Health Organization classification, nearly a third of 5- to 17-year-old Canadians are estimated to be overweight or obese. Between the late 1970s and the turn of the 21st century, the prevalence of excess weight and obesity rose among children and adolescents in Canada. Recent research has indicated that this prevalence has plateaued during the last decade, but it continues to be a public health concern given the tendency to persist into adulthood with negative health outcomes (Roberts, Shields, de Groh, Aziz, & Gilbert, 2012). Clear links have been made between excessive weight in childhood and ill health involving insulin resistance, type 2 diabetes, hypertension, emotional problems, and poor social well-being.

A variety of factors contribute to obesity, including lack of exercise, excessive sedentary behaviour, lack of nutritional knowledge, food marketing, and easy availability of over-processed foods with high caloric content. The factors implicated in obesity and overweight

Obesity is not a mental health disorder though it does have emotional connections for some.

for children and youth are complex (see Roberts et al., 2012). For some, food can become a way of soothing emotional discomfort. Eating to regulate emotions can become a negative game of approach-avoidance, or not eating to avoid weight gain, which can lead to cravings for fatty foods and impulsive binge eating, followed by feelings of guilt and purging. Emotional self-regulation is often needed to support behavioural self-regulation and responsible decision-making.

Author and therapist Karen Koenig (2005) has developed a popular cognitive behavioural approach that promotes guidelines for normal eating. These include eating when hungry or experiencing a craving, selecting satisfying foods, maintaining awareness and focus on eating behaviour to promote enjoyment, and stopping when full or satisfied. Taking this approach reduces a preoccupation with "good" and "bad" foods, increases more relaxed social eating, and ends cycles of fasting and binging.

Koenig's approach is impressive in that it teaches individuals to stop and reflect on their emotions when they experience a craving. The goal is to help them handle difficult emotions such as shame, guilt, anxiety, helplessness, and loneliness rather than holding them inside, and then to focus on normal eating guidelines.

Comprehensive Strategies and Approaches

Two other comprehensive approaches that can be applied in the classroom include the Roots of Empathy program and restorative justice practices.

Roots of Empathy

Roots of Empathy is an inclusive program for K to 8 classes pioneered and developed by teacher Mary Gordon. The program is designed to help students develop and understand empathy, and build a culture of caring within schools and classrooms.

Through the program, a parent from the school community visits classrooms with an infant once a month over the school year. The infant is typically two to four months old. The children observe the infant's expressions of emotion—crying, cooing, smiling, and wriggling. They talk about what they think the infant is feeling, share their own feelings, and offer suggestions for soothing the infant when the baby is upset, for example. They also see how the parent cares for the infant, responding and connecting. The instructor, teacher, and parent help students learn about their own emotions and deepen their understanding of empathy as they observe the infant and his or her interactions. The classroom teacher continues to refer back to the experiences, prompting students to apply the social emotional skills they have learned throughout the school day.

Roots of Empathy is most often delivered in a school system through a partnership with parents, service agencies, school staff, and board consultants. The program provides detailed training to a facilitator/instructor, a curriculum for different grade levels, specific materials, health and safety routines, and monitoring to ensure consistency of application. Between 1996 and 2014, more than 600 000 children participated in the Roots of Empathy program on three continents, including more than 540 000 students in Canada. Research by Santos, Chartier, Whalen, Chateau, and Boyd (2011) suggests that the program results in effective and enduring outcomes. The research base of the program and the care taken to deliver it effectively within the curriculum in partnership with the teacher and parent make it a model program for positive mental health promotion.

Roots of Empathy

Restorative Justice Circles

School systems in North America and elsewhere originally modelled their discipline practices after the restitution-by-punishment principles of the penal system: big on protection mentality and small on the psychology of learning or community development. Students who got caught up in school discipline systems were often made to feel like they did not belong in the school community. Ironically, this put many at risk for behaviours that led directly back into involvement with the law and the penal system.

An alternative to this punitive approach, and one that can help to develop students' social and emotional learning skills, is restorative justice. Restorative justice practices have been used by First Nations in Canada and other Indigenous peoples (such as the Maori of New Zealand) for thousands of years (see Lockhart & Zammit, 2005). Through restorative justice practices, small communities of people resolve conflicts and offences by sitting in a circle to sort out what happened, how people were affected, and what should be done to repair the harm.

Restorative justice circles have been used in the military and some criminal justice cases since the 1970s. They are now being used in school classrooms and systems of care to build a sense of community and create norms of behaviour for getting along together effectively (Costello, Wachtel, & Wachtel, 2010).

Several high schools and elementary schools have made major strides in changing the social and disciplinary culture of their school using a whole-school restorative justice approach and deepening the practice one classroom at a time. These results have also been seen in several North American schools where administrations reported high rates of violence and suspension. School climate improvement information, published by the International Institute for Restorative Practices (IIRP), shows impressive results.

International Institute for Restorative Practices Canada (IIRP Canada)

S P O T L I G H T

Restorative Justice in Action: Kawartha Pine Ridge

The Kawartha Pine Ridge School Board in Ontario may have been the first board in North America to systematically institute a restorative justice practices framework across its 95 schools. One outcome was that total suspension days dropped in elementary and in secondary schools by more than 50 percent over just two years. According to IIRP director Bruce Schenk:

> "What we are doing here in the Kawartha Pine Ridge District School Board is cutting-edge and setting a trend in the manner that inappropriate behaviour is handled. This is achieved in a manner that facilitates repair of harm (victims, schools, others), builds empathy, promotes student accountability, responsibility and reintegration, and sees misbehaviour as an opportunity for learning, not punishment. Probably one of the greatest impacts of this initiative is when teachers and students utilize this approach in the classroom. Not only do many fewer issues come to the office, but the classroom environment is healthier and students are more productive."

Source: Schenk (2008, pp. 8, 10).

©P

When a circle is used to deal with a classroom conflict or discipline issue, each student involved is given a chance to talk while the others listen. Conflicts are usually dealt with in small subgroups rather than with the whole class. The circles focus on a sequence of questions:

- What happened?

- What were you thinking at the time?

- How did that make you feel?

- Who else is affected by your actions?

After everyone has had a chance to talk, the teacher asks each individual these questions:

- What do you want to do about this situation?

- How will you fix it?

The use of restorative justice circles for conflict resolution is becoming more common as a key part of progressive discipline procedures in school systems (see, for example, a 2010 Ontario Ministry of Education publication, *Caring and Safe Schools in Ontario*, page 36). They are also an excellent way to promote social emotional skills and the caring, inclusive environment that promotes positive mental health.

Checklist for a Mentally Healthy Classroom

√ Students are encouraged to become aware of their emotions, share as appropriate in a safe and caring environment such as circles, and recognize how their emotions affect others.

√ Teachers provide explicit teaching of SEL skills across the curriculum, including self-awareness of emotions, strategies to up-regulate and down-regulate, listening and reflecting back to others, verbalizing appreciations, and conflict resolution strategies.

√ Students understand how self-regulation, positive relationship building, and other social emotional skills support their overall mental well-being.

√ Many tools are available to up-regulate and down-regulate, and the classroom is arranged to allow students different ways to self-regulate. Students agree to respect each individual's space and differences.

√ Students take responsibility for their own social emotional management by up-regulating and down-regulating using personal strategies they have found effective.

√ Students learn to recognize stress in their bodies and triggers for their stress, and develop strategies for dealing with their stressors.

√ The class contributes to positive school climate with safe and inclusive practices, such as the immediate reporting of aggression, and restorative justice practices.

Centre for Addiction and Mental Health [CAMH]. (2010). *Stress*. Retrieved from
http://www.camh.ca/en/hospital/health_information/a_z_mental_health_
and_addiction_information/stress/Pages/info_stress.aspx

Collaborative for Academic, Social, and Emotional Learning. (2012). *2013
CASEL guide: Effective social and emotional programs—Preschool and elementary
school edition*. Chicago, IL: Author. Retrieved from the CASEL website:
http://wwww.casel.org

Costello, B., Wachtel, J., & Wachtel, T. (2010). *Restorative circles in schools: Building
community and enhancing learning*. Bethlehem, PA: International Institute for
Restorative Practices.

Durlak, J. A., Weissberg, R. P., Dymnicki, A. B., Taylor, R. D., & Schellinger, K.
B. (2011). The impact of enhancing students' social and emotional learning:
A meta-analysis of school-based universal interventions. *Child Development,
82* (1), 405–432.

Durlak, J. A., & Weissberg, R. P. (2011). Promoting social and emotional
development is an essential part of students' education. *Human Development,
54,* 1–3.

Eckman, P. (1999). Basic emotions. In T. Dalgleish, & M. Power, *Handbook of
cognition and emotion,* 45–60. Sussex, UK: John Wiley.

Goleman, D. (1995). *Emotional intelligence*. New York, NY: Random House.

Goleman, D. (1998). *Working with emotional intelligence*. London, UK: Bloomsbury.

Goleman, D. (2006). *Social intelligence: The new science of human relationships*.
New York, NY: Bantam.

Hockenbury, D. H., & Hockenbury, S. E. (2007). *Discovering psychology*. New
York, NY: Worth. Retrieved from http://psychology.about.com/od/
emotion/f/what-are-emotions.htm

International Institute for Restorative Practices Canada [IIRP Canada] [List of
articles]. http://canada.iirp.edu/featured-articles.html

International Institute for Restorative Practices Graduate School. (2009).
Improving school climate: Findings from schools implementing restorative practices.
Bethlehem, PA: IIRP Graduate School.

Joint Consortium for School Health [JCSH]. (2010). *Schools as a setting for promoting positive mental health: Better practices and perspectives*. Retrieved from http://
www.jcshcces.ca/upload/PMH%20July10%202011%20WebReady.pdf

Koenig, K. (2005). *The rules of "normal" eating: A commonsense approach for dieters,
overeaters, undereaters, emotional eaters, and everyone in between*. Carlsbad, CA:
Gürze Books.

Kuypers, L. (2011). *The zones of regulation*. San Jose, CA: Social Thinking.

Lantieri, L. (2008). *Building emotional intelligence: Techniques to cultivate inner strength in
children*. Boulder, CO: Sounds True.

Lockhart, A., & Zammit, L. (2005). *Restorative justice: Transforming society*. Toronto, ON: Inclusion Press.

Nummenmaa, L., Glerean, E., Hari, R., & Hietanen, J. (2013). Bodily maps of emotions. *Proceedings of the National Academy of Sciences of the United States of America [PNAS]*. Retrieved from www.pnas.org/cgi/doi/10.1073/pnas.1321664111

Ontario Ministry of Education. (2010). *Caring and safe schools in Ontario*. Retrieved from http://www.edu.gov.on.ca/eng/general/elemsec/speced/caring_safe_school.pdf

Paglia-Boak, A., Adlaf, E. M., & Mann, R. E. (2011). *Drug use among Ontario students, 1977–2011: OSDUHS highlights* [CAMH Research Document Series No. 33]. Toronto, ON: Centre for Addiction and Mental Health. Retrieved from www.camh.ca/en/research/news_and_publications/ontario-student-drug-use-and-health-survey/Documents/2011%20OSDUHS%20Docs/2011OSDUHS_Highlights_DrugUseReport.pdf

Roberts, K., Shields, M., de Groh, M., Aziz, A., & Gilbert, J. (2012, September). Overweight and obesity in children and adolescents: Results from the 2009 to 2011 Canadian Health Measures Survey. *Health Reports, 23*(3). Statistics Canada, Catalogue no. 82-003-X.

Salovey, P., & Mayer, J. D. (1990). Emotional intelligence. *Imagination, Cognition, and Personality, 9*, 195–211.

Santos, R. G., Chartier, J. C., Whalen, J. C., Chateau, D., & Boyd, L. (2011). Effectiveness of school-based violence prevention for children and youth [Special issue]. *Healthcare Quarterly, 14*.

Schenk, B. (2008). Restorative practice and our schools: A visionary journey [A report to the Kawartha Pine Ridge District School Board]. In *Improving School Climate: Findings from Schools Implementing Restorative Practices*. Retrieved from the International Institute for Restorative Practices Graduate School website: http://www.iirp.edu/pdf/IIRP-Improving-School-Climate.pdf

Shanker, S. (2013). *Calm, alert, and learning: Classroom strategies for self-regulation*. Toronto, ON: Pearson Canada.

Shanker, S. (n.d.). *Self-Regulation*. Retrieved from www.self-regulation.ca/download/pdf_documents/magforbooklet.pdf

Smith, M., Segal, R., & Segal, J. (2014, October). *Stress symptoms, signs, and causes*. Retrieved from http://www.helpguide.org/articles/stress/stress-symptoms-causes-and-effects.htm#signs

Smith-Fowler, H., & Lebel, M. (2013, April). *Promoting youth mental health through the transition from highschool—Literature review and environmental scan*. Ottawa, ON: Social Research and Demonstration Corporation.

Zelazo, P. D. (2014, May). Executive function, reflection, and neuroplasticity: Implications for promoting empathy in childhood. Keynote address presented at the *Roots of Empathy Research Symposium 2014*, Toronto, ON.

A Strengths-Based Approach

"Children and youth have inner strengths and gifts that support their capacity to initiate, direct, and sustain positive life directions."

—JOINT CONSORTIUM FOR SCHOOL HEALTH, 2010, p. 8

Key Principles of a Strengths-Based Learning Approach

1. Everyone has inner strengths, capabilities, and resources.
2. Everyone has the potential to learn and develop or enhance their strengths and capabilities.
3. People can use their strengths and capabilities to address their own concerns and recover from adversity.
4. People and environments interact and change each other; each has the ability to build the other's capacity.

I once coached a peewee hockey team in rural Alberta. The parent group for our team did fundraising so that we could afford to travel and participate in tournaments. At the end of the year we still had some money left, and I met with the parents to decide how to spend it.

One of the first suggestions was to purchase plastic trophies for the higher achieving players—typically the ones who scored the most goals or got the fewest penalties. I cringed at this idea, as I anticipated some players would get many trophies and some would only get to applaud. I also knew that there is a correlation between hockey success and age (birthdates) that gives some children advantages from the outset—not to mention the impact of such factors as family income and better equipment. But my main point was that I wanted to find a way to appreciate each player, rather than exalting a few (yet again), and then do something special with all of the players, as a team.

There was one child on the team who had not played hockey much in the past. His dream was to play goal (a coach's nightmare). This boy's father and I had a conversation about this dream, and I promised to give him some experience and a fair chance. We worked him into the netminder role more and more as the year went on, and gave him lots of goalie experience at the weekly team practices. Meanwhile, this boy would play any position we offered to him at games when he was not in net. When it came time to work out his contribution, it quickly became clear that he was the only player on the team who had played every position, and with enthusiasm too. If you haven't guessed it already, this boy was recognized for his "versatility." Eventually, we had parent consensus on the special contribution of every child.

Toward the end of the hockey season, I phoned the Edmonton Oilers promotion office to book tickets for my team. Just before the game started, an announcement came over the speaker system for everybody to welcome our "peewee Oilers team, with us here tonight!" A huge spotlight shone on the young players, with thousands applauding. It was real a team-building moment—a perfect complement to the individual recognition the boys had received from the parents.

Some More Than Others: Celebrating Diversity

I like to think we are all unique—just like the players on that peewee hockey team. It is also true that it takes self-esteem to be comfortable with our differences, especially if we are in groups or environments where our unique characteristics are not understood or appreciated.

In a mentally healthy classroom, diversity and uniqueness are appreciated and celebrated, and all students feel they are a valued part of a team. The teacher, supported by the school community, plays a vital role in making this happen. Students *can* develop a mature appreciation of differences through a process of social education.

It is worth noting that we all find ourselves at the far ends of distribution charts of one form or another. Some of us are taller than the norm; others are shorter. In addition to height, there is weight. And then there is intelligence. What about emotional IQ? How about athleticism? Let's not forget wealth. The list goes on.

What is important to appreciate for the sake of mental health promotion is that children and youth at the ends of various continua often have elevated levels of stress and a concomitant need for understanding and support—they are the "some more than others." This can be true, it is interesting to note, even when their unique attribute is seen as a gift, such as high intelligence or heightened sensitivity.

Strengths-Based Learning

A strengths-based learning approach is one way to understand and nurture all students, while acknowledging and supporting their differences and unique gifts. A strengths-based approach is a perspective more than a set of rules, procedures, or teaching techniques, although there are classroom strategies that can support a strengths-based learning environment. Essentially, strengths-based learning leads with the positive and is based on the values of trust, respect, intentionality, and optimism.

As educators, we all have an ultimate goal: to help children and youth fulfill their potential and achieve their dreams. But as we all know, problems and risks often cry loudest to be addressed, and

It is important to note that social emotional learning and a strengths-based perspective are not two different models that have to be added to what you are already doing—they are closely integrated and complementary approaches for healthy development and mental well-being.

they certainly need to be addressed. It is natural to want to identify concerns and remedy them. However, when we start with a problem-orientation and a primary focus on risks, discipline, and what children lack, we can easily lose sight of the need to build the positive foundations that will prevent problems, promote strengths, and give all students the skills to deal with adversity and achieve well-being.

Strengths-based learning has been gaining increased attention with the more holistic focus on positive youth development, including positive mental health. A **strengths** perspective starts with "what is right" with a person and "what can be," recognizing struggles as opportunities to learn and grow. It seeks to avoid the unintended effects of labelling that may limit the options of a child or youth and obscure the student's capabilities or strengths. The focus is less on intervention to "fix" problems or shortcomings, and more on acknowledging strengths and supporting children and youth to find their own solutions. In other words, the goal is to create positive experiences and provide key developmental supports and opportunities—ultimately, teaching and learning for healthy development.

A strengths perspective does not deny that children and youth have issues or problems that need to be addressed; however, it does not allow those issues to define the child. It does not approach learning from the problem first. Instead, it seeks to build a solid foundation for all and target specific issues within that context. Perhaps a helpful way to think about it is "strengths first."

A strengths perspective acknowledges that everyone has the potential to use their strengths to achieve personal goals. This concept is key because it affirms that students can achieve positive life goals, even if the strengths they use are not what we consider conventional knowledge, capacities, and resources (Saleebey, 2006). Later in the chapter, we will look at how unconventional gifts such as high general intelligence, introversion, and high sensitivity can be sources of stress for students and negatively affect their mental well-being if they are not viewed from a strengths perspective.

Strengths
inner characteristics, virtues, and external relationships, activities, and connections to resources that contribute to resilience and core competencies (Resiliency Initiatives, 2012, p. 18)

"The strengths approach as a philosophy of practice draws one away from an emphasis on procedures, techniques, and knowledge as the keys to change. Instead, it reminds us that every youth holds the key to his or her own transformation and meaningful change process."

—*Resiliency Initiatives, 2012, p. 3*

Figure 4.1: Strengths-Based versus Deficit-Based Concepts

Strengths-based learning, essentially a perspective based on key values, requires a different language from a deficit-based approach.

at-potential	at-risk
strengths	problems
engage	intervene
persistent	resistant
understand	diagnose
opportunity	crisis
celebrate (i.e., successes)	punish/discipline (i.e., non-compliance)
time-in	time-out
adapt to	reform
empower	control
process-focused	behaviour-focused
avoids imposition	focuses on dominant knowledge
validates people's experiences	diagnoses based on norms
support	fix
child-determined	expert-oriented
inclusive	exclusive
dynamic	static
flexible	rigid

Source: Excerpted from Resiliency Initiatives (2012, p. 16).

Principles of Strengths-Based Teaching Practice

Resiliency Initiatives is an independent consulting organization aligned with the University of Calgary in Alberta. It collaborates with academic institutions, health organizations, community service providers, and government agencies to promote a strengths-based approach to best practices that support well-being and healthy development. In *Embracing a Strengths-Based Perspective and Practice in Education*, Resiliency Initiatives (2012) sets out key evidence and research-based principles for guiding and implementing strengths-based practice in schools.

Keep an absolute belief that every student has potential. It is a student's unique strengths and capabilities that will determine his or her evolving story as well as define who the student is—not what the student is not (not: *I believe when I see*; rather, *I believe and I will see*).

What we focus on becomes a student's reality. Focus on what a student can do as the starting point, not what the student cannot do. See challenges as opportunities to explore, not as something to avoid. Start with small successes and build upon them to create a foundation of hope and optimism.

Be mindful that the language we use creates a reality—both for educators and for students. Compare these two variations: "It looks like you tried doing this exercise another way—let's see how it worked for you." "Did you not hear what I told the other students?"

Believe that change is inevitable and that all students can and will be successful. All students have the urge to succeed, to explore the world around them, and to contribute to others and their communities.

Positive change occurs in the context of authentic relationships. Students need to know that school staff care and will be there for them unconditionally.

What students think about themselves and their reality is primary—it is their story. Therefore, educators must value and start the change process with what is important to each student. It's the student's story that is important, not the expert.

Students have more confidence and comfort to journey to the future (or to the unknown) when they are invited to start with what they already know.

Capacity building is a process and a goal. Effective and sustainable change is a dynamic process one supports in cumulative ways that lead youth to write the next chapters of their life stories in meaningful ways.

It is important to value differences and the essential need to collaborate. Transformational change is a collaborative, inclusive, and participatory process—"It takes a village to raise a child."

Sourced from: Resiliency Initiatives (2012, p. 4).

Resiliency Initiatives

Recognizing and Building Strengths

When students are supported in recognizing their strengths, and those strengths are acknowledged by those around them, they gain confidence to achieve their goals and tackle challenges using strengths-based solutions. Positive change comes by connecting students' strengths with their aspirations. As a teacher, you have seen the power that connecting a child's passion with a goal can have to overcome difficulties or find new paths. It is equally important to acknowledge that recognizing and developing strengths or capacities is a dynamic and developmental process, and strengths can develop out of students' everyday life experiences.

In my peewee hockey team, "Mr. Versatility" discovered strengths by being given opportunities to explore and to follow his dream. He may not have become a professional goalie, but he discovered his enthusiasm to try different things. Flexibility is an inner strength he could nurture and apply in other aspects of his life if he recognized it as a strength and used it consciously to help him deal with adversity.

Children and youth often do not know what their strengths are and may be caught in their own negative self-concept or conditioned thinking (e.g., *I'm not good enough* or *I'm the odd one out*). Or they may believe they have strengths without completely understanding what those capacities involve (e.g., effective listening). As a teacher, you can help your students identify and understand their strengths by giving them opportunities to explore, and once they have recognized their strengths, by allowing them to apply and build on those capacities. You can help them become aware of what they can use their strengths to achieve, accomplish, and overcome.

Classroom Strategies

Some classes have had wonderful success with a Strengths Wall, started early in the school year and added to as students discover new strengths both in themselves and in their peers. In one Grade 4 class, the teacher started by having students consider the strengths of characters in stories they were reading, as well as in their own lives. Research has shown that exploring characters in stories helps students to consider how their own knowledge, capacities, and resources can be used to help them achieve their goals and find solutions to problems in their own lives (Saleebey, 2006).

The class began by listing the strengths of the story characters and how they used their strengths. In pairs, after a short discussion, they then listed a strength of their partner, and then the strengths of anyone in the class. They took care to identify a strength for everyone, including a student with special needs.

The students listed characteristics such as "intelligent, kind, funny, cheerful, a great friend, a go-getter, responsible, positive, a leader, and respectful." They also recognized that everyone had different strengths, but they were all equally important. They were keen to take the next step to use and grow their strengths (Brownlee, Rawana, & MacArthur, 2012).

A Strengths Wall is one strategy to help build self-worth, inclusivity, and a positive sense of community in the classroom. In one case, for example, a student who had been in a behavioural class and was finding adjustment to a regular class challenging discovered that reminders of her strengths posted on the wall allowed her to steer away from conflict and frustration, and to focus on positive action based on her strengths. She strove to live up to the statements that she heard about herself and found a new self-image. In another case, a young student did not want to miss a day of school because she did not want to let down her reading buddy from Kindergarten. Her classmates had recognized her special ability with younger children as a strength. She began volunteering with the Kindergarten class and loved it (Brownlee, Rawana, & MacArthur, 2012).

If we think back to the story of Charley in the last chapter, it is not difficult to see how her teacher was already applying a strengths perspective by not labelling her hyperactivity and anxiousness as deficits, but rather building on her ability to draw and her athleticism—drawing out inner strengths and character traits that would help her overcome her nervousness and create positive relationships. As her classmates supported her and she recognized her own capacities, Charley would be able to identify with her positive qualities rather than declaring herself a "freak" to gain attention and recognition.

Other strategies can be applied to reinforce and deepen students' exploration and understanding of their own strengths and those of others (see Strategy Focus box, pages 102–103). All support social emotional competencies and the goal of a caring, inclusive classroom and school environment: keys to mental well-being.

"It is proposed that if youth experience success, they would prefer the benefits of success to the natural consequence of non-constructive coping."

—Resiliency Initiatives, 2012, p. 10

Strengths-Based Strategies for the Classroom

Strengths Wall—Students post strengths in a visual place, such as a bulletin board, where they can be viewed every day. Students could post what they believe are their top three strengths at the beginning of the year and continually add to their list as new strengths are recognized. Classmates can be encouraged to identify and add strengths for their peers. Another option is for each student to have a strengths profile sheet, with name, picture, or self-portrait, and continually update it throughout the year. The visual display builds self-worth and serves as a communication focal point for the whole school. Students also have a sense of discovery, growth, accomplishment, and social recognition.

Strengths-Sharing Circle—A sharing circle can be used as a way for students to hear others' perspectives on their strengths, building self-awareness and understanding. Students could also respond to strengths posted on the Strengths Wall, offering suggestions to one another on how to build on strengths and share experiences, furthering a positive sense of caring and community.

Strengths Assessment Inventory (SAI) or Log Book of Strengths Observations—Researchers from Lakehead University have developed a Strengths Assessment Inventory tool for Grades 4 to 8, based on seven domains in a student's life: strengths at school, during leisure time, with friends, from knowing themselves, from involvement in community activities, from their faith or culture, and from their goals and dreams. Students self-assess to create a strengths profile. A less formal option is a log book of strengths observations to build a profile. Both can be used as points of discussion with the students and families, to inform learning and instruction, and to plan community involvement.

Literature (e.g., stories, films, dramas)—Research shows that reading about characters who use their strengths to overcome difficulties and fulfill their dreams helps students to consider how they can use their own strengths in their own lives. Discussion and response groups can focus on strengths-based stories or other media.

Strengths-Based Journal or Portfolio Activities—Some journal or portfolio activities could be focused on a strengths-based theme to document feelings and ideas about self-concept, personal strengths, and progress in developing strengths ("What makes you special in relation to your strengths?" "Where could you use your strengths in and outside the classroom?")

Mutual Strengths Contract—A class can collaboratively develop and agree to a contract of rules for the classroom that are related to class strengths and allow them to get back on track quickly. For example: "One of our strengths as a class is our ability to communicate appropriately.... If we become too noisy, we agree that our teacher will signal us to communicate quietly."

Planning with Strengths in Mind—It can be very powerful to plan with student strengths in mind, not only to build the students' self-confidence but to allow students to learn from one another and appreciate how their strengths can work together to build a stronger class community.

Source: Rawana, Latimer, Whitley, & Probizanski (2009, November).

Community Connection

A Strengths-Based Culture for Mental Health

Promoting a strengths-based approach throughout the school environment and in collaboration with community organizations and agencies is key to building the caring, inclusive culture that is foundational to student mental health.

1. Model and encourage setting clear goals, perseverance, and positive and critical thinking.

2. Promote opportunities for caring relationships built on trust, respect, and non-judgment.

3. Emphasize cooperation and collaboration over competition and relational communities rather than authority-based hierarchies.

4. Communicate about student strengths, their discoveries, and their experiences in the school and classroom.

5. Select community collaborations and resources that provide opportunities for students to explore, apply, and build on strengths (e.g., structured programs, information, decision-making resources).

6. Be mindful not only of the types of resources provided, but how and when they are offered so that they complement and are meaningful for students' strengths and goals (rather than compensate for deficits).

7. Provide engagement in challenging activities in which students are active participants rather than passive recipients of services and supports. Participating in their school and community in ways that reflect their interests and strengths helps students develop a sense of pride, acceptance, positive contribution, and optimism.

8. Share with families so that they can support students' discovery, exploration, and nurturing of strengths.

Promoting Strengths for Mental Health

Now let's consider how a strengths-based perspective can help us to support the positive mental health of students who are the "some more than others"—those on the ends of continua whose unique characteristics can be the sources of stress, feelings of not fitting in, and unhealthy coping strategies, such as withdrawing or acting out if their strengths are not understood and nurtured. Recognizing their unique qualities as "gifts" rather than as problems or concerns allows for a strengths-based approach that is inclusive, supportive, capacity-building, and focused on positive well-being.

It is also worth noting that, in many ways, the challenge of teaching children with these gifts is similar to the challenge of teaching all children. Helping students to discover and develop their strengths, and to use those strengths to reach their goals, is the basis of all teaching. We will see that many of the strategies suggested for students with special gifts can benefit all students, and in a classroom that values diversity and celebrates strengths, the children will learn from and support one another. They can enjoy finding their comfort zone and being stretched to learn new skills when they feel safe and encouraged, rather than feeling that they don't fit in.

"It is through caring and supportive relationships that students develop their personal values and sense of hope and optimism—not because they were just told they should."
—*Resiliency Initiatives, 2012, p. 19*

The Gift of High General Intelligence

Strengths

Some students who are gifted with high general intellectual capability are blessed with the capacity to understand many things readily. They are often curious, want to know the details, and want to touch, explore, interact, and learn. As they acquire knowledge and experience, they become increasingly adept at seeing abstract relationships among concepts, and they are often able to make creative applications to new learning. They may have striking powers of concentration and enjoy long hours alone focused on their interests. Their advanced intellect is likely to provide them with more opportunities for effective participation in social, recreational, artistic, economic, or scientific pursuits. But these benefits sometimes come at a cost.

Some key characteristics of high general intelligence:

Curiosity

Intensity

Creativity

Capacity for abstract thought

Independent thinking

Long attention span

Challenges

As many parents and teachers will attest, *some* students with significantly higher-than-average general intelligence struggle socially in their relationships with their peers. Other children may not connect with what the advanced child talks about because of their disparate levels of abstract thought. The intense curiosity and focused interests of some highly intelligent children may seem odd to their peers. The advanced child also may not enjoy the humour of other children, being inclined to more complex irony or offbeat wit. As a result, the child with advanced intellect may feel different, out of place, and uncomfortable. Even though the child may be recognized for intelligence, he or she may be not be valued for it, particularly among adolescent peers where fitting in with the group is paramount. We all know it is not uncommon for these youth to be labelled as "nerds" or "geeks."

Teachers of very bright and inquisitive students often find it challenging to keep up with the demands of these children for intellectual stimulation and meaningful participation in activities. Some intellectually gifted children become academic underachievers to gain acceptance from their same-aged peers. Some become uninterested in academics as a result of their experiences with a curriculum primarily geared to the average range of student ability—often several years below the advanced child's level. In many provinces and states, children functioning in the top few percentiles of cognitive ability can be formally identified as exceptional and provided with an individual education plan for differentiated instruction.

Children who are exceptionally bright can find life at school quite stressful and may develop negative behavioural patterns to compensate for their stress. They may become argumentative, apathetic, or socially withdrawn. For some, their advanced intelligence may be a factor in their becoming clinically depressed (The Ontario Curriculum Unit Planner, 2002) and wanting to leave school early.

Strategies for Well-Being

In a classroom that values each child's worth and that offers a flexible environment, children with high general intelligence can feel a sense of belonging and support. It is useful to consider the following strategies:

- **Help them to recognize and value their intelligence to build a strong self-concept.** Even with a caring and inclusive classroom environment, our society often places limited value on intellectualism and academic achievement, and tends toward instant gratification and an ever-shortening attention span.

- **Teach social emotional skills.** Learning these will help the students relax, relieve tension, and establish and sustain positive relationships.

- **Ensure that they understand there are options for learning.** Provide choice in activities and assignments and tap into their interests and strengths; co-create learning opportunities.

- **Allow them to explore any concept or field of information in more detail, and in more or innovative ways.** In so doing you will provide challenge and feed their curiosity.

- **Teach skills for how to learn.** Although these students have the curiosity, interest, and motivation to work independently, they need skills for setting goals, organizing and evaluating information, using appropriate methodology, doing effective research, and engaging in critical and creative thinking.

- **Allow incubation time.** Let these students formulate answers to divergent questions—they need time to figure things out.

- **Use group work judiciously.** Groups may not provide the intellectual challenge many need and may lead to frustration; small groups based on common interests may be more successful.

- **Provide opportunities to work independently in quiet spaces.** Enable the students to use their powers of intense concentration and self-motivation, and to work on the tasks they find most challenging and meaningful.

- **Be aware that striving for perfection, high self-criticism, a fear of failure, and too much value on superior achievement may be issues.** Encourage and model safe risk-taking, setting high but realistic goals, accepting and laughing at mistakes, reframing mistakes and failures as learning opportunities, cultivating some playfulness and pleasure in work, and engaging in leisure activities for pure enjoyment.

- **Encourage community connections that offer opportunities to learn beyond the school and curriculum.** Skills students may be able to learn include specific technical skills and concepts; communication, social, and leadership skills; and creative and problem-solving skills.

- **Arrange for mentorships in the community or online.** Having a professional, a university student, a teacher, or an expert as a mentor can be especially effective with gifted students.

Howard Gardner and the Gift of Multiple Intelligences

The concept of Gardner's multiple intelligences is not new, but it takes on a fresh significance when we consider it in the context of strengths-based learning, the valuing of diversity, and positive mental health. Although Gardner's theory diverges from the usual construct of intelligence, it can still serve as a useful heuristic model for teachers.

Howard Gardner (1943–) redefines *intelligence* as what could be considered a set of specific abilities or aptitudes, rather than as one general level of ability. In other words, he encourages us to ask *how* young people are smart, rather than *which* young people are smart, and allows us to look beyond the traditional focus on linguistic (verbal) and logical (mathematical) abilities to recognize that students have multiple and diverse aptitudes. Figure 4.2 summarizes the eight multiple intelligences Gardner identifies.

Gardner notes that everyone has a mix of aptitudes, with often one or two being dominant. Furthermore, these aptitudes are not fixed; it is possible to develop abilities and skills in less dominant styles. People also may use different styles in different circumstances.

This approach invites us to consider each child's special strengths and capacities and underlines the importance of differentiated instructional strategies and multimodal teaching approaches. It also allows us to appreciate those students who develop abilities and skills in their less dominant styles through persistence and a special interest. They are demonstrating important learning skills, development, and growth.

As a teacher, you can watch for personal strengths among the list of "multiple intelligences." Knowing and celebrating your students' gifts instills self-confidence and a greater sense of belonging. Learning is more meaningful for students when it is tied to personal strengths and goals, when students can celebrate and learn from each other's strengths, and when they can explore, discover, and build their capacities.

Figure 4.2: Gardner's Multiple Intelligences

Students who are relatively or exceptionally	Tend to think more with	Show preferences for	Engage well with
Linguistic	words	reading, writing, story telling,	books, discussions, journals, stories
Logical-mathematical	reasoning, analyzing patterns, critical thinking	solving puzzles, experiments, statistics	science projects, charts, detective stories, data interpretation
Visual-spatial	images and pictures, mind maps	drawing, mapping, visualizing, graphic organizers	graphic arts, picture puzzles, videos
Bodily-kinesthetic	physical and sensory experiences	touching, tasting, actions	sports, drama, hands-on learning
Musical	rhythm, pitch, lyrics, rhyme	singing, listening, tapping, poetry	musical instruments, musicals, rap
Naturalistic	classification, natural phenomena	growing plants, animal care	outdoor activities, nature study
Interpersonal	body language and feelings	cooperative learning, meetings	peer mentoring, teaching, role play, shared journals
Intrapersonal	reflection, contemplation, self-talk	quiet, independent work, self understanding	research, reading, metacognition, journal writing

Source: Gardner (1983).

The Gift of High Sensitivity

Strengths

About 15 to 20 percent of students are highly sensitive. Highly sensitive students process sensory information very thoroughly. They seem to have highly tuned nervous systems. They are observant and reflect deeply on what they encounter in their environment. They may notice subtle changes in their surroundings or in others' moods, and they are often intuitive, empathetic, and creative. They feel emotions powerfully and can have rich inner lives.

They may also be remarkably bright, careful, and conscientious, but their feelings are easily hurt and they may cry when the teacher reads the sad part of a story or when another child is being teased. To some, they may seem overly fussy. They may take more time than others considering alternatives before making a decision. They may be more sensitive to loud sounds, bright lights, rambunctious groups, and sharp criticism. They tend to get overwhelmed when their senses have too much to process and filter.

Their empathetic and caring nature means they are often seen as kind and cooperative, and others feel comfortable opening up and sharing with them. Compassion and a strong conscience also mean they may care deeply about social justice issues, violence, and irresponsibility.

Challenges

Sensitive students can easily be misunderstood and thereby overstimulated, which can provoke tantrums, obstinacy, avoidance of enjoyable group activities, and sometimes a high level of school absence. They may be cautious about new situations, people, and places, and so react strongly to transitions from one activity to another or to unfamiliar environments.

It is helpful to understand that they often feel very vulnerable because they are easily hurt and overwhelmed. When they feel overwhelmed, they may withdraw or act out, but this does not necessarily mean an inability to relate to others. They can do well in small, more intimate groups and with large groups in smaller doses. What appears outwardly as a poor attitude or lack of motivation may be a withdrawal from painful overstimulating situations. They may feel especially nervous when they are being evaluated, particularly in a group situation.

While these deeply reflective and conscientious children are not shy by nature, they can become very shy and even fearful as a result of their environmental experiences and how we respond to their gifts. In addition to being at risk for experiencing more anxiety, these children tend to feel sad more readily and deeply.

It is probably an understatement to say that the gift of high sensitivity has not been recognized in our North American culture. Author and psychologist Elaine Aron (2002) has described this phenomenon in her book *The Highly Sensitive Child: Helping Our Children Thrive When the World Overwhelms Them*. Aron explains what these children need in order to develop their gifts successfully, for their own healthy adjustment and for the benefit of those around them.

SPOTLIGHT

Sensitive Boys

High sensitivity can be very painful for boys, who are being raised in a culture where the popular myth of masculine toughness, aggression, and repressed emotions conflicts with the fact that there are many strong, sensitive men (Zeff, 2010). In his recent book *The Strong, Sensitive Boy*, psychologist Ted Zeff talks about the social risks for boys in exposing these extraordinary gifts of heightened compassion, gentleness, and vulnerability in an intolerant environment.

Sensitive boys are likely to have a keen appreciation for beauty and a capacity to feel love deeply. At the same time, they have a heightened capacity for hurt. When they are forced to deny their true selves, they are likely to experience fear, anxiety, and low self-esteem—all factors that can seriously undermine their mental well-being. For these boys, parents, educators, and peers who understand them and respect their unique form of masculine strength are particularly important.

Strategies for Well-Being

Ross Greene (2013) has developed a unique psychological approach for supporting highly sensitive children and youth who do not yet have the skills to manage their sensitivity. Greene's focus is on collaborative problem-solving—talking to these students so that parents and teachers can come to understand how they become overwhelmed

Lives in the Balance
—collaborative problem-solving approach by Dr. Ross Greene

and how we can support them. Greene emphasizes that young people do well *if they can*, not just *if they want to* (see Greene, 2010). This latter philosophy allows us to "blame" the child for being sensitive and overwhelmed, and to overlook the flexibility skills they need to manage stressful situations effectively.

Greene's approach fits well with Aron's and Zeff's research, which shows how important it is for parents and teachers to understand these gifted, sensitive learners. The ability to experience empathy deeply and to be extremely conscientious are clearly needed in our world and in our school communities. With understanding and support, highly sensitive students can use their deep-thinking capacity and observation skills to produce highly creative outputs.

- **Minimize visual and auditory distractions and harsh stimuli in the classroom.** Gongs or other more calming sounds can be used to signal transitions in place of buzzers or loud claps; scattered posters can be organized into more focused visual centres. Avoid seating highly sensitive students in the middle of the classroom, near the door, or in other areas of higher traffic or noise.

- **Provide quiet personal spaces.** These students need to be able to pull away from high-stimulation environments or situations and ease transitions. For young children, this space may be a tunnel or a "cave"; for older children, it may be a small couch or chair tucked into the corner of the classroom. Wearing headphones may also work well for some children to block out outside stimuli.

- **Build trust.** Highly sensitive children often do not respond well to top-down authority whereby they are given orders and no choices. If you ask for their thoughts, their opinion of how they think an activity went, or ideas on what could be improved to help them, they will often do much better.

- **Give choices.** These students need to know that they have a voice and choices at school. This knowledge helps to ease their anxiety and sense of vulnerability; it appeals to their sense of fairness and conscientious nature. They will feel better able to succeed.

- **Check-in frequently.** It is not always easy to interpret why a highly sensitive child is reacting in a particular way to a situation, or how the child is perceiving what is going on. By checking-in often to understand how the child is feeling, you can develop the nurturing collaborative relationship needed.

- **Encourage engagement in, and expression through, the arts.** Engaging in the arts can reduce stress and anxiety, increase self-awareness, and provide opportunities for expression and creativity. These students can be encouraged to use their talents to express their keen observations, reflections, and insights.

- **Teach social emotional skills.** Like all students, these students can benefit from the self-regulation and social skills to help them flourish. Their empathy and prosocial development may be particularly helpful to other students.

The Gift of Introversion

Strengths

Carl Jung was the first to introduce the concept of two personality types he called introverts and extroverts. He described introverted individuals as drawn to an inner world of thought and feeling, and focused on making meaning of the events around them. They tend to be quiet, contemplative, deep thinkers, comfortable with solitude. Extroverts he described as more focused on an external world of people and activities; they are talkative, comfortable in the spotlight and taking risks, and energized by groups. Contemporary psychologists have added to and refined Jung's descriptions.

It has been argued that, in our market economy, we have developed a cultural bias in favour of extroversion as a desired personality trait. Extroverts stand out as business leaders, salespeople, and celebrities. They may make a better impression as politicians, speaking in the spotlight. Those who are more comfortable observing, listening, and thinking may be less admired, even though they may at times be more astute.

Susan Cain (2012) can be described as the modern-day champion of introverts. In her book *Quiet: The Power of Introverts in a World That Can't Stop Talking*, she asserts the value of those inclined to be introverted where caution, moral sensibility, and deep thinking are required, such as in financial investing and global politics. She points out that some of our greatest innovations, ideas, and acts of courage have come from quiet, thoughtful, and determined people, including Rosa Parks, Steve Wozniak, Eleanor Roosevelt, Charles Darwin, Vincent van Gogh, and Mahatma Gandhi.

Figure 4.3 summarizes some of the main qualities associated with introversion. Introverted individuals may work more slowly, deliberately, and conscientiously than others, with a strong sense of conviction, determination, and persistence. They can be insightful problem-solvers and effective leaders. Cain (2012) tells us that one-third to one-half of the population is introverted. That means that at least one in three students in a classroom may be an introvert.

Introversion is a different concept from sensitivity. An individual may be introverted, without being highly sensitive and responsive to external stimulation. However, research shows that approximately 70 percent of highly sensitive individuals are introverted.

SPOTLIGHT

Introverts and Extroverts

It is important to recognize that there are no all-purpose definitions of introverts and extroverts and that introversion and extroversion is a continuum. This notion of a continuum was something that Carl Jung postulated. He believed it impossible for one person to have attributes that could be ascribed only to being either an introvert or an extrovert. We are all wonderfully complex individuals with multiple personality traits and personal histories. There are many different kinds of introverted and extroverted people. Contemporary psychologists, however, generally agree on some important characteristics that can inform educator understanding of strengths and ways to promote the mental health of our students with these tendencies.

Figure 4.3: Characteristics of Introverts and Extroverts

Characteristics	Introverts	Extroverts
Level of stimulation to function well	Less stimulation—"geared to inspect and reflect" More prone to becoming distracted, unfocused in very stimulating situations	More stimulation—"geared to act and respond" Reduces chance of boredom
Natural inclination	Focus on internal feelings, thoughts, reflections May be uncomfortable in large groups	Seek experiences in the exterior world Tend to avoid personal reflection
Social style	Prefer small groups of close friends May not enjoy small talk; prefer deep discussions Listen and observe more than talk in groups May expend energy in social situations	Often gregarious, assertive, sometimes dominant Talk more than listen in groups Comfortable with conflict, less so with solitude May gain energy from social situations
Communication	Think before they speak May be more comfortable writing than speaking Have difficulty speaking "off the cuff"	Comfortable speaking "on the fly" Think on their feet Sometimes speak before they think

Characteristics	Introverts	Extroverts
Work and leadership style	Prefer work based on individual performance Don't require extrinsic praise or reward Tend to remain private at work Have difficulty expressing their ideas As leaders, lead by example	Prefer positions that involve working with others (e.g., sales) Like to think as they talk— work through problems with others Can speak easily in public As leaders, lead by action

Sources: Cain (2012), Cherry (2014), Diamond (2012), Kahnweiler (2014).

Challenges

"…The bias against quiet can cause deep physic pain…I have seen firsthand how difficult it is for introverts to take stock of their own talents, and how powerful it is when they do." (Cain, 2012, pp. 6, 7)

Students with more introverted personalities may struggle to fit in among their more outgoing peers and may be an easy target for social bullying. Being quiet, and in this way different, they exert less social power, despite their independent thinking. People who don't talk in our North American society can sometimes be perceived as weaker or lacking and can appear aloof, disconnected, or unfriendly. When they are quiet in groups, introverts are following their nature and applying their strengths—observing, thinking, and carefully reflecting. When they do speak, their contributions are often carefully considered and incisive.

On the school report card, the more introverted student may get poor class participation ratings. Although the student may be an astute observer, listener, and thinker, that student might be overlooked in a classroom that values instant ideas from outspoken peers.

Introverts prefer to develop close relationships with a few people, rather than compete to be popular with large groups. Many do enjoy lively group activities, but they need quiet downtime alone to recharge. They may avoid and withdraw from conflicts rather than confront issues immediately. In small groups, where they are comfortable, however, they may be as talkative and open as anyone.

Introverts are not always easy to identify. Even at a young age, some introverts become adept at acting like extroverts and hide or deny their natures. While introverts need to develop skills to compete in an extroverted world, we do not want to create environments that cause these children to experience mental health struggles. We can all stretch ourselves, but only so much before the stress and anxiety compromise our health.

Strategies for Well-Being

So, how can we create positive environments for quieter and more sensitive students to develop their unique strengths? The suggestions below, as in all of these cases, are not meant to be comprehensive, but rather, offer some key strengths-focused strategies.

- **Provide quiet personal spaces where these students can recharge, think, and create.** For young children, the space may be a tunnel or a "cave"; for older children, a small couch or chair tucked into the corner of the classroom. Wearing headphones in these spaces may also work well for some children who need to block out outside noises.

- **Help these students to find like-minded friends who share their interests and passions.** Close relationships with a few friends are very nurturing for introverts. Help them to understand the value of these few close relationships—number of friends is less important.

- **Provide opportunities for work in small structured groups.** These students are comfortable talking with one or two peers, and if they've already expressed their ideas with a partner or in small groups, they may be more comfortable sharing with the class. Even if they don't speak up for the class, they have still participated in the discussion. It is important for them to have the opportunity to translate their thoughts into spoken language. They are also most comfortable in groups when they know and can choose their role.

- **Wait 5 or 10 beats after asking the class a question.** This time gives introverted students a chance to think through their ideas and process them, so they may feel more comfortable about raising their hand and sharing.

Shyness and introversion are not the same, though they sometimes overlap. "Shyness is the fear of social disapproval or humiliation, while introversion is a preference for environments that are not over stimulating. Shyness is inherently painful; introversion is not."

—Cain, 2012, p. 12

- **Consider using social media as a way for introverts to express their ideas.** In a discussion on Twitter, students can write their answers instead of speaking up in class, and the rest of the class can still see what they are thinking.

- **Help students play to their strengths in groups.** If they are not comfortable making assertions, perhaps they are good at asking thoughtful questions. Help them see that their unique point of view has value and how it could benefit the discussion.

- **Coach them to push through their walls of discomfort.** Let them know it is okay to take time to gather their thoughts before speaking, even if it seems everyone else jumps in quickly. Help them see that contributing earlier is easier than waiting until everyone else has spoken and their anxiety builds.

- **Encourage intense engagement in interests and activities that allow them to unleash their passions.** When they are fully engaged, they may forget their inhibitions and find bravery even in large social situations because of the rewards and enjoyment the activity gives them.

- **Teach social emotional skills.** Doing so will help these students develop self-awareness, self-management, confidence, and assertiveness: skills that will both help them value their strengths and compete in an extrovert environment.

In school and in business, it will be the job of those in leadership positions to recognize and allow for the input of quieter individuals who are disinclined to fight for airtime.

The Gift of High Activity

Strengths

Individuals with high energy and heightened activity levels can be a real asset for various environments such as the workplace or a sports field. Providing these students with learning environments grounded in what they enjoy and can succeed in—in other words, their strengths—can positively support their mental health.

Consider for a moment what happens when we look first for strengths rather than deficits—we may see high energy, spontaneity, divergent thinking, playfulness, a focus on action, curiosity, and imagination. Remember, as R. W. Greene's 2010 video title puts it, *kids do well if they can*. The high energy of these individuals can be a real asset when channelled to lead or complete a task quickly, or in sports and other active pursuits. People who tend to be restless and constantly moving also have an advantage in situations that require "going with the flow" and being flexible, rather than sticking to a routine.

Likewise, high energy and fast output can propel a career that requires fast talking and immediate action, such as salesperson, courier driver, real-estate agent, or hotel manager. If these individuals learn to take the time to calculate risk versus advantage, their nature may also help them to take advantage of business opportunities.

Challenges

Children with high activity levels may easily become distracted, have trouble focusing and sitting still for long periods of time, and sometimes act impulsively. Their attention may be easily diverted away from schoolwork when they become restless. They may act out in sometimes inappropriate ways when they cannot find an outlet for their pent-up energy. Some may appear frequently nervous, jumpy, and agitated.

These individuals will need positive outlets for their energy, activity breaks, and strategies for down-regulating and maintaining focus. When their energies are channelled in productive ways, they can be positive assets in the classroom.

Strategies for Well-Being

- **Seat students away from areas that are potentially distracting.** These areas may be near the door or pencil sharpener or near noisy vents or activity areas. Don't put more students than are necessary in their line of vision.

- **Minimize visual and auditory distractions in the classroom.** For example, attach felt or tennis balls to the bottom of desk and chair legs, and avoid visual clutter by organizing wall posters and other pin-ups into clearly labelled areas.

- **Provide areas and tools that enable students to be active and integrate physical activity throughout the day.** For example, arrange for fidget tools, physical activity centres in the classroom, floor cushions, outdoor physical activities and involvement in sports, high-stimulation learning resources, and expressive arts and creativity centres.

- **Allow students to play to their strengths and interests.** This strategy applies to assignments, group work, active projects, and physical activities where their energy, imagination, and curiosity are most focused and beneficial to those around them.

- **Use multiple teaching strategies and frequent state changes.** For example, use dynamic demonstrations, graphic organizers, appropriate technology, small-group discussion, options in terms of assignments, learning contracts, and movement from sitting to standing to group work and then individual work.

- **Establish clear and consistent rules, routines, and transitions through mutually developed contracts.** Put a focus on positive contributions and immediate feedback (e.g., they may choose to water the plants or maintain the art supplies).

- **Model and teach specific organizational skills.** These include setting clear goals, creating a plan before they start, chunking assignments into clear, sequential, and achievable parts, and using checklists.

- **Engage students with effective decision-making skills.** Students need to know skills such as reasoning and critical thinking and the steps in decision making.

- **Teach and practise relaxation skills and positive self-talk.** Measures include deep breathing, progressive muscle relaxation, yoga exercises, and telling themselves to stop and think before acting or answering a question.

- **Teach and model social emotional skills.** The goal is to foster self-awareness, social awareness, and relationship skills. These students benefit particularly from learning self-regulation skills, mindfulness and visualizing techniques, perspective taking, and how to read non-verbal signals.

The Gift of High Excitement

Strengths

If it were not for our ability to become scared, physiologically aroused, and otherwise excited about situations we sense are potentially dangerous, we would not survive long. Anxiety is adaptive, and we all experience it from time to time, in various situations. Excitement and adrenaline allow us the motivation and focus to accomplish goals and meet challenges we may not otherwise be able to achieve.

Excitement becomes problematic anxiety when we become physiologically, emotionally, and cognitively agitated about situations that are not really dangerous, and our capacity to function is reduced. Psychology researchers showed some time ago that anxiety intensity and performance can be plotted as an inverted U (Yerkes & Dodson, 1908) (see Figure 4.4).

Figure 4.4: The Inverted U of Anxiety

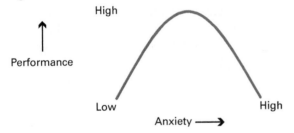

The Yerkes-Dodson Law, originally set out in 1908, shows that high levels of anxiety can enhance performance for simple learning tasks, but impair performance of more complex tasks.

Challenges

Heightened anxiety is one of the most common mental health challenges in the school setting. Anxiety is not always obvious, because individuals often develop avoidance behaviours to escape stress-provoking circumstances, numb their experience, or disguise their anguish.

Social and performance anxiety are especially common. Parents may notice quite early that their children have anxieties about appearing or performing in public. As early as Kindergarten, some children become very upset just walking through the classroom door because they feel that everyone is looking at and evaluating them. Most of the time, this social anxiety resolves itself. However, some students still carry around great levels of social anxiety during the high-school years, when adolescents can be very self-conscious.

Some students may live in constant fear of being singled out in class to answer a question. During the elementary years, they may learn to avoid eye contact with teachers so that they will not be called upon. They may experience no problem speaking to other students or teachers outside class, but will receive poor grades for class participation. Typically, anxious students are hesitant to discuss the problem with their teachers or to ask for accommodations. Teachers may think these students are merely shy, obstinate, or not motivated to learn.

Some teachers catch on to a student's discomfort, recognize existing talent, and are sympathetic to the apparent shyness. Others may try to engage the student by calling on him to answer the occasional question and encouraging him to speak up. This encouragement may be helpful in some cases. On the other hand, it can become increasingly distressing for the student with profound social anxiety. I have met students who were able to work out a deal with their teacher to do some form of written assignment as an alternative to an oral presentation. Some anxious students agree to read their prepared oral presentations to their teacher in private. These are viable alternatives as long as the student is encouraged to gradually take risks and overcome anxiety in small, brave steps.

Strategies for Well-Being

Stress Lessons Toolkit

Kids Have Stress Too!
program

It is unfortunate that many students experience the anguish of anxiety throughout their elementary and secondary years. It is also very unfortunate when students do not pursue post-secondary opportunities because of their anxiety over formal presentations and class seminars. Compounding the situation is the concern that without coping skills, students will seek to blot out their pain with substances of one form or another.

As with all forms of stress, students can learn to detect the physiological sensations of anxiety in their bodies and understand that their response is a form of conditioning. Thinking about and visualizing fearful situations are what set off these conditioned anxiety responses. To bring the anxiety under control, they can unlearn these conditioned reactions. It is also important that they are given the opportunity to voice their feelings and concerns to a trusted teacher, friend, or other caring adult (e.g., their anxiety that only whispers would come out of their mouth if they tried to speak in class; their fear that their classmates will laugh at their answers and their nervous mannerisms if they try to speak up in class).

So, what strategies and tools can help students overcome anxiety?

- **Intentional relaxation skills.** Deep breathing techniques, progressive muscle tensing and relaxing, slow breathing, and relaxing visualizations are useful for reducing the feelings of anxiety. The goal is to become adept at becoming deeply relaxed in a short time, so that they can calm down when they find themselves starting to get anxious.

- **A process of systematic desensitization.** The intense physiological conditioning that causes bodily symptoms of anxiety can be gradually undone. This process can involve speaking to a trusted teacher while sitting in an empty classroom, then having one of their best friends sit in the classroom for a question-and-answer session to expand their zone of comfort and use relaxation skills. They can then progress to smaller groups of trusted friends, and eventually the teacher could help the student become more comfortable in a regular classroom setting by calmly asking a question or two.

- **An attitude of bravery.** Adopting this will help the student to stick with the program, one step at a time, while inching closer to success.

- **Reframing of anxiety.** Students can come to realize that a certain amount of anxiety can be useful to bring energy and enthusiasm to the situation. They can use their anxiety positively and calmly.

- **Sense of humour.** In dealing with anxiety management, the student need not stick to a totally serious journey. Teachers, friends, and the student involved in the process can all be encouraged to see the lighter side of their activities.

- **Basic public speaking skills.** Learning these will build confidence in their abilities. Students can be taught to seek out eye contact while presenting and to look for interest expressed in others' eyes for support and encouragement. Projecting their voices and using presentational supports such as visuals, graphics, or video clips are also helpful.

- **Visualization of success.** Based on this work, the student will be able to visualize being successful, and use these positive visualizations to replace earlier visions of failure and embarrassment. (This cognitive rehearsal strategy is commonly used by elite athletes.)

A Caveat
Small groups can have big impacts, but groups that are not supportive can hinder performance and challenge mental health.

Strengths Versus Discouragements

If they are not accommodated properly, the gifts described here—as well as the challenges—can be factors in discouragement. Our best hope to help prevent students from becoming discouraged is to promote positive mental health and to develop tighter communities of care in which children and youth feel connected and valued for who they are.

Clinical depression may be thought of as a severe form of discouragement. Like many other mental health illnesses, depression often has multiple pathways. Genetics can be a factor. Life experiences and disappointments can also play a role. Sometimes, people become depressed when they experience serious setbacks or losses, such as the death of a loved one. When depression sets in for seemingly no reason at all, there may be an inherited chemical imbalance related to the brain's neurotransmitters.

Although all of us are familiar with sadness and discouragement from normal and unavoidable losses or grief, a clinical depression is more significant and long-lasting. In my clinical practice over the years, I have witnessed profound suffering by youth and adults with clinical depression. An individual with severe depression can feel helpless and lose all hope for the future. Suicidal thoughts and fantasies may visit the mind of the depressed person, with the allure of potential peace and relief from emotional pain.

Depression in Children and Youth

Students who are significantly discouraged may complain of poor concentration and feel incapable of finishing their work. Oftentimes, younger children express depression with defiance and angry outbursts. Children, youth, and adults with depression will usually report tearfulness over minor issues. At a deeper stage of depression, they may report an inability to cry anymore, even over big issues. Friends and acquaintances will often notice significant social withdrawal. Teachers may notice plummeting grades.

Children and youth with depression may try to hide it. Flett and Hewitt (2013) published a paper showing that many students become adept at "flying under the radar" to avoid detection of mental health ailments. A lack of mental health literacy, combined with the stigma of a diagnosis, can cause youth to hide a dark secret of despair. The reality of this problem hits home when there is a death by suicide, and many friends, family members, and other close acquaintances had no clue about the pain that the student was experiencing.

The challenges brought on by the normal developmental transition through adolescence in a complex society are significant. Adolescence, beginning between the ages of 10 and 12 years, is a time of rapid change involving the journey into adulthood with its many responsibilities. Physically, there are increases in height and weight, along with the development of sexual functions and hormonal change. Significant psychological development occurs as well, involving the need for independence and to seek out an individual identity. Adolescents develop increased capacity for abstract thought as well as logical, idealistic thought and moral reasoning based on imposed societal standards. Simultaneously, there is a tendency for egocentrism or self-absorption.

Fortunately, the last decade has produced a number of highly effective therapies for depression. According to a study published in the *American Journal of Psychiatry* (March & Vitiello, 2009), for adolescents, the best evidence supports a combination of cognitive behavioural therapy (CBT) and medication. It is worth noting that positive psychotherapy (PPT) is being developed and has shown positive results (Rashid, 2014). Positive psychotherapy focuses on cultivating character strengths, positive emotions, and positive relationships, and on pursuing meaningful, intrinsically motivated accomplishments to help deal with psychiatric stress. Various models of school applications are being put forward: these use resources such as positive emotions, a growth mindset, engagement, relationships, a sense of meaning, and accomplishment to support student well-being (Anjum, 2014). So, before discouragement becomes serious, prevention by promoting positive mental health is a pathway we can forge in our schools and classrooms.

Diversity and Well-Being in the Classroom

There is strength in diversity. As we acknowledge and nurture the various gifts of unique individuals, we can come to appreciate team and community strengths in diversity. We all know that every team needs members with complementary skills and talents to be successful. Students will recognize the same is true in their classroom, and many will identify class strengths as a result of the diverse mix of individuals.

In a classroom that puts strengths first and where individuals understand and value their own strengths and those of others, relationships are stronger and more caring, the focus is on positive experiences and goals, and there is a greater sense of optimism and energy. Students will support and learn from one another.

A flexible and balanced classroom environment can bring us closer to the goals of optimal learning and positive mental well-being for all students. No one is denying that there will be conflicts, issues, and daily problems—some serious and all that need to be addressed. But mistakes, issues, and adversity can be seen as learning opportunities. As we will see in Chapter 5, how we deal with adversity is one of the keys to positive mental health.

Anjum, A. (2014, July). *Strength based resiliency program* [SBR]. Pre-conference workshop presented at the 2nd Canadian Conference on Positive Psychology, Ottawa, ON.

Aron, E. (2002). *The highly sensitive child: Helping our children thrive when the world overwhelms them.* New York, NY: Crown.

Brownlee, K., Rawana, E. P., & MacArthur, J. (2012). Implementation of a strengths-based approach to teaching in an elementary school. *Journal of Teaching and Learning, 8*(1). Retrieved from http://ojs.uwindsor.ca/ojs/leddy/index.php/JTL/article/download/3069/pdf

Cain, S. (2012). *Quiet: The power of introverts in a world that can't stop talking.* New York, NY: Crown.

Cherry, K. (2014). 5 signs you are an introvert. In *About.com*. Retrieved from http://psychology.about.com/od/personalitydevelopment/fl/5-Signs-You-Are-an-Introvert.htm

Diamond, S.A. (2012, May 26). Essential secrets of psychotherapy: Jung's typology, eudaemonology, and the elusive art of happiness. In *Evil Deeds*. Retrieved from http://www.psychologytoday.com/blog/evil-deeds/201205/essential-secrets-psychotherapy-jungs-typology-eudaemonology-and-the-elusive-

Flett, G. L., & Hewitt, P. L. (2013). Disguised distress in children and adolescents "flying under the radar": Why psychological problems are underestimated and how schools must respond. *Canadian Journal of School Psychology, 28*(1), 12–27.

Gardner, H. (1983). *Frames of mind: The theory of multiple intelligences.* New York, NY: Basic Books.

Greene, R. W. (2010). Kids do well if they can [Video]. Retrieved from http://www.youtube.com/watch?v=jvzQQDfAL-Q

Greene, R. W. (2013). *The explosive child: A new approach for understanding and parenting easily frustrated, chronically inflexible children* (5th ed.). New York, NY: HarperCollins.

Joint Consortium for School Health [JCSH]. (2010). *Schools as a setting for promoting positive mental health: Better practices and perspectives.* Retrieved from http://www.jcshcces.ca/upload/PMH%20July10%202011%20WebReady.pdf

Kahnweiler, J. B. (2014). Advice for introverts: How to thrive in the business world. In *American Management Association*. Retrieved from http://www.amanet.org/training/articles/Advice-for-Introverts-How-to-Thrive-in-the-Business-World.aspx

March, J. S., & Vitiello, B. (2009). Clinical messages from the Treatment for Adolescents with Depression Study [TADS]. *American Journal of Psychiatry, 166*(10), 1118–1123.

Ontario Ministry of Education. (2002). *The Ontario curriculum unit planner: Special education companion*. Toronto ON: Queen's Printer for Ontario.

Rashid, T. (2014, July). *Positive psychotherapy [PPT]*. Pre-conference workshop presented at the 2nd Canadian Conference on Positive Psychology, Ottawa, ON.

Rawana, E., Latimer, K., Whitley, J., & Probizanski, M. (2009, November). Strength-based classroom strategies for teachers. *Canadian Teacher Magazine*.

Resiliency Initiatives. (2012). *Embracing a strengths-based perspective and practice in education*. Retrieved from the Resiliency Initiatives website: http://www.resil.ca

Saleebey, D. (2006). Power in the people. In D. Saleebey (Ed.), *The strengths perspective in social work practice* (4th ed.). Toronto, ON: Pearson Education.

Yerkes, R. M., & Dodson, J. D. (1908). The relation of strength of stimulus to rapidity of habit formation. *Journal of Comparative Neurology and Psychology 18*, 459–482.

Zeff, T. (2010). *The strong, sensitive boy*. San Ramon, CA: Prana.

CHAPTER 5

Resilient, Active, and Flourishing

"…Happiness, flow, meaning, love, gratitude, accomplishment, growth, better relationships… constitute human flourishing. Learning that you can have more of these things is life changing."

—SELIGMAN, 2011, p. 2

Key Aspects of Optimal Mental Health

- Resilience—a combination of skills and attributes that help us solve problems, deal with disappointments, learn from challenges, and bounce back from adversity

- An active lifestyle—enjoyable physical activity as an integral part of daily life that improves interpersonal relationships, self-image, self-worth, cognitive functioning, and overall life satisfaction and well-being

- Flourishing—the experience of positive emotions (fun and enjoyment), passionate engagement, a sense of meaning and accomplishment, self-realization of strengths and talents, and positive relationships that create a deep sense of well-being

It is worth beginning this chapter by considering this anecdote.

My friend Jack was small for his age when he started school. Photographers for class pictures always placed him at the front and at one end of the row to symmetrically compose the pictures, as if Jack belonged in only a marginal way. Jack also had a problem with anxiety, as did his father and several uncles. At one point, his father had a breakdown, staying off work for a long time to regain his confidence and make some major career changes. At another point, Jack's father was hospitalized for several months.

Jack was self-conscious about others seeing his work or hearing him answer a question. He seemed to come out of himself at fun events like a birthday party, where there was lots of excitement and he could act silly without being the centre of attention. Most people didn't know that Jack worried a lot and felt scared for no particular reason that even he could identify at first.

In Grade 3, Jack began worrying about the inevitability of death. Sometimes, he felt so scared that he told his teacher he felt sick and asked if he could call home. Most of the time, Jack hid his fears well. He never shared his secret about being afraid of dying until he was an adult.

Jack could recall some very distressing experiences from his childhood. He remembered the day his mother got the call that his grandfather had died in a car accident. Not only did it feel like the world had caved in because he realized he would never see his grandfather again, but his mother cried with grief on the phone. That propelled Jack's anxiety into a full panic attack. He cried even harder than his mother, and he could not be consoled for some time.

There was also an incident when his brother tried to make French fries and the vegetable oil caught fire. The flames licking up the wall told Jack that all would be lost, and someone was going to get seriously hurt, or die. This belief triggered another panic attack consisting of intense fear, screams, difficulty with breathing, and a feeling that he was going to collapse. After that, Jack could not be around when his mother or anyone else made French fries.

In the early years at school, Jack lacked confidence and didn't compete hard in games or athletics. His schoolwork was mediocre. He loved his summer holidays more than going to school because he could help out on his uncle's farm. His uncle really appreciated his help, and Jack felt happiest when he was helping his uncle— throwing hay down to the cows or spreading straw around for the other animals to sleep on. Sometimes, he could go to the family farm for an overnight stay. During early adolescence, farming experience increased Jack's strength and agility.

In Grade 8, Jack's teacher, Mr. Speck, took an interest in Jack, recognized his strengths, and encouraged him to try out for track and field activities.

Mr. Speck always stopped to talk to Jack, and he listened attentively and smiled when he talked to him. He told Jack that he had quick legs and with practice, he could become even faster. Jack was almost stunned with disbelief, but he was also thrilled with the idea of being fast and being noticed for those supposedly quick legs.

Mr. Speck was steady with encouragement and guided Jack to set running goals and to develop a safe and gradual program to further develop his skills. Jack ran daily for several months. He started feeling comfortable around the others involved in track and field and gained a stronger sense of belonging than he had ever felt at school before. He became less inclined to shrink away during social interactions.

In the final weeks of Grade 8, Jack competed in races at school and was proud to place third in one event. Mr. Speck encouraged Jack to get involved in track and field in high school. Jack describes high school as a much better experience than his early years in elementary school, and university was better still.

As an adult, Jack has continued to run for about 30 minutes, two or three times a week, for more than 30 years. He has a number of friends with whom he occasionally runs after work or on the weekends. He also plays pick-up hockey in the winter. He loves his work and has developed strong skills in his profession. Jack says that running keeps him sane when his work life becomes overly busy and challenging. If he misses running for several days in a row, he begins to feel lethargic and cranky.

I asked Jack if he still has panic attacks. He told me that he sometimes gets reminders, or "little ones." If Jack gets tired and has a lot to deal with, he experiences a sense of "impending doom" and is reminded of the terror he felt at times many years earlier. He responds to these uneasy feelings with a combination of rest, running, and relaxation. He went to a psychologist in his early twenties and learned a progressive muscle relaxation technique, combined with deep and slow breathing exercises to reduce stress. Jack also uses positive self-talk as soon as he begins to feel anxious. He gets a run in as soon as he can and finds a way to get a good sleep. These tactics work for him.

Jack wishes that he had thanked Mr. Speck for the impact he had on his life, but he can't—Mr. Speck has passed away. Jack now volunteers as a hockey coach. He keeps his eyes peeled for quiet kids who may need a little encouragement.

Achieving Optimal Mental Health

It is helpful to keep Jack's story in mind as we go through this chapter. Jack came to be resilient, active, and flourishing. He represents the difference a teacher, or a school, can make in a child's mental health—not through expensive or sophisticated interventions, but through compassion, inclusion, and encouragement. By encouraging Jack to join the track team, Mr. Speck taught Jack the value of physical activity not only as a way to control anxiety, but also as a way to develop resilience: the ability to deal with the ups and downs that come our way.

For other individuals, the strengths, resources, and methods they bring to dealing with challenges and adversity may be different. The pathways to optimal mental health are diverse and individual, but it is worth acknowledging that one of the most powerful and life-changing gifts we can give children and youth is the *goal* of positive well-being. *It is possible to overcome adversity and engage in worthwhile striving to be the best we can be. There are skills, attributes, and resources that we can all cultivate not only to meet life's challenges, but to flourish.*

Recall that we defined positive mental health as "the capacity of each and all of us to feel, think, and act in ways that enhance our ability to enjoy life and deal with the challenges we face. It is a positive sense of emotional and spiritual well-being that respects the importance of culture, equity, social justice, interconnections, and personal dignity" (Public Health Agency of Canada [PHAC], 2006).

There are three fairly independent areas of research with powerful findings that ought to be considered together to really understand what is important to ensure positive mental health in our children and youth. These three areas incorporate what we have considered so far about social emotional learning (SEL) and a strengths-based approach. Indeed social emotional learning and a strengths-based perspective work to lay the foundations for optimal well-being and a balanced life. The research I am referring to is in the areas of

- resilience

- the importance of physical activity for mental health

- the concept of "flourishing"

My experiences as a psychologist, parent, and educator have led me to the conclusion that resilience, an active lifestyle, and the experience of flourishing through self-realized talents are the true expression of positive mental health and well-being. Together, they represent what well-being really looks like. At the centre of all three is relationships. Strong, caring relationships can be seen as the most

That children should grow up in community environments of happiness, love, and understanding to develop their personalities, abilities, and talents to their best potential is enshrined in the United Nations *Convention on the Rights of the Child* (1990). Some 193 countries have signed the agreement to this convention, which has a total of 54 parts, or articles.

reliable factor in, and indicator of, positive well-being. Figure 5.1 shows this model of well-being (first seen in Chapter 1). In this chapter, we will look at each component in more depth.

Figure 5.1: A Model for Well-Being

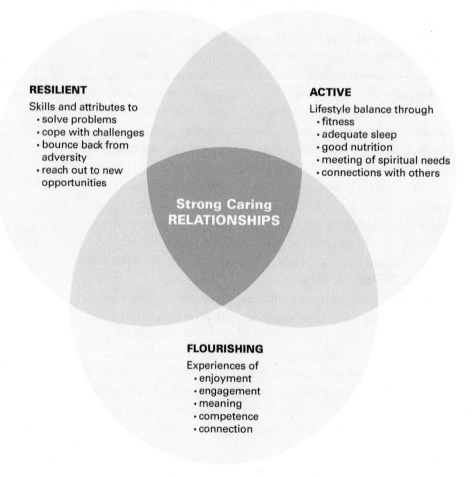

RESILIENT
Skills and attributes to
- solve problems
- cope with challenges
- bounce back from adversity
- reach out to new opportunities

ACTIVE
Lifestyle balance through
- fitness
- adequate sleep
- good nutrition
- meeting of spiritual needs
- connections with others

Strong Caring RELATIONSHIPS

FLOURISHING
Experiences of
- enjoyment
- engagement
- meaning
- competence
- connection

School-Based Approaches for Promoting and Supporting Well-Being

A whole-school, whole-community approach
- actively promoting positive mental health and creating a healthy, caring, inclusive class and school environment

A social emotional learning approach
- developing self-awareness, self-management, social awareness, relationship skills, and responsible decision-making

A strengths-based approach
- recognizing and cultivating the inner strengths, capabilities, and resources we all have for well-being

Worth considering are other definitions and models that incorporate similar ideas and offer a holistic perspective on well-being. These include the concept of the Medicine Wheel (Figure 5.2). The Medicine Wheel is a symbol in the form of a circle that expresses belief in the endless cycle of life in many Indigenous cultures. It is based on knowledge of the rhythm of life and the observation of Nature. While not all First Nations, Inuit, and Métis cultures in Canada use the Medicine Wheel, for many it represents "The Great Everything," as well as each individual's own personal universe.

Medicine in Aboriginal worldviews is energy, or the vital power that is in Nature and in each individual to become more whole or balanced. The wheel is sometimes shown with the cardinal directions (east, west, north, south), each representing a path to knowledge and energy that can bring self-realization, meaning, purpose, and fulfillment to life.

Health in many First Nations, Inuit, and Métis worldviews encompasses both healing and wellness. Healing goes beyond the treatment of sickness; it is holistic, encompassing all four domains represented in the Medicine Wheel, and focuses on creating a safe and positive environment for becoming whole and balanced. Wellness is also more than mental or physical health. It is holistic, representing a balance of all dimensions—physical, emotional, mental, and spiritual—of the individual, family, and community (Stewart, 2008). Although a person can focus on each dimension individually, they are all connected and affect one another.

With this focus on positive well-being rather than on deficits or disorders, the Medicine Wheel can enrich our understanding of mental health promotion and pathways to well-being—not only for First Nations, Inuit, and Métis children and youth, but for all children and youth, their families, and teachers.

Best Start Resources: Holistic Support Wheel

A Child Becomes Strong: Journeying Through Each Stage of the Life Cycle

As a resource by the Ontario Secondary School Teachers' Federation (2012, p. 3) puts it:

> For many, the medicine wheel is used as part of a healing process. This process has been described in the following way. 'I begin my healing journey in the South, where my anger, sadness and pain force me travel to the North where I learn more about what happened. That learning leads me on my journey to the West to gather more information from the spirits of my ancestors. With my spirit healed and my new knowledge I travel to the East to share my findings and my knowledge. I have come full circle. If I'm challenged or need more, I will return to the South and begin the journey again.' The circle is often seen as whole and never ending. It can be balanced or unbalanced, depending upon what is placed on or in it.

Figure 5.2: One Representation of a Medicine Wheel

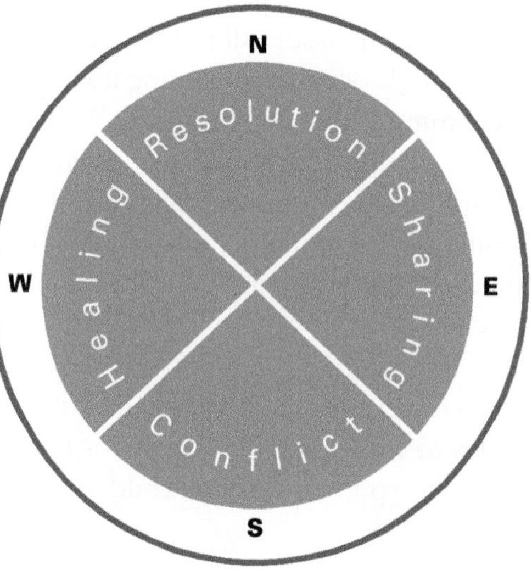

This example of a Medicine Wheel is based on cardinal directions.

Resilience

What Is Resilience?

The Psychology Foundation of Canada has defined *resilience* as "a combination of skills and positive attributes that people gain from their life experiences and relationships. These attributes help them solve problems, cope with challenges, and bounce back from disappointments."

All of us want to be happy and successful. In other words, we want to develop our skills to be competent at handling adversity, and we want to experience kindness and support in our relationships with others. Resiliency research has a long history of studying people who seemed to defy the odds and do well despite trying circumstances. As such, resiliency research emphasizes strengths over deficits. Each individual draws upon unique learning experiences, strengths, and resources to overcome challenges. The research also shows, however, that some common skills and attributes underlie resilience.

> "Resilience helps people deal with stress and adversity, overcome childhood disadvantage, and reach out to new opportunities. More than thirty years of research shows that people who are resilient are healthier, live longer, are more successful in school and at work, are happier in relationships, and are less prone to depression."
>
> —*Pearson & Hall, 2006, p. 1*

Developing Resilience

Before we consider resiliency skills and attributes, it is worth emphasizing that resilience is not something we either have or don't have. *Developing and maintaining resilience is a lifelong process.* Moreover, resiliency skills can be learned. The learning and nurturing process can begin with very young children. Children as young as two and three can reflect what their caregivers model, and during the early elementary years, children can develop the thinking skills, attitudes, and emotional regulation skills that are key elements of resilience.

Resilience is especially important for youth making the transition into high school, where students need to navigate social relationships with various groups of excitable and competitive peers in what is often a much larger school. In adolescence, hormonal changes also complicate life and a rapidly developing limbic system, which processes emotions, tends to override the executive command and logic control of the prefrontal cortex—in other words, the part of the brain responsible for complex planning, decision making, moderating social behaviour, and even personality expression (Yang & Raine, 2009). The emotional highs and lows of adolescence and the high rates of teenage depression underline the importance of positive mental health promotion and resiliency skills development for this age group.

What Makes Us Resilient?

In his book, *Duct Tape Isn't Enough: Survival Skills for the 21st Century*, Ron Breazeale (2009) provides an evidence-informed list of skills and attitudes that constitute resilience in children and youth. The five *skills* he identifies are as follows:

- developing effective relationships
- showing flexibility
- doing realistic action planning
- listening and problem solving
- managing emotions

Breazeale's list of resiliency traits includes *attitudes* that help make us resilient:

- having self-confidence
- seeing meaning and purpose
- holding an optimistic perspective
- keeping a sense of (appropriate) humour
- keeping balance and fitness
- nurturing empathy and making a social contribution

Perhaps you have noticed that the lists of skills and attitudes reflect key elements of the social emotional competencies. Let's take a closer look at Breazeale's list of skills.

©P

What Kids Say

The research findings on resilience and social emotional skills are also reflected in what kids say has helped them bounce back. Their advice:

- Ask for help.
- Talk it out.
- Focus on the positive.
- Get active and have fun.
- Learn to know how you feel.
- Try something new.
- Keep trying.

We all need someone to help us when we are going through a tough time.

Think about one person you can tell things to when you are down.

Remember to help friends when they need help. We are stronger together!

Source: Student Support Leadership Initiative (Oxford, Elgin, London/Middlesex) (2014, p. 6).

Reaching In...Reaching Out (RIRO)—resiliency skills training

Developing Effective Relationships

We have seen the powerful influence that even a single caring adult can have on a child or youth, and this is especially so when a child comes from a disadvantaged background and experiences high levels of adversity (Ungar, 2013). Likewise, negative relationships that misunderstand behaviour, focus on shortcomings or mistakes, impose decisions, and thus increase anxiety—however innocently or well intentioned—can have damaging effects.

Children and youth need to know that they can reach out for help to someone they trust and who understands them. They also need the social emotional skills to build positive relationships, resist negative peer pressure, and develop the self-awareness and self-confidence to deal with conflict and adversity in relationships. Ultimately, the goal is to develop the close relationships built on trust, caring, and empathy that will sustain them through the bumps in the road and help them be ready to take on new challenges. Breazeale notes that relationships that can provide support and caring are one of the primary factors in resilience.

Flexibility

Flexibility involves a willingness to try new things and to learn from our mistakes. Thomas Edison is said to have made more than 10 000 attempts to develop the first viable electric light bulb. Before he succeeded he was asked by a reporter about whether he felt like a failure and should give up. Edison apparently replied that he now knew more than 9000 ways that an electric light bulb would not work. The reporter looked at Edison's efforts as failures; Edison considered them to be learnings. This example underlines the value of flexibility and persistence. Celebrating efforts rather than correct end products only can help students understand and develop flexibility. Flexibility is key not only in academic pursuits, but also in interpersonal relationships and in strategies to manage emotions.

Being able to analyze a problem and consider various alternative and realistic solutions is another form of flexibility—flexible thinking. We all have deeply held beliefs and thinking habits that can affect our ability to assess situations accurately. Children and youth (and adults as well) can get stuck in **thinking traps** that prevent them from moving toward positive change. Or, they may act impulsively without thinking, particularly when under stress.

Taking a moment to stop and assess a situation accurately can make a significant difference. Considering the source of the stress or problem, whether it is temporary or permanent, and how much of our lives it really affects can ease stress and help us feel less overwhelmed and more able to find solutions. "It's all my fault" can become "I'm only one member of the team." "This is never going to end!" can become "Once this test is over, I'll be able to hang out with my friends." "I can't do anything right" is replaced with "I'll get better at this once I have more experience" (Pearson & Hall, 2006).

Bouncing back is easier when we see that a situation affects only part of our lives. When the problem is deeper and more permanent, flexible and resilient thinking can help us avoid getting stuck and instead move toward positive solutions.

Realistic Action Planning

Realistic action planning is a key tool for jumping the hurdles of life. By this assertion, I do not mean to condemn the joy of spontaneity, although spontaneity can sometimes reduce our ability to make realistic choices. Coasting along or making haphazard choices means we might end up with holidays that don't work out or run out of time to study for that exam. I have counselled bright, but upset young high-school students who found they could no longer coast like they did in elementary school and still get good grades. When I ask what grades they would like to get and what their planning strategy is, we soon end up in a conversation about realistic action planning.

Realistic action planning also means that when children and youth are in trouble, they understand they can get help and they know where to get it. They can realistically assess whether actions or situations are feasible or healthy for them, and if not, they can say no. They can learn to set realistic and achievable goals that support their well-being. Realistic action planning means recognizing that positive outcomes do not happen automatically. They require planning, effort, and action. If we approach obstacles with flexibility, we can generate and assess alternatives, and plan realistic solutions. We can ask: "What else can happen now? How else could I think about this? What can I do about it? Which action is best?"

Listening and Problem Solving

It is probably obvious to say that good communication skills are extremely useful for overcoming most challenges. But it is notable that, in his list of skills, Breazeale highlights listening. Without active and effective listening, communication does not happen. Active listening is mindful—it involves making a conscious effort to hear and understand, and it includes awareness of the situation or context, non-verbal cues, and what we know about the person or people we are listening to. It is only when we really take in what others are trying to tell us that we can move toward effective and collaborative problem solving.

Working effectively as a team member in their community is a way for youth to build resilience. More and more projects involve teamwork by individuals who bring different skill sets to the table. Consulting with others is often important with individual projects, as well. Cooperative work groups provide students with opportunities to develop listening skills and engage in teamwork for problem solving. Teachers can promote listening and joint problem-solving skills among their students so that they achieve group work synergy.

Managing Emotions

> "Resilience does not involve avoiding one's feelings; it involves confronting and managing them."
>
> —Breazeale, 2009, p. 3

Resilience requires emotional control. How we manage our emotions affects the way we relate to others, view situations, solve problems—and ultimately, look at the world.

A friend of mine once got a flat tire in rush hour on a busy road when he was late for an appointment. He told me he could feel his face flushing, his chest tightening, and some unusual language crossing his mind. He was about to lose control. Then, he took a step back and managed to switch his perspective. He turned the situation into a positive challenge, rather than an overwhelming trauma. In 21 minutes, the funny little biscuit tire was on, and with only slightly dirty hands, he was on his way. He told me he laughed all the way down the highway, aware of the irony of being in a hurry while moving like a turtle. Nonetheless, he made it to his destination about half an hour later and even managed to spot a garage on the way that agreed to fix his tire while he was at his meeting.

What is illuminating about this anecdote is how a switch in mindset can change a situation and make us more resilient to change. I have used this story in talking with students. Generally, students are able to grasp the related concepts of mindset and perspective. They can see that a positive mindset can change their view or perspective on a situation. I often see enthusiasm for the notion of emotional self-regulation when we discuss these ideas in times other than in the heat of a crisis. With practice, students are able to use this skill of reframing with minimal prompting, and it becomes a self-management tool for them.

If we think about it, it's clear that the various skills and attitudes associated with resilience work together. Developing good relationships, communicating effectively, as well as being flexible and able to plan, help to produce a positive self-image and the confidence to tackle a problem with success in mind. These skills also help us to maintain an optimistic perspective and even find humour in a situation. When we feel confident and competent, and we enjoy good relationships, we are more likely to take care of ourselves with exercise and a reasonable diet. Likewise, when we reach out to others in our communities, we feel empowered, confident, and more optimistic about ourselves and our relationships.

SPOTLIGHT

Flexible and Resilient Thinking

We know that stress, adversity, and challenge are parts of life that we often cannot avoid or control. The way we think about adversity, however, is within our control and is a major factor in resilience. We can learn to be more resilient by changing how we think about adversity.

Pessimists see adversities as permanent and catastrophic, feel helpless, don't look for solutions, don't take action for improvements, give up easily, get stuck in distress, and have a sense of meaninglessness.

Realistic optimists see adversities as temporary and as problems that can be solved. Without denying the negative aspects, they feel confident, consider other perspectives, look for realistic options, take action for positive outcomes, move on and keep trying, and feel there is purpose and meaning in life.

In their guidebook on resilient thinking, Pearson and Hall provide a description of a resilient view: "A resilient view is characterized by accurate and flexible thinking and consists of creative problem solving, the capacity to see other points of view and to challenge one's own views, and the ability to move on with daily life despite obstacles" (Pearson & Hall, 2006, p. 1). They note that children can develop accurate and flexible thinking from an early age, contributing to their resiliency development.

"Studies show that people who manage stress and adversity best have what can be referred to as 3 Cs in common.

Control: a belief in their ability to take charge of the controllable aspects of a situation and 'influence a more positive outcome'

Challenge: a view of mistakes as opportunities for new learning, and change as potential for growth

Commitment: an active engagement in work and other pursuits that provides a basis of meaning for their lives."

—Pearson & Hall, 2006, p. 1

Barriers to Flexible and Resilient Thinking

Psychologist Martin Seligman's research (1991) points to other thinking concepts that can affect resiliency development—what he calls "iceberg beliefs" and "thinking traps." These can develop early in childhood and stay with us into adulthood.

Iceberg beliefs are deeply rooted beliefs about how we think the world should operate, and they may be passed on from generation to generation or be culturally rooted. Iceberg beliefs often work subconsciously and can be problematic when they interfere with our relationships or our resilience. For example, "Never let them know you are hurting" can prevent people from reaching out to others for help, and "Things should always be fair" can be an unrealistic perspective that may prevent people from moving on. Not all iceberg beliefs are problematic (some are important values that support our resilience), but they can cause us to react out of proportion to a situation.

Thinking traps are common thinking errors, often automatic and largely unconscious, that trap us into drawing conclusions prematurely. Thinking traps can cause us to see a situation inaccurately and unrealistically because we use only information that supports what we already believe and filter out what does not support our belief. Thinking traps include overgeneralizing, exaggerating or catastrophizing, minimizing or downplaying, personalizing, mind-reading (assuming we know what others are thinking without asking), and engaging in emotional reasoning (making false conclusions based solely on how we feel rather than on the facts).

Our Explanatory Thinking Styles

Iceberg beliefs and thinking traps can contribute to what Seligman calls our "explanatory styles." Seligman's research shows that people unconsciously look for answers to three questions when they try to explain a problem they are experiencing.

Personalization: Who caused the problem? Me/Not me

Permanence: How long will this problem last? Always/Not always

Pervasiveness: How much of my life does this problem affect? Everything/Not everything

Because our explanatory styles can cause us to react out of habit and jump to conclusions that may not be accurate, we need to challenge our beliefs and be aware of our explanatory styles with each situation we face. Our explanatory styles can lead to negative depression or aggression if they are constant, or they can promote the realistic optimism that reflects more flexible and resilient thinking.

Figure 5.3: Explanatory Styles and Their Effects on Resilience

Explanatory Style	Depression	Aggression	Unrealistic Optimism	Realistic Optimism (Flexible and Resilient Thinking)	Questions to Realistically Assess a Situation
Personalization	Me	Not me	Not me	Me/Not me	How much is my responsibility? How much is due to circumstances outside my control? What parts of the situation can I do something about?
Permanence	Always	Always	Not always	Not always/ Sometimes long-lasting	Can I see an end to this situation? How long will it really last? Do I need to reach out for support?
Pervasiveness	Everything	Everything	Not everything	Not everything/But recognize serious issues	Does this problem really affect everything in my life? What parts of my life does it affect? What can I do?
Examples	*"Everybody hates me. I'm never going to have any friends."*	*"Maria always gets invited to Sasha's parties. I never do. They are such snobs."*	*"Sasha must have just forgotten to invite me. I'll be able to go to the party."*	*"I'm disappointed I wasn't invited, but I don't know Sasha very well. Maybe I'll be invited next time after we know each other better."*	

Explanatory Style	Depression	Aggression	Unrealistic Optimism	Realistic Optimism (Flexible and Resilient Thinking)	Questions to Realistically Assess a Situation
Results	• take things personally • believe negative situations are permanent and affect many areas of their lives • lose hope and experience depression	• blame others; take little responsibility • believe negative situations are permanent and affect many areas of their lives • have sense of futility, feel trapped and angry, may lash out at others	• optimistic but may not be an accurate or realistic view of a situation, particularly if see all situations this way • may ignore difficult issues and therefore have difficulty in relationships or with asking for help when a real problem emerges	• take appropriate personal responsibility but also recognize she or he is not always at fault • feel optimistic but do not deny negative aspects of a situation or pervasive elements • think as accurately and flexibly as possible about each situation they face	• catch thinking traps and biases • have a more realistic view of a situation or problem • consider other perspectives • assess and focus on positive action

Source: Pearson & Hall (2006).

Strategies for Building Resilience

There are a number of practical strategies that can help students develop their resiliency skills. Below are a few examples.

Positive Self-Talk—Encourage students to pay attention to their self-talk, or the thoughts they say to themselves without speaking out loud. Help them to identify thinking traps and to recognize their explanatory style. If their self-talk is primarily negative, guide them to challenge their negative thinking and focus on realistic and flexible thinking, coping statements, or positive self-statements. Questions such as these can help turn thinking around: "Have I confused a thought with a fact? What would I tell a friend if he or she had the same thought? What is the worst that can happen? If this did happen, what can I do to handle it?"

Coping Cards—Keeping coping cards can help children and youth remember their personal coping strategies when they need them most, in the heat of the moment, when it is often difficult to think straight. Coping cards can be small cards with short statements or reminders, including positive coaching statements, notes on personal coping skills, and calming facts.

Sample Coping Card

My Coping Card to Beat Anxiety!

1. Anxiety is not dangerous. It can't hurt me. It's just a bully.

2. I can boss back my anxiety. I have done it before!

3. If my heart is racing, I get sweaty, and my tummy/stomach hurts. That means that my anxiety is acting up. I'm not in danger.

4. I could do some relaxation now.

5. Am I falling into a thinking trap?

Source: ADABC Parenting Project © Anxiety BC anxietybc.com

Literature—Stories, other literature, and media can be a powerful resource for promoting critical resiliency abilities and thinking skills. Talking about stories allows children to express their beliefs; exposes them to other thoughts, feelings, and experiences; and offers a way to challenge assumptions. Stories allow children to discover ways to overcome obstacles and deal with challenges in life.

Mindfulness strategies—Susan Kaiser Greenland (2011) has defined mindfulness as "the capacity to be alert and open to life experience as it occurs in a non-reactive, resilient, and compassionate way." Mindfulness encourages reflection, emotional balance, and clarity. Children can understand mindfulness as quieting our minds and being fully aware of what is happening in the moment—without worrying or judging. Mindfulness strategies have been shown to reduce stress, develop attention, and increase resilience. Strategies that have been successful with children and youth include these:

- **mindful breathing:** Students can practise focusing on their breathing and using it as an anchor. Thoughts and feelings can wander, but our breath is constant and rhythmic. Sitting upright and relaxed with feet flat on the floor and hands resting in our laps, we can pay attention to our breathing, letting it flow in and out, noticing that our chest or stomach moves. If our mind wanders, we can gently notice and name what has caught our attention, listen for a while and then bring our attention back to our breathing. We can notice how we are feeling, thoughts crossing our minds, and keep bringing ourselves back to our breathing. Afterwards, we can talk about and perhaps share insights.

- **mindful eating:** Students can try eating a raisin or grape in slow motion—first looking at it, touching it, describing it with all of the senses, then slowly putting it in the mouth without biting it, closing their eyes and just feeling it, then biting it and chewing slowly noticing taste and texture, and what the tongue is doing, and finally slowly swallowing. Then ask what this was like, what they noticed, if there were any surprises, and whether this was hard to do and why.

Some teachers have had success with yoga poses and tai chi as well. Students can come to understand that we can do many things mindfully every day. With practice, mindfulness can provide the calm, alert, reflective moments that can help us find balance and perspective.

Mindfulness Without Borders—educational programs and resources based in best practices for social emotional learning and mindfulness-based education

Reaching In...Reaching Out Resiliency Guidebook—"Bounce back" thinking skills for children and adults

Recognizing Resilience

Many years ago I was asked to consult about a student who had defied his teacher (yet again) and would not line up to come in from recess with the other students. The student seemed very upset. Earlier in the day, he had been in an altercation with another student, and his teacher had to intervene.

Recess was over and all of the students filed in to line up—except this young boy. In talking to him a few days later, I learned that he had been having difficulty fitting in and he felt as though some other students were picking on him. During recess, one of the other students had knocked off his hat. His teacher intervened before he could physically react, but he was angry. When the teacher asked him to line up with everyone else, he felt the only way he could control the rage he was experiencing was to hang onto the tetherball pole with all his might.

This young boy was actually demonstrating good emotional control and resiliency skills. His decision to hang on tight to control what adrenalin was doing to his body was quite constructive compared to a list of alternatives I could think of—which might have involved someone getting hurt.

His teacher was most understanding when we talked, and the two of them were able to plan what they would do the next time something similar happened. They came to an agreement that the teacher would hear him out if he talked to her, and the two students would be prompted to hold a conversation to clear the air, share how each felt about the incident, and decide what could be done to resolve the problem to the satisfaction of both. In other words, there would be accountability and an effort to get to the bottom of any incident, a chance for both sides to express their feelings, and an opportunity to resolve issues to promote good relations. However, until this young boy was able to control his emotions enough to safely talk to his teacher, he was free to clamp onto the tetherball pole, and his teacher would understand. His teacher also came up with the idea of supervising some structured activities with this group of children at recess, so that they would learn skills for getting along.

This anecdote provides a good reminder that when we look closely, we may often see that a child is, in fact, demonstrating terrific

Strength Based Resilience assessment tool

resilience at getting his or her developmental needs met, though in what we might call socially inappropriate ways. More desirable resiliency skills and attitudes can develop when a caring adult steps up to help the child access what he or she needs in order to do well.

Community Connection

Working with Parents to Support Resiliency Development

Parents and other adults can play a key role in supporting a child's resiliency development by role modelling and applying the same strategies and expectations at home that are learned in the classroom. Parents and other caregivers can do the following:

Encourage Helpful and Positive Thinking

- Look on the bright side of things.
- Laugh at minor mistakes and see them as learning opportunities.
- Avoid exaggerating problems or jumping to conclusions.
- Provide congratulations for sticking with something (even when it gets tough).
- Be reassuring and talk about alternative solutions to problems.
- Give praise for being resourceful and solving problems or getting through sticky situations.

Stop, Think, and Plan

- Practise stopping to think before acting, especially when feeling anxious, angry, or overexcited.
- Help identify situations that cause anger, worry, or upset.
- Talk about ways of dealing with strong feelings.
- Help recognize what others (e.g., siblings, friends) might be feeling.
- Talk about how to predict and deal with difficult situations.
- Encourage not being afraid to ask for help when it is needed.
- Plan fun and engaging events together.

A Social-Ecological Perspective on Resilience

Other recent resiliency research further supports the pivotal role an adult and school can play in helping students gain access to resources for success and well-being. Ungar, Brown, Liebenberg, Cheung, and Levine (2008) conducted research with a diverse population of Canadian youth coping with a range of personal challenges and cultural circumstances. This research was also part of an international study.

Results showed the importance of understanding each youth's individual context, culture, and circumstances to truly assess how behaviour relates to a youth's best efforts to be successful. The research also showed the need to take into account an interactive system of factors, including material resources, sense of belonging, relationships, and values.

The researchers were able to identify seven common mental health–enhancing experiences (see Figure 5.4). They described these experiences as "tensions" to emphasize that young people have variable access to these elements and that efforts to gain access to one affects access to the others in a dynamic fashion. The researchers concluded that each youth seeks to negotiate a balance among the seven tensions simultaneously. For example, when a teacher invites a student to try out for the track team, the student has an opportunity to make new friends at the expense of old friendships. She may also experience a change in self-concept, feeling more like she fits in at school. These dynamics produce unique patterns of coping for each individual.

Ungar's (2013) research led him to develop a social-ecological perspective on resilience. In his view, resilience is a quality of both individuals and their environments. Individuals do develop skills for resilience when they are successfully engaged in school activities, have a chance to build positive relationship skills, and develop confidence at problem solving. However, not all students make the varsity team, understand the hip language of the dominant cultures, or can afford the latest personal technology devices. Ungar's approach suggests that, if the school environment does not ensure that all students become engaged in school activities, then that school environment does not ensure opportunities for all students to develop resiliency skills. It is encouraging to know that a key relationship with even one adult educator can help a student access important resources, such as support to find a part-time job for personal spending money, or a counsellor or health nurse when needed.

This social-ecological approach makes resilience possible for *all* children, provided the resources are available. Focusing on youth who are disengaged or on the periphery of social cliques and connecting them with others will set in motion many opportunities for resiliency skill development. This approach also encourages school staff to think about what a school can do to enhance the resilience of youth who are disadvantaged and at-risk for mental health difficulties.

Figure 5.4: Ungar's Seven Tensions for Resiliency Development

Tensions	What Schools Can Provide
Access to material resources • availability of financial, educational, medical, and employment assistance and/or opportunities • access to food, clothing, and shelter	• Students all need access to basic services, from dental care and health services, to transportation and satisfying recreation. • Students may also need access to material goods, such as clothing, books, equipment, and food, so that they can focus on their studies. Breakfast programs, clothes cupboards, and other services made available through the school can help to alleviate some of the pressure on students whose material needs are not being met at home. • Schools need to ensure that all students have access to school facilities and recreational opportunities. These should not be reserved for a minority of students who make the cut for varsity teams, are able to afford the uniforms and equipment, or have a parent with time and means for transportation.
Supportive relationships • relationships with significant others, peers, and adults within one's family and community	• Those students who lack effective relationships elsewhere require some level of consistent attachment to a particular individual who will serve as an advocate or mentor. • This relationship should be one that invites the students to engage with activities in the safe school environment, where they will be able to develop and express their personal strengths and talents. • A mentor can also help students learn how to access the other core elements they need to develop, and will know when a student requires access to community resource help.

Tensions	What Schools Can Provide
Development of a desirable personal identity • sense of having a personal and collective purpose • ability to appraise one's own strengths and weaknesses, aspirations, beliefs, and values, including spiritual and religious identification	• The elementary and early high-school years are a time when students try on and develop a sense of identity. This search needs to be appreciated and supported. • Students who are connected at school are more likely to develop more socially responsible identities, rather than connecting with unhealthy alternatives.
Power and control • caring for oneself and others • the ability to effect change in one's social and physical environment	• A satisfying sense of identity contributes to a sense of self-efficacy, a sense that "I can." School can support caring environments in which students have choice and are involved in decision making. • Students with a strong sense of identity in relation to their peers are more likely to be assertive about getting their physical and social needs met, rather than being pessimistic and becoming discouraged or depressed.
Cultural traditions • adherence to, or knowledge of, one's local and/or global cultural practices, values, and beliefs	• Students need to know that their culture is celebrated and congruent with what they are learning. Often, their cultural heritage will be relevant to their spirituality and sense of identity.
Social justice • experiences related to finding a meaningful role in one's community that brings with it acceptance and social equality	• Social justice includes not just fair treatment, but also social and cultural acceptance of every student. It also includes a sense of belonging in the school environment and support for taking an active role in the community.
A sense of cohesion with others • balancing personal interests with a sense of responsibility to the greater good • feeling part of something larger than oneself, socially and spiritually	• Students need to feel that they are contributing members of the school community. • Students need to know that their lives matter to others and to acquire a sense of purpose or meaning for their personal existence.

Sourced from: Ungar et al. (2008, p. 6).

It is easy to imagine how some students who are not connected and engaged at school might gravitate toward less fortunate choices. A student who lacks basic material resources will look for opportunities to satisfy those basic needs however and whenever possible. If children do not have adequate, supportive relationships at home, they will look for a sense of connection elsewhere, either in the school environment or beyond. Developing a personal identity with a collective sense of purpose is a necessity for all youth. It is unfortunate if students feel their best opportunities to get ahead and gain power and control come from undesirable groups and through antisocial or illegal patterns of behaviour.

Sports, clubs, and other extracurricular activities are also important to keep students engaged. Students will be tempted to drift away from, and perhaps disown, the traditions and values of their cultural heritage if these are not valued. Students who lack the money or equipment to access school activities that reinforce a sense of belonging may begin to behave outside the norm and may lack a sense of fairness or social justice. The social cohesion that Ungar describes will not develop.

Discovering Strengths toolkit—resources for reaching disengaged Aboriginal youth

Supporting Resilience for Children and Youth at-Risk

For children and youth facing significant adversity, Ungar sees resilience as both

- the capacity of individuals to *navigate to* the psychological, social, cultural, and physical resources that sustain their well-being, and

- their capacity individually and collectively to *negotiate for* these resources to be provided and experienced in culturally meaningful ways (Ungar, 2008, p. 225).

With this in mind, he has identified five principles that schools can incorporate to make the development of resilience more likely for children and youth who are at-risk (Ungar, 2012).

1. **Shape the students' environment to support their development.**

   When we understand the individual needs of children and youth, we are better able to set them up with the conditions for success. We can change the school and classroom environment to support their development, rather than try to change the children. Our actions can positively increase their chances of success.

2. **The most disadvantaged students in our schools need the most help and support.**

The children from the most challenged environments benefit the most from what we give them. Children who do not have adequate caring from adults outside school will benefit most from caring relationships with adult role models in the school environment. Students from chaotic environments will also benefit most from opportunities such as smaller classes, where relationships can be stronger and the opportunity to learn social emotional skills is more purposeful.

3. **Early intervention is better, but it is never too late to help or intervene.**

Ungar points to research evidence that providing services for young adolescents can change life trajectories. He reminds us that the efforts put into children early on eventually pay back. Earlier is always better, but it is never too late.

4. **Complex problems require complex solutions.**

This principle stresses the importance of a whole-school approach. Successful strategies used in the classroom have greater power when schools share them with students' families and other community partners.

5. **More is not necessarily better.**

Far too often, disadvantaged youth can be bounced around to various service providers, where the documentation can be heavy but the relationships brief. Feedback from youth indicates that consistency and connection with one advocate or resource person is more effective than a chain of individuals who come and go over time.

These research-based principles are reassuring and empowering: they affirm that, as educators, we can make a difference.

Being Active

Physical Activity and Mental Health

Adjacent to Notre Dame Basilica (circa 1647) in old Quebec City, and just outside the courtyard for the old seminary, stands a plaque which reads:

Bouncing balls, gliding pucks...the Children's Courtyard has been a student playground for over 300 years. And though it has seen some major transformations over the years, the lively sounds of ball games, hockey matches, and winter sledding have never faded. No matter what the surface—dirt, gravel, or asphalt—the courtyard has always helped ensure a vital balance between physical exercise and intellectual activity.

Few of us would dispute that the struggle to maintain a "vital balance" between physical exercise and *all* other activities has become a serious issue. Technology from cars to cellphones has reduced the number of physical movements students and adults alike make each day.

And yet, the importance of regular exercise in helping to sustain mental and physical health is supported by a robust base of evidence (Otto & Smits, 2011; Ratey, 2008). Likewise, a growing body of research supports the use of physical exercise to help manage a wide range of mild to severe psychological difficulties among adolescents and adults (Richardson et al., 2005). These include anxiety symptoms, depression and mood challenges, anger, stress, serious mental illness, and alcoholism and drug abuse. Research also tells us that individuals with common mental health disorders tend to have reduced physical activity (Oeland, Laessoe, Olesen, & Munk-Jorgensen, 2009).

In healthy individuals, regular physical activity has been associated with

- improved interpersonal relationships (Parfitt, Pavey, & Rowlands, 2009)

- social skills, self-image, self-worth, and cognitive functioning (Ratey, 2008)

- brain composition changes (Kilpatrick, 2008)

- better psychological functioning (Johnson & Krueger, 2007)
- overall life satisfaction and happiness (Stubbe, de Moor, Boomsma, & de Geus, 2007)

In *Spark: The Revolutionary New Science of Exercise and the Brain*, John Ratey (2008) provides compelling evidence for the effects of exercise on the brain. Ratey cites research showing that exercise increases levels of the neurotransmitters serotonin, norepinephrine, and dopamine, all important for the functions of thought and emotion. He also describes how psychological stress hinders the connections among the billions of nerve cells in the brain—the opposite of what exercise does when it causes a release of neurochemicals that bolster the brain's infrastructure. Inactivity causes the brain to wither, while physical exercise allows the brain's interconnections to replenish.

It is hard to argue that aerobic activity is not critical for well-being. Ratey's book includes a description of an exemplar school outside Chicago called Naperville Central High School. Naperville successfully developed a daily exercise curriculum for all students. Results included observable increases in student attentiveness in class, reported improvements in mental health, and gains in achievement levels.

Promoting Physical Activity in Schools

Creating a Safe Environment

It takes skilled teaching to create a safe environment where students feel comfortable regardless of body shape, athletic ability, gender identity, or sexual orientation. Considerations also include ethnocultural, racial, and religious backgrounds. Students may avoid participation in physical activities because they are self-conscious about their physical appearance. As teachers, we can be sensitive to the privacy arrangements students are offered for changing into appropriate clothing for physical activities. Students need to feel accepted to participate in physical activities and comfortable to discuss important physical and mental health topics.

Effective teaching is a key component to student success in adopting a physically active lifestyle. Classroom teachers are important role models for their students. Our attitudes toward health and physical education can have a significant influence on student behaviour.

Taking an Integrated Approach

The Health and Physical Education curriculum plays a key role in shaping students' attitudes to a healthy lifestyle. We can reinforce physical education concepts, skills, and attitudes by effectively integrating them with other areas of the curriculum. Students can come to understand the vital connection between physical health and mental health—and essentially, overall well-being.

With a whole-school approach, the school and classroom environments can provide multiple and rich opportunities for engaging in physical activities. As we have seen, a flexible classroom environment can include centres for physical engagement, allow stretch breaks, and incorporate physical movements into many instructional practices. Yoga, tai chi, and some martial arts movements are also effective calming and mindfulness strategies that can be incorporated into daily practice.

As part of mental health promotion, physical activity needs to be an integral and meaningful part of everyday routines and interactions within the whole school community. It also needs to become an essential part of students' daily lives outside school. Integral to an active lifestyle is adequate sleep, good nutrition, and attention to spiritual needs, which may include participation in family, cultural, community, faith-based, and personally enriching activities. While our focus here is primarily on physical activity, it is important to realize that an active lifestyle encompasses these broader health and spiritual aspects of our lives. They are all interconnected and vital for a balanced life and our well-being. We will struggle to be resilient or flourishing if we do not have a balanced active lifestyle—and an active life also involves cultivating the positive relationships that are at the centre of the well-being model.

Canadian Physical Activity Guidelines for Children and Youth

Canadian Society for Exercise Physiology (CSEP) guidelines

The Canadian Society for Exercise Physiology (CSEP) is a recognized scientific research authority on physical activity, health, and fitness. The CSEP's Physical Activity Guidelines for children (5–11 years) and youth (12–17 years) indicate that they require at least 60 minutes of moderate- to vigorous-intensity activity per day. The Canadian Society for Exercise Physiology also notes that only 9 percent of boys and 4 percent of girls meet this minimum requirement (CSEP, 2011). This startling statistic, based on four years of research, underlines the critical importance of mental and physical health promotion.

Children should be physically active daily as part of play, sports, transportation, recreation, physical education, or planned exercise, in the context of family, school, and community (e.g., volunteer employment) activities. This should be achieved above and beyond the incidental physical activities accumulated in the course of daily living. (CSEP, 2011)

Benefits of Physical Activity

Moderate activity includes bike riding and playground activities. Vigorous-intensity activities, such as running and swimming, raise a real sweat and cause laboured breathing. Following the CSEP guidelines has been shown to improve measures of cholesterol, blood pressure, body composition, bone density, cardiorespiratory function, muscular fitness, and certain aspects of mental health. Being active for at least 60 minutes daily can help children and teens

- improve their health
- do better in school
- improve their fitness
- grow stronger
- have fun playing with friends

- feel happier

- maintain a healthy body weight

- improve their self-confidence

- learn new skills

Source: CSEP, 2012, p. 5.

Issues with Sedentary Behaviours

On the other hand, Canadian children and youth spend approximately 62 percent of their waking hours engaged in sedentary activities, including an estimated six to eight hours per day in screen viewing (CSEP, 2011). Sedentary behaviours include sitting for lengthy periods of time, using a computer, playing passive video games, using motorized transportation, and TV watching. CSEP evidence shows a direct correlation between higher levels of sedentary time and decreased fitness, poor self-esteem, weak academic performance, obesity, and increased aggression. The CSEP guidelines recommend limiting recreational screen time and other sedentary activities to promote overall health.

Adopting an Active Lifestyle

No matter who you are, it is much easier to stick to an activity program if you actually enjoy the activities (McCague & Carney, 2011). Research also shows that well-structured exercise programs can produce positive mood states (Kilpatrick, 2008). Experienced exercisers have discovered how to create enjoyable and positive exercise sessions—either through trial and error or because they received good counsel from a health and fitness professional.

In *Exercise for Mood and Anxiety*, Otto and Smits (2011) point out that most exercise programs fail because they ask people to work only for some *future* goal, such as improved fitness or weight loss, rather than promoting an active lifestyle because it can make you feel good *now*. Noticing positive mood effects during and after exercise, and limiting the intensity so it doesn't hurt, are both ways to support success. If we think back to Jack, we'll remember that he reported feeling "energized" when he jogged, and "lethargic and cranky" when he missed his run for several days in a row. Most people I know who have developed an active lifestyle report similar feelings.

New exercisers, however, often lack the skill or intuition to make optimal choices, and poor choices can limit their ability to stick with the program. Physical education teachers can help students plan the frequency, intensity, duration, and mode of activity that works best for them, is sustainable, makes them feel good, and provides lasting benefits. Finding activities that they enjoy doing regularly and feeling more energized without the pressure or stigma of having to lose weight or change their bodies can help students make activity an integral part of their lives.

Setting Reasonable Goals

A first step toward helping students adopt a more active lifestyle is encouraging them to set attainable goals, including the immediate goal of feeling good *now* (Raphael, 1998). Goal setting is, in itself, motivational. The SMART or ABCD model for goal setting can be very useful.

Figure 5.5: Useful Models for Goal Setting

The SMART Method	The ABCD Method
Specific	**A**chievable
Measurable	**B**elievable
Achievable	**C**lear
Realistic	**D**esirable
Time-limited	

Source: Raphael, 2008; Martin, 2008.

Goals need to be specific, observable behaviours that the student truly wants to achieve (Kilpatrick, 2008; Sharkey & Gaskill, 2007). Jack, for example, wanted to race, and Mr. Speck no doubt helped him set specific goals to gradually increase practice so that Jack would be ready to compete on a set date and also enjoy his workouts along the way. His goals would have included specific, realistic, and achievable practice intervals for running, distances, and speeds.

Maintenance

The fear of failure can be strong enough to deter many students from beginning a program or activity. They are more likely to maintain a newly adopted activity if they find

- the activity meets a need

- they have fun

- they have social or psychological support

- they see evidence of change (Sharkey & Gaskill, 2007)

These factors will help students move from being extrinsically motivated to being intrinsically motivated, so that they can become more independent of a teacher or coach and do the activity without prompting. Students also need strategies to deal with those days or situations when they really don't feel like it or something gets in the way—we have all been there! Teachers can help students anticipate and plan for threatening factors (e.g., cold weather) and possible lapses, to avoid getting derailed.

A supportive social network is also crucial. Whether it is family, friends, interest groups, mental health professionals, clubs, publications, organizations, or programs—all of these support systems have the potential to encourage and enhance any individual's self-efficacy and motivation for change (Sharkey & Gaskill, 2007). For students who may be experiencing anxiety or mood difficulties, teachers can work together with mental health professionals to encourage effective physical activities (see Figure 5.6).

Figure 5.6: Physical Activities and Mood Responses

Recommendation	Main Idea
Limit competition	• Competition can undermine positive mood responses during exercise, especially for inexperienced individuals. • Competition can provoke anxiety and frustration.

Recommendation	Main Idea
Concentrate on moderate intensity	• The old adage of "go hard or go home" has limited applicability because high-intensity exercise can compromise positive mood responses. • Noticing heavy exertion can act as biofeedback to lower exercise intensity for more positive mood effects.
Encourage self-selection	• Imposed prescriptions decrease feelings of control and autonomy and negatively affect mood. • Self-selecting frequency, intensity, duration, and mode produces a sense of empowerment that positively affects mood.
Focus on in-task feelings	• Negative moods during exercise seem to more strongly influence future behaviour than positive feelings after exercise. • Activities that make participants feel good both during and after should be encouraged.
Avoid overtraining	• Excessive training at high intensities, frequencies, and/or durations can lead to negative mood responses and depression. • Too much of almost anything is not a good idea, and moderation in exercise is a useful reminder to some individuals with very high training volumes.
Consider individual differences	• Ironclad rules for maximizing mood benefits with exercise are not possible because of individual differences. • Recommendations for improving mood responses have great value, but all efforts must be customized to the individual's unique personality and circumstances.

Sourced from: Kilpatrick (2008, p. 18).

Flourishing

What Does It Mean to Be "Flourishing"?

Psychology and brain research have shown that we can learn new ways to think, emote, and behave to improve our mental health. Martin Seligman has been a prolific contributor to the area of positive psychology that focuses on understanding and creating well-being. In his book, *Flourish*, Seligman (2011) expands his earlier work on "authentic happiness" into a more comprehensive theory of well-being. He believes *happiness* has become a rather hackneyed term that creates confusion. Happiness alone does not give life meaning. In his revised theory, "flourishing" is the gold standard for measuring well-being—for individuals, communities, and nations.

Seligman's Concept of Well-Being

So what does it mean to be "flourishing"? How can we all work toward that goal and how do we know when we are there? Beyond that, how do we sustain it?

Seligman describes five distinct and measurable elements that contribute to well-being:

- positive emotion (fun and enjoyment)
- engagement (passionately absorbed; in the flow)
- meaning (sense of purpose)
- accomplishment (competency)
- positive relationships (connection; valued; belonging)

He also believes that no one element by itself *defines* well-being. In other words, a person might choose to engage in an activity for reasons related to any one or more elements, but true well-being comes from experiences involving all five elements. When an individual or community has all five of these elements, that individual or community is flourishing.

Interestingly, once again, we can see that these elements reflect aspects of our definition of positive mental health, the social emotional competencies, and a strengths perspective. In fact, Seligman stresses that these elements of well-being need to be based in our strengths and that we can actively choose to cultivate these elements in our lives and in our communities. He also stresses the need to develop our ability to measure results so that we can effect change.

> As our ability to measure positive emotion, engagement, meaning, accomplishments, and positive relations improves, we can ask with rigor how many people in a nation, in a city, in a corporation are flourishing. We can ask with rigor when in a lifetime an individual is flourishing. We can ask with rigor if our school systems are helping our children flourish.
>
> —*Seligman, 2011, p. 28*

Let's take a closer look at these elements of well-being.

Positive Emotion

Fun, pleasure, comfort, and joy—these are all positive emotions we can experience in the course of our lives. For students, having hobbies, friends, and social media connections; enjoying comfortable surroundings; and engaging in fun activities can produce these emotions and a level of happiness. Seligman describes a life where these emotions are predominant as the "pleasant life." In the long run, however, pleasurable experiences seem to have a relatively minor contribution to authentic life satisfaction.

Engagement

More effective for producing a deep feeling of satisfaction and well-being are experiences that create a sense of engagement. When we are engaged in something that truly uses our strengths or talents, and for which we have a real passion, we can be completely absorbed. We can experience "flow," where time seems to stand still and we lose self-consciousness. As educators, we have witnessed students deeply engaged in what fascinates them, whether it is science and opportunities to experiment; literature, or the dramatic or expressive arts; athletics; or a passion outside the school environment. They are experiencing "flow." I can remember a very young student with a specific learning disability for reading who was a genius at running his dad's backhoe, and he loved it!

Meaning

Seligman (2002) describes "meaning" as using our strengths to belong to and be in the service of something bigger than ourselves. In the largest sense, this element can be a life of social contribution, as epitomized by such individuals as Mother Teresa and Nelson Mandela. But meaningful endeavours can include volunteering, taking part in environmental movements or social reform organizations, and engaging in activities related to religion, belief system, or cultural tradition.

Gratitude Visits

Seligman (2004) cites impressive examples of positive psychology research. He talks about the enduring feelings of well-being that people experience from "gratitude visits." People think about someone who has changed their life for the better, but who they were never able to truly thank. They write a letter or testimonial for that person, conveying thoughtful and purposeful gratitude, and then arrange a surprise visit. Sharing and talking about the content of their letter, which expresses what the person did for them, how it affected their life, and how they think about it now, bring highly emotional reactions. People have reported positive feelings for weeks, even months afterwards. The research suggests that personal satisfaction from altruistic actions lasts much longer than that from more fleeting "fun" activities.

When I think about examples from our school systems, I wonder at the deep sense of meaning many students feel when they get involved in social justice activities, such as the popular Me to We events. I hear educators talk about life-altering experiences for some students who have flown to countries such as South Africa to build schools and dig wells with a community of villagers. Providing volunteer support for seniors or younger students with learning difficulties in their own communities can produce profound effects, as well.

Accomplishment or Competency

Developmental psychologists have long described a basic, unlearned drive to acquire competency. As educators, we have seen how children from a young age are driven to learn skills and master exercises—often for no other reason than to become good at something. In children, curiosity and exploration facilitate the development of competency, but as competency increases, children will often look for new challenges. Once children master a video game, they will look for the challenge of a new game to gain that same sense of achievement or accomplishment once again.

As teachers, we can ignite a student's natural drive to acquire competency by stirring his or her curiosity and using differentiated instructional practices so that learning always involves a degree of appropriate challenge. We can also provide rich and meaningful opportunities for exploration. Technology has greatly expanded the possibilities for exploration and investigation.

Seligman points out, however, that competency and accomplishment that lead to well-being do not involve becoming good at something—such as basketball, for example—to win or make money. If we don't win or make money, there would be no sense of well-being. The competency and accomplishment come from the activity for its own sake. If we lose the championship, we will still enjoy basketball and keep playing to become even better. We have a sense of competency or accomplishment that contributes to our well-being.

Positive Relationships

Positive relationships are fundamental for well-being. Without at least a few good friends, we experience loneliness and even illness. Families can be a vital source of positive relationships. We also seek out relationships within our schools and communities, through clubs, recreational centres, faith-based or cultural organizations, and other pursuits. The cellphone and the internet have expanded the possibilities for developing and maintaining relationships, and make it easier to keep in touch with old friends.

Schools provide a wonderful opportunity to expand a child's positive relationships from the home and the neighbourhood to an environment packed with individuals from many backgrounds and cultures. Ungar's social-ecological perspective of resilience puts positive relationships at the top of core needs: see Ungar et al. (2008) and Ungar (2012, 2013).

In Seligman's theory of well-being, all of the strengths (e.g., wisdom, courage, justice) and virtues (e.g., creativity, persistence, love) discussed and investigated in positive psychology research underpin the five key elements of well-being. When people deploy their highest strengths, they experience increases in positive emotion, sense of meaning and accomplishment, and improved relationships (Seligman, 2011). They flourish.

SPOTLIGHT

Applying Positive Psychology and Strengths-Based Education: Two Projects

Geelong Grammar School

Examples of schools that have wholeheartedly embraced positive mental health and the concept of "flourishing" do exist. The Geelong Grammar School in Australia has been collaborating with Dr. Martin Seligman for a number of years to teach students skills that increase resilience, positive emotional engagement, and meaning (Institute of Positive Education, 2014). Educators from Geelong believe that the synergy between positive emotion and learning skills, and the prevalence of mental health struggles, make the systematic teaching of emotional well-being in the school environment critical and speak well for success.

Institute of Positive Education

The Geelong demonstration project teaches positive psychology skills and principles both implicitly and explicitly. The goal is to provide implicit teaching at each year level, at every campus, and across all aspects of school life, including subject teaching, pastoral life, and the co-curriculum program. Explicit teaching is delivered in Grade 7 and Grade 10, through specific positive psychology programs written by the world's leading research psychologists and developed in collaboration with experienced classroom teachers.

The stated aims of positive education at Geelong are as follows:

- to increase the experience of positive emotions in their students

- to encourage students to engage their signature strengths for personal and community goals

- to engage students to live meaningful lives, to find purpose, and to make a difference to the community at large

The implicit program comprises seven overarching topics that are explored from entry to Grade 12:

- emotion
- gratitude
- strengths
- creativity
- self-efficacy
- resilience
- mindfulness

The explicit positive psychology programs taught in Grade 7 and Grade 10 teach students the following empirically based skills to help them tackle life's challenges:

- thinking and explanatory styles
- thinking traps
- detecting icebergs (underlying and surface beliefs)
- challenging beliefs
- putting it into perspective
- real-time resilience

Geelong asserts that research studies over the past 20 years provide evidence that these explicit positive psychology programs have the following impact on students:

- increased levels of creativity
- better critical thinking skills
- increased levels of positive emotion
- positive effects on depressive symptoms
- improved explanatory style for negative events
- significant impacts on depression, anxiety, and adjustment disorders

Dr. Seligman and his team have provided intensive training for more than 160 Geelong staff. The goal is for each of these teachers to use this learning in their classes and activities so that positive education reaches every student—in the classroom, on the sports field, and in their living quarters—every day.

Strengths in Education Project

One Canadian project that embraces positive psychology is under way in the Wellington Catholic District School Board in collaboration with York University, the University of Guelph, and community partners. The project focuses on strengths-based education with the goal of building a strengths-based school system.

Strengths in Education Project

The strengths-based philosophy implemented in the schools is based on the character traits model. It affirms that all youth have inherent value and strengths despite any difficulty they may be experiencing. The goal is to promote a positive self-image, which is shown to be a protective factor against depression, and to support positive well-being, student engagement, and academic achievement.

Teachers and principals from participating schools in the board created a "Strengths in Motion" working group. A leading researcher in the field, Dr. Edward Rawana, led a workshop for teachers to lay the foundation for the approach. Schools also worked with researchers Dr. Margaret Lumley and Dr. Jennine Rawana to review student engagement, conduct a survey of students' personal strengths, and observe results on positive emotional and educational functioning, and academic achievement.

Each participating school has its own applications of the strengths-based philosophy. One school created a Strengths Wall for teachers. Another school implemented a link leaders program that pairs strengths-trained leaders with incoming students. In another school, rather than focusing on bullying, the school took a strengths-based "Kindness Matters" approach.

Teachers and researchers involved in the program are working together to develop a strengths-based curriculum.

Flourishing, Mental Health, and Mental Illness

We can all flourish. Corey Keyes (2002) has used the term *flourishing* to describe individuals who show an optimal level of mental health, regardless of mental illness. His research affirms that the absence of mental illness does not necessarily imply positive mental health, just as the absence of disease does not imply physical health (Smith-Fowler & Lebel, 2013). People experiencing mental illness can flourish (Figure 5.7). When we use our strengths to be the best we can be, we can *all* experience well-being: this concept is key in our understanding of mental health and mental health promotion.

It is significant, however, that in Keyes's study sample, less than 40 percent of the adolescents met criteria for being mentally healthy to a degree that might be described as flourishing.

Figure 5.7: Mental Health, Mental Illness

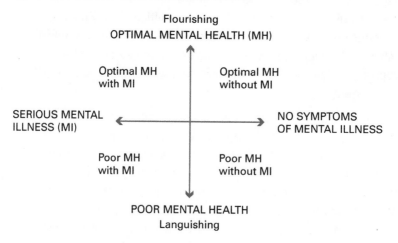

Source: Smith-Fowler & Lebel (2013, p. 6).

Resilient, Active, and Flourishing in Today's Classrooms

The model of well-being we have explored in this chapter focuses on resilience, an active lifestyle, and the experience of flourishing. With this model in mind, we can look at mental health promotion in a school setting as an endeavour to develop resiliency skills, promote an active lifestyle, and support opportunities for *all* students to flourish.

This point is emphasized by Smith-Fowler and Lebel (2013, p. 7) and has become a cornerstone in the Mental Health Commission of Canada's mental health policy.

The Mental Health Commission of Canada (MHCC, 2012) identified the need for Canada to do more to promote positive mental health and prevent mental illness throughout childhood, in addition to early intervention. The MHCC's new mental health strategy for Canada calls for comprehensive home-based approaches to support parents, and school-based programs to promote healthy social and emotional development, build resilience, reduce bullying and stigma, in addition to targeted programs for children and youth at greatest risk.

With this in mind, we define "student mental health" as a positive concept—akin to **flourishing**—for the subgroup of youth currently engaged in any kind of school or academic learning.

Checklist for a Mentally Healthy Classroom

√ Students understand and appreciate the value of positive mental health for feeling good and being resilient in the face of life and challenges ahead.

√ Students understand the important links between positive mental health and self-care, including sleep, nutrition, and daily exercise.

√ Students know recommended daily levels of activity and sedentary behaviour limits and are enthusiastically engaged in self-monitoring.

√ The teacher promotes the value of an active lifestyle to feel good "in the now" as well as for any health goals in the future.

√ Students understand links between positive mental health and positive thinking, including realistic optimism, awareness of thinking traps, use of stepping back to take another perspective when discouraged, and realistic goal setting.

√ Students understand links between positive mental health and interpersonal skills, including empathy, kindness, and inclusion, which maximize positive relationships and well-being.

√ Action is taken to celebrate the cultural heritage of each child.

√ Opportunities are provided for each student to use interests and talents for deep learning engagement (flow).

√ Students have opportunities to use their interests and strengths to contribute to the greater good, to achieve a sense of affiliation by helping others, to take leadership roles, and to be involved in social justice activities (e.g., promoting a healthy environment).

√ There is an assurance that all children have developed a sense of competency related to their learning achievement. Students can state what they are able to do as a result of what they are learning.

Anxiety BC®. (2014). *ADABC Parenting Project*. Retrieved from http://www.anxietybc.com

Best Start Resource Centre. (2012). *Building resilience in young children* [Booklet for parents of children from birth to six years].

Breazeale, R. (2009). *Duct tape isn't enough: Survival skills for the 21st century*. Portland, ME: Bounce Back USA.

Canadian Society for Exercise Physiology [CSEP]. (2011). *Canadian physical activity guidelines and Canadian sedentary behaviour guidelines*. Retrieved from http://www.csep.ca/guidelines

Canadian Society for Exercise Physiology [CSEP]. (2012). *Canadian physical activity guidelines and Canadian sedentary behaviour handbook*. Retrieved from http://www.csep.ca/english/view.asp?x=804

Centre for Social Innovation. (2013). *Mindfulness without borders*. Retrieved from http://mindfulnesswithoutborders.org

Greenland, S. K. (2011). *A whole new world*. Retrieved from http://www.susankaisergreenland.com/blog/a-whole-new-world.html

Institute of Positive Education. (2014). *Geelong Grammar School, exceptional education*. Victoria, Australia. Retrieved from http://www.ggs.vic.edu.au/School/Positive-Education/About-Positive-Education

Johnson, W., & Krueger, R. (2007). The psychological benefits of vigorous exercise: A study of discordant MZ twin pairs. *Twin Res Hum Genet, 10*(2), 275–283.

Keyes, C. L. M. (2002). The mental health continuum: From languishing to flourishing. *Journal of Health and Behavior Research, 43*, 207–222.

Kilpatrick, M. W. (2008). Exercise, mood, and psychological well-being: A practitioner's guide to theory, research, and application. *ACSM'S Health & Fitness Journal, 12*(5), 14–19.

Martin, A. (2008). *Motivation and engagement scale: Test user manual*. Lifelong Achievement Group. Retrieved from http://www.lifelongachievement.com

McCague, E., & Carney, P. J. (2011). The "magic" drug: A research base and how-to-approach in implementing physical activity in clinical and non-clinical populations. Poster session presented at the annual convention of the Canadian Psychological Association, Toronto, ON.

Mental Health Commission of Canada [MHCC]. (2012). *Changing directions, changing lives: The mental health strategy for Canada*. Retrieved from http://strategy.mentalhealthcommission.ca/pdf/strategy-text-en.pdf

Oeland, A., Laessoe, U., Olesen, A., & Munk-Jorgensen, P. (2009). Impact of exercise on patients with depression and anxiety. *Nordic Journal of Psychiatry, 64*(3), 210–217.

Ontario Secondary School Teachers' Federation. (2012). *Full circle: First Nations, Métis, Inuit ways of knowing. A common threads resource.* Toronto, ON: Author.

Otto, M., & Smits, J. (2011). *Exercise for mood and anxiety: Proven strategies for overcoming depression and enhancing well-being.* Oxford, England: Oxford University Press.

Parfitt, G., Pavey, T., & Rowlands, A. V. (2009). Children's physical activity and psychological health: The relevance of intensity. *Acta Pædiatrica, 98*(6), 1037–1043.

Pearson, J., & Hall, D. K. (2006). *Reaching in…reaching out resiliency guidebook.* Toronto, ON: Child & Family Partnership [YMCA of Greater Toronto, The Child Development Institute, University of Guelph, George Brown College]. Retrieved from http://www.reachinginreachingout.com

Public Health Agency of Canada (PHAC). (2006). *The human face of mental health and mental illness in Canada.* Ottawa, ON: Author.

Raphael, R. (1998). Physical activity can relieve symptoms of depression and anxiety, improve mood, and may even reduce the risk of developing depression. *ACSM'S Health & Fitness Journal, 2*(2), 18–20.

Ratey, J. J., with E. Hagerman. (2008). *Spark: The revolutionary new science of exercise and the brain.* New York, NY: Little, Brown.

Richardson, C. R., Faulkner, G., McDevitt, J., Skirinar, G. S., Hutchinson, D. S., & Piette, J. D. (2005). Integrating physical activity into mental health services for persons with serious mental illness. *Psychiatric Services, 56* (3).

Seligman, M.E.P. (1991). *Learned optimism: How to change your mind and your life.* New York, NY: Pocket Books.

Seligman, M.E.P. (2002). *Authentic happiness: using the new positive psychology to realize your potential for lasting fulfillment.* New York, NY: Free Press.

Seligman, M.E.P. (2004). The new era of positive psychology [Video]. Retrieved from http://www.ted.com/talks/martin_seligman_on_the_state_of_psychology.html

Seligman, M.E.P. (2011). *Flourish: a visionary new understanding of happiness and well-being.* New York, NY: Free Press.

Sharkey B. J., & Gaskill, S. E. (2007). *Fitness and health* (6th ed.). Champaign, IL: Human Kinetics.

Smith-Fowler, H. & Lebel, M. (2013) *Promoting youth mental health through the transition from high school - Literature review and environmental scan.* Social Research and Demonstration Corporation [SRDC].

Smits, J., & Otto, M. (2009). *Exercise for mood and anxiety disorders.* Oxford, UK: Oxford University Press.

Stewart, S. L. (2008). Promoting indigenous mental health: Cultural perspectives on healing from Native counselors in Canada. *International Journal of Health Promotion and Education, 46*(2), 49–56. Retrieved from http://www.tandfonline.com/doi/abs/10.1080/14635240.2008.10708129#.U-jpg51zbcs

Stubbe, J. H., de Moor, M. H. M., Boomsma, D. I., & de Geus, E. J. C. (2007). The association between exercise participation and well-being: A co-twin study. *Preventative Medicine, 44*, 148–152.

Student Support Leadership Initiative (Oxford, Elgin, London/Middlesex). (2014). *Bounce back...again* (2nd ed.). Retrieved from http://www.mentalhealth4kids.ca

Ungar, M., Brown, M., Liebenberg, L., Cheung, M., & Levine, K. (2008). Distinguishing differences in pathways to resilience among Canadian youth. *Canadian Journal of Community Mental Health, 27*(1), 1–13.

Ungar, M. (2008). Resilience across cultures. *British Journal of Social Work, 38*, 218–235.

Ungar, M. (2012). *Understanding resilience in schools and school systems* [Video produced as part of the Learning Partnership for building capacity for resilience]. Retrieved from http://www.youtube.com/watch?v=XJ482GgfZTs

Ungar, M. (2013). The impact of youth–adult relationships on resilience. *International Journal of Child, Youth and Family Studies, 3*, 328–336.

United Nations Human Rights, Office of the High Commissioner for Human Rights. (1990). *Convention on the Rights of the Child* (Overview). Retrieved from http://www.unicef.org/crc/files/Rights_overview.pdf

Wellington Catholic District School Board. Strengths in Education project. Retrieved from www.strengthsineducation.ca

Yang, Y., & Raine, A. (2009, November). Prefrontal structural and functional brain imaging findings in antisocial, violent, and psychopathic individuals: A meta-analysis. *Psychiatry Research, 174*(2), 81–88.

CHAPTER 6

What About Me? Educator Well-Being

"The quality of relationships in a school…impacts on teacher well-being and their ability to cope well with the many and varied stresses that are the hallmarks of the profession…. How teachers feel makes a difference to their ability to respond effectively to the challenges they face."

—ROFFEY, 2012, p. 8

Indicators of Teacher Well-Being

Teachers who have high levels of well-being

- have positive relationships within and outside the classroom
- are responsive, flexible, and empathetic
- have a positive sense of autonomy and self-worth
- are proactive and positive about engaging in new initiatives
- have well-developed solution-finding skills
- have a sense of meaning, purpose, and future goals
- have good social emotional, communication, and resiliency skills
- are part of a caring, inclusive, and respectful professional environment

We have focused on students—but what about you? Our ultimate goal is to promote the well-being of each and every child. But few of us would deny that how we feel about our work, the school environment, and our relationships at school, and how effective we believe our efforts are significantly influence our ability to meet that goal. Teacher well-being is a critical part of the learning equation. Research shows that *teacher well-being promotes student well-being* (Roffey, 2012).

Often, teacher well-being is seen through a deficit-only lens—with a focus on stress, burnout, and problems with teachers leaving the profession. These issues are real. But, a problems-first orientation can limit the view on solutions and overlook the foundations for positive well-being. In this chapter, we will look at the strengths, skills, and resources that can actively promote your mental well-being and allow you to be the best you can be. You may still face significant challenges, stresses, and relationship difficulties, but you can feel better prepared to manage these hurdles by drawing on personal resources and external supports. Much of what we have looked at in terms of student well-being can become part of your wellness toolkit as well—viewed through a different lens.

Teacher Well-Being Matters

The calling to be a school teacher involves many things. For most teachers it involves a relatively high "social" interest. How else could we spend over 1000 hours per year with 20 or more students at a time? A high social interest is likely to work well with other interest personality areas, such as artistic, enterprising, conventional, investigative, and realistic. We are all diverse individuals with personal strengths and talents that we bring to our teaching. The teacher who is highly social and artistic is likely to provide a different experience for learning enrichment than a teacher who is highly social and investigative. One teacher will take art to a new level for students; the other might take science to a new level. Most teachers also enter teaching with a sense that helping children to develop and flourish matters—what we do makes a difference to the future of each individual and to the kind of community or society we live in.

When we flourish as educators, the concept of teaching as "a calling" becomes very clear. We experience passion and enjoyment, we feel we have a meaningful career that contributes to the greater good, we have a sense of competence, and we enjoy positive relationships with our students and fellow educators. We are effective in our profession, which contributes to a positive sense of overall well-being. Likewise, when we see improvement in our students' learning and well-being, our feelings of efficacy and satisfaction increase. In many ways, that is the heart of teaching and a worthy goal to strive for. We can make positive well-being a conscious goal for ourselves, just as we have done for our students. Our well-being matters.

The Value of Social Emotional Skills

Teacher well-being involves a number of factors—personal, social, and environmental. Consider this for a moment: what other profession requires as much emotional and social intelligence as teaching children? Managing your relationships with 20 or more students at a time so that you are tuned in to their emotions as well as your own in order to maintain an ideal emotional space for learning is wizardry. Research demonstrates that *learning is greatly enhanced when teachers recognize the emotional component of the teaching–learning exchange and apply this information purposefully.*

"Social and emotional competencies influence everything from teacher–student relationships to classroom management to effective instruction to teacher burnout."

—Jones, Bouffard, & Weissbourd, 2013, p. 62

Recall that Goleman defined emotional intelligence as "the capacity for recognizing our own feelings and those of others, for motivating ourselves, and for managing emotions well in ourselves and in our relationships" (Goleman, 1998, p. 317). Social emotional intelligence includes five key competencies: self-awareness, self-management, social awareness, relationship skills, and responsible decision-making. It follows, then, that social emotional intelligence in teaching involves

- recognizing and responding to your own feelings and those of the students in the classroom in order to make you both more effective in your respective roles

- teaching social emotional skills, and inspiring actions to ensure optimal emotional states for learning, development, and positive relationships

- fostering resilience, physical activity, and the elements of positive mental health that allow both you and your students to flourish

Let's consider for a moment how Sarah, a Grade 7 student, described her favourite teacher, Ms. Moreau.

Ms. Moreau seemed to like teaching us. She didn't get crabby much and she smiled a lot. She came around and helped you when you got stuck. Some of the kids got stuck more than the others, but she could help you without making you feel bad. Sometimes, she took us outside to play games, even when it wasn't recess. My favourite was "scrub baseball." The whole class got to play, and you got to play every position as you rotated through all of the positions, including batter. Sometimes, Ms. Moreau played too. We did a lot of reading together in Ms. Moreau's class. She would read first and get us really interested in a story, and then she would get each of us to take turns reading. Most of all, I think I liked Ms. Moreau because I think she liked me.

It is not difficult to see that Sarah's teacher was in the habit of preparing herself emotionally for her teaching role each day. Sarah sensed that her teacher "liked teaching us." We don't know what Ms. Moreau did to self-regulate, but we do know that it worked. She "didn't get crabby much." Sarah also noticed that her teacher had a sensitive manner when assisting students: that "she could help you without making you feel bad." Ms. Moreau looked after her relationships with her students. Sarah notes, "Most of all, I think I liked Ms. Moreau because I think she liked me." Somehow, I can picture Sarah's teacher going out of her way to greet the more discouraged students each morning by making eye contact, smiling, and commenting that she was glad to see them again this morning. I can also imagine that she was able to navigate most crises and behavioural challenges with the same calm and compassionate demeanour and with a focus on finding positive solutions. Her positive feelings are reflected in her relationships with her students.

It is no surprise that teachers who are more adept at regulating their own emotions and building positive relationships with their students experience higher rates of job satisfaction and lower rates of burnout. They also report higher levels of positive emotion while engaged in teaching (Brackett, Palomera, Mojsa-Kaja, Reyes, & Salovey, 2010). Opportunities for teachers to develop their social emotional skills create a more positive and effective learning environment (Durlak, Weissberg, Dymnicki, Taylor, & Schellinger, 2011).

"Teachers with stronger SEL competencies have more positive relationships with students, manage their classrooms more effectively, and implement SEL programs targeted to students with greater fidelity."

—*Jones, Bouffard, & Weissbourd, 2013, p. 64*

"Teachers with high self-efficacy (and high EI) appraise and interpret teaching-related job demands as more of a challenge rather than a threat, which can certainly aid in the management of negative [emotional] experiences."

—*Vesely, Saklofske, & Leschied, 2013, p. 76*

Community Connection

A Whole-School Approach

Like student well-being, the promotion of positive teacher well-being requires a whole-school approach. Building social emotional skill development and practices into daily teacher, staff, and administrator interactions can promote a positive and healthy school environment.

Encourage emotional awareness. Make talking about and exploring the emotions involved in teaching and learning a regular part of staff meetings, non-evaluative video reviews, and logs or journals. Find out what SEL training opportunities and professional development opportunities are available and best suit you and your school. In addition to CASEL workshops and RULER (a program of the Yale Center for Emotional Intelligence), CARE (Cultivating Awareness and Resilience in Education) and SMART (Stress Management And Resilience Training) are two mindfulness programs for educators that aim to build emotional regulation skills, increase job satisfaction, and promote effective relationships with students.

Incorporate reflection into daily routines. Take time for regular reflection—even if it is several minutes at the beginning and end of the day. Set up partners or teams for regular reflective discussions, and make these discussions part of school meetings. Reflection focuses on understanding what is happening, why, and what might need to change. It is a critical skill for dealing with challenging situations and taking advantage of new opportunities.

Tackle stressors. Talk about circumstances and situations that are sources of stress, such as scheduling and resource issues. Focus on finding solutions or ways of managing to ease stress and frustration. We can't eliminate stress, but we can find ways to deal with it. Practise personal stress-reducing strategies, such as taking deep breaths and stopping to assess before reacting, keeping active, and catching negative thinking traps.

CASEL Guide

RULER program information and evaluation

CARE (Cultivating Awareness and Resilience in Education)

SMART (Stress Management And Resilience Training)

Create a culture of continuous improvement and mutual support. Work together to encourage an environment of positive collaboration and support, respect for differences, acknowledgment of effort, a voice in decision making, and positive goals for improvement.

Source: Jones, Bouffard, & Weissbourd (2013).

Resources for Educator Social Emotional Learning

In a review article, "Teachers—The Vital Resource: The Contribution of Emotional Intelligence to Teacher Efficacy and Well Being," Vesely et al. (2013) suggest that emotional intelligence is foundational to improved psychological health and teaching success, at the same time as producing positive student outcomes. Training for social emotional skills can decrease stress and job dissatisfaction, while increasing teacher efficacy.

The Collaborative for Academic, Social, and Emotional Learning (CASEL) promotes social and emotional skills training for teachers as well as students. "The Emotionally Intelligent Teacher" is a workshop presented in four sections. It covers the perception, use, understanding, and management of emotions. The workshop provides teachers with strategies to increase social emotional intelligence skills in personal and professional relationships. It also involves activities designed to increase school effectiveness through skills for improving interactions within the school community.

Vesely et al. (2013) also highlight the evidenced-based approach to social emotional learning known as RULER. The RULER acronym refers to the five key skills of recognizing, understanding, labelling, expressing, and regulating emotions. This school-based program involves students, teachers, family members, and school leaders. Goals include skill development to improve decision making, relationship building, academic achievement, and personal well-being in the school environment (Brackett, Rivers, & Salovey, 2011). Research-based outcomes include more positive and respectful interactions in classrooms, more prosocial behaviour, greater enthusiasm for learning, fewer bullying instances among students, and less anger and frustration expressed by teachers. The authors conclude that how educators and students feel, and how they use and respond to their feelings, influences the school environment in ways that support learning and development.

Lifestyle Balance

As educators, we need to manage our lifestyle balance across work, family, finances, recreation, social life, spirituality, personal growth, health, and fitness. It can be useful to draw a circle like that shown in Figure 6.1, and rank your level of satisfaction from 0 to 10 in each segment by drawing an inner outline. The new perimeter can provide an indicator of where you might set goals for maximizing balance. If you are not devoting time to each segment of your lifestyle, you may be a little "out of balance." Excessive time devoted to any one segment can have repercussions in the other segments. The Medicine Wheel described in Chapter 5 (pages 135–136) is another model for considering and working toward life balance.

Figure 6.1: Lifestyle Balance

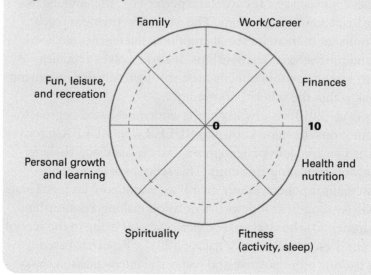

©P

Teacher Resilience and Personal Competency

Opportunities to develop social emotional intelligence can be broken down into the five areas of personal competency originally described by Goleman (1998). These areas became the basis for the five social emotional learning competencies used with students. It is useful to think about these original personal competencies—self-awareness, managing emotions, self-motivation, empathy, and managing relationships—in relation to the role of teaching.

Self-Awareness

Self-awareness is about knowing and integrating your internal states, preferences, resources, and intuitions for your role as a teacher. It involves recognizing your emotions and their effects on your performance, as well as knowing your strengths and limits. Of course, too, self-awareness involves attention to your lifestyle balance.

A personal competence for self-awareness also implies a strong sense of self-worth and capability as a teacher. Further developing self-awareness, for any of us, may require reading, reflection, and supportive emotional relationships with particular family members, friends, colleagues, or counsellors who will listen with care and help reflect on important feelings and perceptions for personal growth.

Most of us will experience times in our lives when we are emotionally "out-of-sorts" or even distressed. At these points, it is more difficult to feel competent, maintain effective relationships, and keep balance. This assessment can be especially true for teachers, who need to navigate the constantly changing emotions of 20 or more students each day, including, at times, dealing with student trauma and distress. Beyond the classroom, teachers need to relate to parents, other teachers, administrators, and people or groups in the larger school community. Navigating through periods of significant loss or change will require considerable emotional resilience and professionalism.

A high level of self-awareness contributes to our resilience. When we have consciously integrated our life experiences, disappointments, traumas, and joys into a strong sense of self-worth and self-understanding, we can better deal with challenges and adversities, and take advantage of new opportunities. This process is not unlike how we integrate all of our sensory learnings in life—from bumps and falls, to touching hot things, to hearing horns honk—so that we can safely navigate our physical world. In the same way, emotional integration allows us to effectively navigate our social world.

Emotional experiences from our past, both good and bad, can function as learning experiences. We can work to understand our strengths, vulnerabilities, and what we need to do to take care of ourselves, rather than carry around heavy stones in our personal knapsacks and suppress issues because of the pain or confusion they evoke. These issues and negative emotions can affect our perspectives and our relationships. With high levels of self-awareness, we can be well grounded and in a strong position to use self-management skills in our relationships with students and others.

Managing Emotions

Managing emotions is largely about self-regulation. I wonder how Sarah's teacher up-regulated or down-regulated so she "didn't get crabby much." Emotional management requires self-control skills. At times, we have to keep disruptive emotions and impulses in check. We also require adaptability and flexibility for handling change, from personal traumas and issues to the varied teaching assignments and environmental conditions that are part of the regular operation and politics of any school.

Like Jack, in Chapter 5, we may need to use strategies such as "rest, running, and relaxation" to get stress under control when anxiety creeps into the work environment. We all need to be able to name emotional states where we find self-regulation is necessary and identify the healthy strategies that we use to find balance.

Self-Motivation

Self-motivation can be described as emotional tendencies or professional attitudes that guide us to reach our goals. Ideally, as teachers, we develop motivational attitudes that enhance our effectiveness in the classroom. For example, a motivational attitude can be an emotional readiness to act on opportunities—in other words, to take initiative. With the advent of technology in the classroom, some educators initially shied away from these tools. Others stepped up and enthusi-astically learned all about the possibilities. In this case, they were moti-vated and demonstrated initiative. Self-motivated teachers are also often innovators. They have a thirst for novel ideas and approaches founded on good evidence.

Another important form of self-motivation is an attitude of opti-mism. In the lunchroom or at a meeting, everyone would like to sit next to a person with an optimistic attitude. That attitude creates a positive atmosphere in the school and classroom. Now contrast that with the experience of being around someone who is pessimistic. Pessimism pulls the individual down, as well as pulling down all those around the pessimist. Can you imagine having a pessimistic coach?

Empathy

Empathy may be described as the heart of social emotional compe-tence. When we have finely tuned empathy skills, we are both aware of, and sensitive to, the feelings, needs, and concerns of others. When we model and teach empathy to students, they are disinclined to put down or bully one another.

It is important for teachers to realize that some students arrive in class with attractive personalities; others are less fortunate. Some are easy to like and they will be popular with other students and with teachers. Empathy will come easily for us in our relationships with these students. Students not gifted with a sunny disposition may not arouse much empathy. When we realize this, we can understand that empathy is a skill. All students have dignity and worth. With a little effort we can get to know and understand a student who has a dour disposition or even presents aggressive behaviour. We can also uncover that student's gifts and talents, and help the child flourish. More than anything, professional teaching involves the development of empathy for the child who is hard to get to know and may, at first, be hard to like.

Teachers who develop high levels of empathy will recognize that aggressive behaviour in children may be an expression of pain and yearning to have their emotional needs met, and that children often express their need through misdirected, dysfunctional behaviour. Unmet needs drive dysfunctional behaviours. Dreikurs understood this idea when he put forward his strategies for positive encouragement. Ungar also knew the importance of empathy in his social-ecological perspective on resilience. Disadvantaged youth can develop effective resiliency skills when caring adults engage them in the school community where their developmental needs can be met appropriately. This development can happen only when these adults communicate empathetic caring.

When we engage in caring relationships with students and foster their successful development, we share empathy and experience the sense of meaning and competence that helps us to flourish as teachers. We can also extend empathy to colleagues and other staff, fostering a more inclusive and caring whole-school environment.

Managing Relationships

Managing relationships depends largely on our development of social skills. The term *managing* suggests a heavier touch than is usually required. There are times when we have to "manage" our relationships, but most of the time, we are "fostering" healthy relationships. Key social skills include influencing others through benevolent and mutually beneficial means of persuasion, rather than adopting more self-serving tactics for getting what we want in a relationship. Active listening, open communication, negotiating and mediating to resolve disagreements, inspiring and guiding individuals and groups, working collaboratively and cooperatively toward shared goals, and initiating or managing change are other key social skills for teaching.

Moreover, in most Canadian schools today, students come from diverse backgrounds and cultures. As teachers, we are expected to understand social and ethical norms for behaviour, and to be aware of family, school, and community resources and supports. We are called on to be societal leaders in understanding cultural perspectives, empathizing with diverse students, and being able to form encouraging professional relationships. We can better handle these expectations when we have developed key social understandings and skills.

This is perhaps easier said than done when the stress of the teaching profession seems to be growing, rather than reducing, in part due to the complexity of the conditions in which many teachers find themselves.

Many teachers' federations have written on the impact of stress and the need for a healthy work-life balance for their members. Kenneth Leithwood (2006), in a publication produced by the Elementary Teachers' Federation of Ontario (ETFO), explored the effects of classroom, school, district, and provincial conditions that impact teachers and teachers' work life. In the study, Leithwood also outlined what actions could mitigate some of the negative effects of the conditions under which teachers must work. He identified five strategies that teachers could implement:

1. Build a professional network.
2. Continue to pursue professional development.
3. Expect leadership from your administration.
4. Exercise a voice in decision making.
5. Control volunteering. (pp. 74–78)

Some of these same points are made in an earlier publication, also produced by ETFO. Hammill (2000) makes the case that teachers should be comfortable saying yes when it is appropriate and equally comfortable saying no when it is appropriate; that teachers not judge themselves so harshly—we all make mistakes; and that we help others as they help us. (p. 9)

Shanker (2012) devotes a portion of the final chapter of *Calm, Alert, and Learning: Classroom Strategies for Self-Regulation* to mental wellness and to the mental well-being of teachers. Shanker states:

> … as teachers we need to attend not only to our students' academic and psychological needs, but also to our own mental health as we try our best every day to keep up with and implement curriculum, assess students, deal with parents, and fulfill many other duties. All this, as no doubt your daily experiences and recent studies attest, is extremely demanding. (p. 151)

On the following pages, one teacher recounts her experiences of implementing self-regulation in her classroom and the unintended benefits she discovered on her ability to manage her personal self-regulation. Whether one tackles personal mental wellness through the lens of self-regulation, mindfulness, or social emotional learning, many of the strategies that we help our students to implement can be beneficial to us.

A Teacher's Journey

I went from feeling stressed out and frustrated to feeling that I am in an exciting and effective partnership with the students in my class. It's been a great experience for me.
—Kate Przybylski

Kate was facing a challenge. She was in a high-needs school, and each day her frustration and stress levels were rising. She was struggling to support the students and wasn't sure where to go. She decided to take a new approach. She realized that trying to focus on academics before she acknowledged and helped her students understand their biological, emotional, social, and inter-personal needs wasn't working. She had to find a better way to connect with her students and help them to understand and express their personal learning styles first.

Kate had heard a presentation by Stuart Shanker on self-regulation that sparked her exploration into his work and similar research, such as Kuypers' Zones of Regulation model and social emotional learning. She began applying some of the strategies with her students.

I literally learned with the kids…and that was a great experience because then it was all of us sort of making mistakes and figuring it out together. And I was always very honest with them…I'm learning this, I'm trying this out. I told my students I wanted to hear from them. I told them that at the end they were going to tell me what they thought, and we would say if it was worthwhile or not.

I was surprised at how little the kids knew—even just vocabulary to label emotions or express themselves. I was also surprised at how much they enjoyed the process and how open they were. I think they really enjoyed talking about themselves.

The journey Kate went on with her students had surprises, struggles, and successes.

There were definitely a lot of surprises—I think we all sometimes think that things like self-regulation and emotional well-being and understanding oneself are innate, and I've definitely found that they need to be taught. It's a skill that we develop and hone over time.

Another surprise was that some of the kids who I would never have thought needed to work on self-regulation—those kids who attend well, are friendly, and can deal with their problems—some of them found it the most valuable. They gravitated to the fidgets and other sensory tools that I had available in the classroom. It helped me to see that all of the students had places to grow.

Kate also found that the growth wasn't only for her students; it was for herself as well.

I found I was less frustrated with them because I wasn't looking at their behaviour as something that needed to be fixed or something that was wrong with them or something that was purposeful.... It was rather hmmm...you do this, let's see what need that would be filling. For example, "let's work together at finding out why you feel the need to shout out in class."

It let me do what I do—teach, rather than try to dictate.... It allowed the kids to see that I was working with them and not against them.

Kate found she started applying the same strategies to self-regulate.

I would share the vocabulary with the kids. I would say...I'm in the yellow zone right now. You can read silently right now. I need to go take a breather and fill up my water bottle. It definitely made me more aware of my own emotional state. So, if I found I was in a hyper-aroused or stressed state, I knew it was not a good time for me to attack a difficult lesson. I developed a heightened level of self-awareness so that I knew how to regulate myself in order to be an effective educator.

I found I was on a very similar journey as the kids in the class.

Kate felt her own sense of satisfaction and efficacy improving.

The level of stress and frustration went down because I felt like I had tools to work with my students.... Sometimes things worked and sometimes they didn't, but if that one strategy didn't work, I wasn't left high and dry trying to figure out what to do next. I had ideas. I had ways to help them, and it was okay for them to come up with the ideas as well. It wasn't all on my shoulders anymore.

I was also more open to changes and more aware of where they were at and where they needed to be and less concerned about my schedule. I was definitely interested to see what we accomplished by the end of the year academically, and I found we did far more than when academics were my primary concern rather than their emotional stability in the classroom.

I'm quite proud of where those kids have come to. You always say you want to make a real difference for at least one or two students each year, and I feel like I succeeded in making a difference with several students, which is very satisfying.

Kate has found renewed excitement and satisfaction in her teaching.

I also really enjoyed the professional learning and sharing with my colleagues. We all make mistakes and we can problem-solve together.

I think I'm more excited in my career right now. I feel like I have all this room to learn and grow, and I'm excited about the journey. After 14 years of teaching with all of the ups and downs, I am excited to continue to grow and learn and help my students become the best they can be in my classroom.

Source: Based on an interview with Kate Przybylski, August 4, 2014.

A Caring, Inclusive Professional Environment

"Supportive school cultures not only enhance staff members' SEL abilities, but, importantly, set the conditions for using them effectively."

—Jones, Bouffard, & Weissbourd, 2013, p. 63

We know how important a sense of belonging and positive relationships are to student learning and well-being. It is no different for us as educators. A supportive professional culture is as important for the success and well-being of teachers as a caring and inclusive classroom is for students.

To be effective as teachers, we need a sense of belonging and commitment—a strong sense of connection to our school and to a professional learning community. We need to feel that what we do matters and that we have an investment in being there. To create that foundation of belonging and commitment, a school environment needs to explicitly foster the values of respect, acceptance, and care, extending both to and from all staff. When these values are discussed, promoted, and practised each day at all levels of the school, they can create a culture that encourages not only student learning, but professional learning and positive collaboration.

A safe and positive professional learning environment acknowledges teachers' diverse and individual strengths. It allows teachers to take risks, try new things, and feel safe that mistakes can be acknowledged, addressed, and seen as learning opportunities. Open communication is encouraged and respected, and teachers feel they have a voice in decision making. A safe and inclusive environment also builds trust among colleagues so that they will openly exchange information, feel confident in one another's abilities, be caring of one another, and share positive rather than negative feelings and experiences. Positive feelings are important and are everyone's responsibility. School leaders and administrators play a key role, but the work of creating a positive culture is both internal (within us as individuals) and external.

In a supportive professional environment, it becomes more possible to achieve shared goals, make positive connections with parents, and take advantage of community resources and opportunities. When the school is then viewed positively within the larger community, commitment and well-being are enhanced further.

We can view a positive working environment for teachers as one that fosters

- explicit values of trust, respect, inclusivity, and caring

- high expectations to create a strong communal identity

- respectful and dignified treatment as professionals

- teacher participation in decisions and a degree of autonomy in their work

- regular opportunities for professional learning, reflection, and intentional social emotional skill development

- opportunities for positive interaction and sharing among colleagues

- acknowledgment of strengths, effort, and achievement

- encouragement for innovation, initiative, mutual support, and shared goals

> "The importance of positive feelings in schools is only just being recognized. Not only do these promote more positive behaviours, but also creativity, problem-solving, and coping skills. Positive emotions are critical for resilience and well-being."
> —Roffey, 2012, p. 14

Managing Stress

The Ontario English Catholic Teachers' Association has produced a guide on managing stress, directed to the teaching profession. The following material is from this publication, *Managing Stress & Promoting Wellness: A guide for teachers on managing stress in the workplace and beyond.*

While we often think of stress as something caused by external factors such as workload, deadlines, or other people, it is our response to these circumstances that produces stress. Stress becomes most problematic when it controls or overwhelms us.

Recognizing Stress-Related Symptoms

Below are some common symptoms associated with stress. The more symptoms you exhibit, the more likely the stress you are experiencing will affect your health and well-being.

Cognitive Symptoms

- Memory problems
- Inability to concentrate
- Poor judgment
- Seeing only the negative
- Anxious or racing thoughts
- Constant worrying

Physical Symptoms

- Aches and pains
- Diarrhea or constipation
- Nausea or dizziness
- Chest pain or rapid heartbeat
- Loss of sex drive
- Frequent colds
- Exhaustion

Emotional Symptoms

- Moodiness
- Irritability or short temper
- Agitation or inability to relax
- Feelings of being overwhelmed
- Sense of loneliness and isolation
- Depression or general unhappiness

Behavioural Symptoms

- Eating more or less
- Sleeping too much or too little
- Isolating yourself from others
- Procrastinating or neglecting responsibilities
- Using alcohol, cigarettes, or drugs to relax
- Nervous habits (e.g., nail biting or pacing)

Managing Stressors

Set realistic expectations for yourself and others.

- **Be clear in your expectations of others and your understanding of their expectations of you.** Set realistic goals for yourself and don't judge yourself harshly when you come up short. When you face multiple expectations seek help about your priorities from senior staff (e.g., your vice-principal). Be flexible—with yourself and with others.

- **Strive to change only what is changeable.** Change is constant in this world, and certainly in education. To deal with change, look for ways you can contribute to providing a solution to a problem.

- **Promote understanding and celebrate differences.** We don't have to like everyone, nor does everyone have to like us. What is important is to be able to see from another's perspective and appreciate their views. A shared ability to appreciate one another can help us deal with a range of problems. If a problem becomes too large then we need to involve trusted others to help us move to consensus.

- **Be decisive and don't procrastinate.** Procrastination can lead to a sense of losing control. Make the best decision you can at the time with the information you have and move forward.

- **Keep a to-do list and prioritize.** Begin by knowing and noting what you need to do and when. Prioritize your responsibilities. Schedules can help you stay on track and provide a sense of control.

- **Be creative and expand your talents.** Think about what you do well and what you enjoy, then introduce it into your classroom. Want to try your hand at something new? Do it and perhaps discover a new skill.

- **Create a positive space.** Make your classroom space comfortable for everyone—clear clutter, ensure that there is good air flow, and look at your lighting. Making physical changes to improve your classroom can have a positive impact on people's well-being and comfort in your space.

- **Connect with co-workers.** Having good relationships with co-workers decreases your stress level at school. When you have peers to confide in answers may appear more quickly and easily.

- **Take workplace training in stress management.** Some districts will offer courses in reducing stress and coping with common problems—both work-related and personal. Take advantage of these programs to help you manage and mitigate the effects of stress.

- **Utilize Employee Assistance Programs.** Check your plan for the types of services offered. Typically EAP plans offer a wide range of short-term services, from financial planning advice through psychotherapy.

Sourced from: Counselling and Member Services Department, Ontario English Catholic Teachers' Association, Managing Stress & Promoting Wellness: A guide for teachers on managing stress in the workplace and beyond.

Teacher Engagement

We have seen how engagement in learning that allows us to apply and develop our strengths and competencies contributes positively to well-being. For teachers who are highly engaged and flourishing in their careers, professional learning occurs every day. They continually improve their practice by reflecting, researching, and hypothesizing—both independently and collaboratively—in the context of both their own classrooms and the whole school environment. They recognize their strengths and want to apply and develop them toward achieving positive personal and professional goals.

Models for professional learning that allow for professional choice and decision making, open-ended investigation, and positive collaboration can work well to promote positive engagement. Collaborative inquiry is an example. **Collaborative inquiry**, in this context, involves one or more teachers working together to address an identified learning need (Timperley, Wilson, Barrar, & Fung, 2008; Ontario Ministry of Education, 2011; Bethke, 2014). Collaborative inquiry models can vary in the number of stages and what constitutes each stage, but there are several crucial elements that characterize any model: a teacher need to solve a student problem or misconception, data gathering and analysis, instruction, and assessment (what worked, what didn't, and how we can improve).

Imagine for a moment that teachers feel students in their classes are off-task much of the time and they identify the need for increased self-regulation. The model below, applied to this problem, has five major stages:

Stage 1: Gather Information

- As a team, discuss evidence, observations of students' current knowledge of self-regulation and language related to emotions.

- Decide on instruments and techniques to gather data to confirm your observations. This could be as informal as observations or as formal as a student survey to determine levels of knowledge.

- Gather data. Analyze and interpret results.

Stage 2: Plan to Implement

- Given students' current level of understanding of self-regulation, determine your needs and requirements around subject knowledge. Consider the question: Do we need to build our personal knowledge of self-regulation before we implement our teaching plans? If yes, then analyze and act on personal learning needs before you set out to design student learning plans.

- Determine learning outcomes for students.

- Plan your lesson design. Include how you will assess effectiveness of the teaching strategies—"How will we know?"

Stage 3: Implement

- Explore themes of self-regulation and emotional language with students.

- Introduce activities students can implement to practise self-regulation, including developing their language around emotions.

- If possible, co-teach self-regulation strategies to your classes.

Stage 4: Observe and Assess

- Observe and monitor student awareness and implementation of self-regulation strategies and understanding of emotional language. Are they able to implement strategies on their own?

- Share observations of colleague practice.

- Apply assessment measures identified in Stage 2. Did your teaching strategies help students to achieve intended learning outcomes?

Stage 5: Reflect and Extend

- Evaluate the learning cycle. Where were you successful? What would you change in the cycle? Determine next steps to support and extend students' understanding and application of self-regulation.

In phase 2, teachers determine what knowledge and skills they need before implementing activities with their students. In our example, teachers may decide that they need to enhance their own social emotional knowledge and self-management skills before they can effectively teach and model self-regulation for their students. They may need to consult resources or collaborate with colleagues to identify research-informed teaching practices.

As every teacher knows, the art of teaching is most pronounced in phase 3, which involves a deepening of professional knowledge and refinement of skills identified in phase 2. Student feedback will help teachers modify and enhance their work (phase 4). Teachers will reflect on the evidence of learning through the inquiry (phase 5), and they will be positioned to share findings with other educators in their larger learning communities of school, school board, or district.

In an inquiry cycle, professional learning occurs in each phase of inquiry regardless of the number of phases. Trial and error is encouraged, and instant success is not expected as activities are first introduced. Learning occurs from risk taking, and refinements are made over time through careful observation and adjustment. Teachers learn from one another and grow together through comparison, collaboration, and understanding. Professional learning models such as these can work to meet the goals of increased teacher efficacy, teacher well-being, and student well-being.

Putting It All Together

In Chapter 1, we talked about the key goal of creating a culture of mental health in all our schools. As we look back on that goal now, we can see that in many ways it starts with us—the educators. If we look after our own mental health and well-being first, we will be in a better and stronger position to understand, advocate for, and support the mental health development of our students. The more we learn and understand about evidence-based mental health strategies and tools, the better we will be able to apply them for ourselves and our students.

It is also important to acknowledge again that we are not alone. Throughout the book we have looked at key community connections—pathways to the whole-school and whole-community approach that is vital to creating a positive culture of well-being. We need the support of government initiatives, school board policies and actions, and the active participation of all staff in schools. But as individuals, we can support the values and work to build the relationships that are the foundations of that culture. As teachers, we are closest to our students and in a vital position to influence their mental well-being. What we do makes a difference.

It may be worth reminding ourselves to take a moment out of each day, as we are caught up in our various tasks and trials, to reflect not on the problems but on the positive elements of mental health and what we are doing to foster it—for ourselves and our students. When we do that, we can remember to keep a positive perspective and focus on what we need to do to be and stay well.

Before that, though, I suggest you revisit the questionnaire in Chapter 2 (page 23). Consider how your understandings and perceptions about mental health have changed and where you have come on your own personal journey.

Checklist for Teacher Mental Health

√ Teacher well-being is recognized as an important and positive goal.

√ The importance of social emotional skills for teacher efficacy and well-being is acknowledged and supported.

√ Teachers give attention to lifestyle balance and personal well-being strategies.

√ A caring, inclusive professional environment encourages belonging, commitment, trust, professional autonomy, and positive collaboration.

√ Individual strengths are recognized, differences are respected, risk taking and effort are acknowledged, and teachers have a voice in decisions.

√ Teachers are engaged in regular opportunities for meaningful professional learning.

Bethke, R. (2014). *Pedagogical Documentation: A Facilitator's Guide* [Working document]. Toronto, ON: Pearson Canada.

Brackett, M. A., Palomera, R., Mojsa-Kaja, J., Reyes, M. R., & Salovey, P. (2010). Emotion-regulation ability, burnout, and job satisfaction among British secondary-school teachers. *Psychology in the Schools, 47*, 406–417. doi: 10.1002/pits.20478

Brackett, M. A., Rivers, S. E., & Salovey P. (2011). Emotional intelligence: Implications for personal, social, academic, and workplace success. *Social and Personality Psychology Compass, 5*, 88–103.

Counselling and Member Services Department, Ontario English Catholic Teachers Association. (2014). *Managing stress & promoting wellness: A guide for teachers on managing stress in the workplace and beyond.* Retrieved from www.oecta.on.ca

Durlak, J. A., Weissberg, R. P., Dymnicki, A. B., Taylor, R. D., & Schellinger, K. B. (2011). The impact of enhancing students' social and emotional learning: A meta-analysis of school-based universal interventions. *Child Development, 82*(1), 405–432.

Hammill, D., & Elementary Teachers' Federation of Ontario. (2000). Be well, beware [Excerpt]. *After the chalk dust settles.* Toronto, ON: Elementary Teachers' Federation of Ontario. Retrieved from www.survivethrive.on.ca/files/upload/resource/11/81_bewell.pdf

Goleman, D. (1998). *Working with emotional intelligence.* London, UK: Bloomsbury.

Jones, S. M., Bouffard, S. M., & Weissbourd, R. (2013, May). Educators' social and emotional skills vital to learning. *Phi Delta Kappan, 94*(8), 62–65. Retrieved from kappanmagazine.org

Leithwood, K. (2006). *Teacher working conditions that matter: Evidence for change.* Toronto, ON: Elementary Teachers' Federation of Ontario.

Ontario Ministry of Education, Student Achievement Division. (2011). Professional Learning Cycle DVD. SS/L-18ITEB.

Roffey, S. (2012). Pupil well-being—Teacher well-being: Two sides of the same coin? *Educational & Child Psychology, 29*(4), 8–17.

Roffey, S. (2014). *Teacher wellbeing: What does the research say?* Retrieved from http://www.sueroffey.com/wp-content/uploads/2014/04/CDU-Teacher-Wellbeing-Relationships-Roffey.pdf

Timperley, H., Wilson, A., Barrar, H., & Fung, I. (2007). *Teacher professional learning and development: Best evidence synthesis iteration* [Report to the Ministry of Education]. Wellington, New Zealand: Ministry of Education.

Vesely, A. K., Saklofske, D. H., & Leschied, A. D. W. (2013). Teachers—The vital resource: The contribution of emotional intelligence to teacher efficacy and well-being. *Canadian Journal of School Psychology, 28*(1), 71–89.

A

acculturative stress—feelings of stress such as anxiety, confusion, and depression that are triggered by the challenges of adjusting to a new culture

active—participating in regular physical activity for fitness, in addition to adequate sleep, good nutrition, and attention to spiritual needs

anxiety—worry, concern, or apprehension related to thoughts of a current or future situation

autonomic nervous system—the system that controls largely involuntary bodily responses such as blood flow and heart rate

B

biodots—small self-adhesive circles that are applied to the back of a person's hand. Circles, or dots, contain a chemical that changes colour based on body temperature. Warm hands mean someone is relaxed, cool hands mean someone is tense. Why? Stress causes our blood vessels to contract, which makes our hands cool.

biofeedback—a technique where, through technology, people are able to perceive normally unconscious bodily processes, allowing them to mentally gain control of such processes. An example would be to become aware of muscle tension and then to employ deliberate relaxation methods.

C

cognitive intelligence—the capacity to make sense of things around us and figure out what to do

collaborative inquiry—two or more professionals working together to find ways to fulfill identified needs. For example, teachers may use collaborative inquiry to address learning needs, while social workers may use it to address coping needs.

conditioning—a form of learning in which a given stimulus becomes increasingly effective at evoking a response

cultural competence—ability to effectively and respectfully deal with people of diverse cultures, which is dependent on continual development of attitudes, awareness, knowledge, and skills; a necessary ability for the acceptance of diversity

D

depression—a condition in which continual feelings of hopelessness, sadness, and helplessness are present

desensitization—a form of physiological conditioning intended to gradually undo bodily symptoms of anxiety

discrimination—the behaviour that results from belief in a negative stereotype

diversity—a state that encompasses differences in racial and ethnocultural background, sexual orientation, special physical, emotional, or behavioural needs, learning needs and strengths, and personal preferences

E

emotion—a complex set of mental, physical, and expressive responses to stimuli. Feelings are the subjective awareness of emotional states.

emotional intelligence—the capacity to use understanding of emotions to guide thinking and behaviour for positive relationships and overall well-being

empathy—the ability to imagine and fully understand the emotions or motivations of another person

encouragement—interaction based on improvement rather than level of achievement, and that motivates students to keep trying

equity—fairness and justice

explanatory thinking styles—three ways in which people try to explain a problem they are experiencing by unconsciously seeking all-or-nothing answers to three questions: personalization asks who caused the problem (me/not me), permanence asks how long the problem will last (always/not always), and pervasiveness asks how much the problem will affect one's life (everything/not everything). Martin Seligman first noted these thinking styles.

extroversion—the characteristics of a personality that needs more stimulation to function well, that prefers to work with others, that may gain energy from social situations, that talks more than listens in groups, that sometimes speaks before thinking, and that is comfortable with conflict

F

flexibility—a willingness to try new things, to learn from our mistakes, and to be able to analyze problems and consider various alternative and realistic solutions

flourishing—an optimal level of mental health, regardless of mental illness

flow—a state of deep engagement in an activity, sometimes to the extent that one loses track of time

H

high sensitivity—ability to process sensory information very thoroughly, often noticing subtle changes, as a result of having a highly tuned nervous system

I

iceberg beliefs—deeply rooted beliefs about how we think the world should operate, that may be passed on from generation to generation or be culturally rooted

inclusivity—respect for diversity, personal dignity, and other perspectives; making everyone feel included and part of the same group

intergenerational trauma—the resulting condition when effects such as acculturative stress and marginalization are passed on from one generation to the next

introversion—the characteristics of a personality that needs less stimulation to function well, that prefers to work independently, that may expend energy in social situations, that listens and observes more than talks in groups, that usually thinks before speaking, and that is uncomfortable with conflict

L

limbic system—the part of the brain that controls physiological responses and emotions that were originally related to survival

M

Medicine Wheel—a symbol in the form of a circle that expresses belief in the endless cycle of life in many Indigenous cultures. It is based on knowledge of the rhythm of life and the observation of Nature.

mental health—the state of well-being encompassing a sense of enjoyment in life, of realizing our potential, meeting challenges, being productive, respecting ourselves and others, and making a positive contribution to our communities

mental health intervention—specific support and referral to mental health professionals provided to students who have mental health disorders

mental health literacy—the understanding of the requirements that allow people to exist in a state of well-being and to be resilient, to be active, and to flourish

mental health promotion—an endeavour to promote lifestyle experiences for all that include regular opportunities for positive emotion, engagement, meaning, accomplishment, and positive relationships

mental illness—an umbrella term for a broad range of conditions that negatively affect mental health

mindfulness—the ability to quiet the mind and focus fully on what is happening in the current moment, accepting the experience without worrying or judging.

P

positive mental health—a state of well-being in which a person is resilient, active, and flourishing

positive self-talk—the encouraging thoughts people say to themselves without speaking out loud

prosocial behaviours—positive behaviours and actions intended to help others, including honesty, empathy, and concern for the rights and welfare of others

R

reframing—a switch in mindset or viewpoint, such as changing a negative into a positive, that assists with managing emotions

resilience—believing in our own strengths, abilities, and worth, and having the ability to cope with life's disappointments, challenges, and pain

restorative justice—a method of conflict resolution in which the involved people gather in a circle where everyone is given a chance to talk, discussing what happened, what they were thinking at the time, how they felt, who was affected by the actions, and how to resolve the situation

S

self-awareness—a state in which you are conscious of your own mental and physical existence. You recognize strengths and weaknesses and are aware of what motivations influence your behaviour and emotions.

self-management—an ability related to self-awareness, in which you are able to control your behaviour, emotions, and motivations in various situations

self-regulation—an ability related to self-awareness, in which you are able to govern recognized mental and physical states in socially acceptable ways

social awareness—an ability to relate to, understand, and empathize with others regardless of socioeconomic, education, or cultural background

social emotional learning (SEL)—the process in which people (especially young people) become able to integrate behaviour, thought, and emotion for successful participation in their immediate community and in society at large

social intelligence—the capacity to effectively navigate and negotiate complex social relationships and environments

social justice—the idea that all people should be equally able to participate in society and the benefits society has to offer

stigma—a negative stereotype resulting in discrimination

strengths—the mental, emotional, and physical characteristics that allow a person to be resilient, to be active, and to flourish

strengths-based approach—a methodology in which a person's strengths are given greater attention than their deficits

stress—the body's alarm response to any situation that we perceive as overwhelming or threatening. It causes a specific set of physiological reactions in the body—our heart rate increases, blood is distributed to our large muscles, our pupils dilate, and digestion shuts down.

T

thinking traps—common thinking errors, often automatic and largely unconscious, that trap us into drawing conclusions prematurely. These errors include overgeneralizing, exaggerating or catastrophizing, minimizing or downplaying, personalizing, mind-reading (assuming we know what others are thinking without asking), and engaging in emotional reasoning (making false conclusions based solely on how we feel rather than on the facts).

three-tiers model—a three-level model of supporting people socially, behaviourally, and emotionally. Tier 1 is promotion and universal support for all, Tier 2 is prevention through targeted support for some, and Tier 3 is intervention and intensive support for a few.

triggers—stimuli, such as sight, sound, or smell, or other experiences that set off a psychological reaction, such as feelings of anxiety or reminders of trauma

V

visualizing—imagining something or some situation in great detail, so that it becomes a mental image

W

well-being—a positive and healthy state characterized by a sense of enjoyment in life, of realizing one's potential, meeting challenges, being productive, respecting self and others, and making a positive contribution to the community

wraparound support—a model of service that encompasses a team of individual and community-based support networks to meet mental health needs

Anjum, A. (2014, July). *Strength based resiliency program [SBR]*. Pre-conference workshop presented at the 2nd Canadian Conference on Positive Psychology, Ottawa, ON.

Anxiety BC®. (2014). *ADABC Parenting Project*. Retrieved from http://www.anxietybc.com

Aron, E. (2002). *The highly sensitive child: Helping our children thrive when the world overwhelms them*. New York, NY: Crown.

Bell Let's Talk Initiative. (2014). Retrieved from http://letstalk.bell.ca/en/end-the-stigma/facts/

Best Start Resource Centre. (2012). *Building resilience in young children* [Booklet for parents of children from birth to six years].

Bethke, R. (2014). *Pedagogical Documentation: A Facilitator's Guide* [Working document]. Toronto, ON: Pearson Canada.

Brackett, M. A., Palomera, R., Mojsa-Kaja, J., Reyes, M. R., & Salovey, P. (2010). Emotion-regulation ability, burnout, and job satisfaction among British secondary-school teachers. *Psychology in the Schools, 47*, 406–417. doi: 10.1002/pits.20478

Brackett, M. A., Rivers, S. E., & Salovey P. (2011). Emotional intelligence: Implications for personal, social, academic, and workplace success. *Social and Personality Psychology Compass, 5*, 88–103.

Breazeale, R. (2009). *Duct tape isn't enough: Survival skills for the 21st century*. Portland, ME: Bounce Back USA.

Brown, B. (2012). *Daring greatly: How the courage to be vulnerable transforms the way we live, love, parent, and lead*. New York, NY: Gotham.

Brownlee, K., Rawana, E. P., & MacArthur, J. (2012). Implementation of a strengths-based approach to teaching in an elementary school. *Journal of Teaching and Learning, 8*(1). Retrieved from http://ojs.uwindsor.ca/ojs/leddy/index.php/JTL/article/download/3069/pdf

Cain, S. (2012). *Quiet: The power of introverts in a world that can't stop talking*. New York, NY: Crown.

Canadian Mental Health Association [CMHA], Ontario. (n.d.). *Stigma and discrimination*. Retrieved from ontario.cmha.ca/mental-health/mental-health-conditions/stigma-and-discrimination/

Canadian Mental Health Association [CMHA]. (n.d.). *Understanding mental illness*. Retrieved from www.cmha.ca/mental-health/understanding-mental-illness/

Canadian Society for Exercise Physiology [CSEP]. (2011). *Canadian physical activity guidelines and Canadian sedentary behaviour guidelines*. Retrieved from http://www.csep.ca/guidelines

Canadian Society for Exercise Physiology [CSEP]. (2012). *Canadian physical activity guidelines and Canadian sedentary behaviour handbook*. Retrieved from http://www.csep.ca/english/view.asp?x=804

Carlson, J., Sperry, L., & Dinkmeyer, D. (1992). Marriage maintenance: How to stay healthy. *Topics in Family Counseling & Psychology, 1,* 84–90.

Centre for Addiction and Mental Health [CAMH]. (n.d.). *Talking about mental illness community guide.* Retrieved from www.camh.ca/en/education/teachers_school_programs/resources_for_teachers_and_schools/talking_about_mental_illness_a_community_guide_for_developing_an_awareness_program_for_youth/Pages/tami_commguide_part1.aspx

Centre for Addiction and Mental Health [CAMH]. (2010). *Stress.* Retrieved from http://www.camh.ca/en/hospital/health_information/a_z_mental_health_and_addiction_information/stress/Pages/info_stress.aspx

Centre for Addiction and Mental Health [CAMH], Dalla Lana School of Public Health, University of Toronto, & Toronto Public Health. (2012). *Best practice guidelines for mental health promotion programs: Refugees.* Retrieved from https://knowledgex.camh.net/policy_health/mhpromotion/Documents/BPGRefugees.pdf

Centre for Social Innovation. (2013). *Mindfulness without borders.* Retrieved from http://mindfulnesswithoutborders.org

Centre for Suicide Prevention. (2013). *FNMI [First Nations, Métis, and Inuit] suicide prevention resource toolkit.* Calgary, AB: Author.

Cherry, K. (2014). 5 signs you are an introvert. In *About.com.* Retrieved from http://psychology.about.com/od/personalitydevelopment/fl/5-Signs-You-Are-an-Introvert.htm

Collaborative for Academic, Social, and Emotional Learning [CASEL]. (2012). *2013 CASEL guide: Effective social and emotional learning programs—Preschool and elementary school edition.* Chicago, IL: Author. Retrieved from http://casel.org/

Costello, B., Wachtel, J., & Wachtel, T. (2010). *Restorative circles in schools: Building community and enhancing learning.* Bethlehem, PA: International Institute for Restorative Practices.

Counselling and Member Services Department, Ontario English Catholic Teachers Association. (n.d.). *Healthy tips for teachers.* Ontario Teachers' Federation, Survive & Thrive.

Cowan, K. C., Vaillancourt, K., Rossen, E., & Pollitt, K. (2013). *A framework for safe and successful schools* [Brief]. Bethesda, MD: National Association of School Psychologists.

Diamond, S.A. (2012, May 26). Essential secrets of psychotherapy: Jung's typology, eudaemonology, and the elusive art of happiness. In *Evil Deeds.* Retrieved from http://www.psychologytoday.com/blog/evil-deeds/201205/essential-secrets-psychotherapy-jungs-typology-eudaemonology-and-the-elusive-

Dreikurs, R., Cassel, P., & Dreikurs Ferguson, E. (2004). *Discipline without tears: How to reduce conflict and establish cooperation in the classroom* (Rev. ed.). Toronto, ON: Wiley.

Durlak, J. A., & Weissberg, R. P. (2011). Promoting social and emotional development is an essential part of students' education. *Human Development, 54*(11), 1–3.

Durlak, J. A., Weissberg, R. P., Dymnicki, A. B., Taylor, R. D., & Schellinger, K. B. (2011). The impact of enhancing students' social and emotional learning: A meta-analysis of school-based universal interventions. *Child Development, 82*(1), 405–432.

Eckman, P. (1999). Basic emotions. In T. Dalgleish, & M. Power, *Handbook of cognition and emotion,* 45–60. Sussex, UK: John Wiley.

Elias, B., et al. (2012). Trauma and suicide behaviour histories among a Canadian indigenous population: An empirical exploration of the potential role of Canada's residential school system. *Social Science & Medicine. 74*(10), 1560–1569.

Evans, T. D. (2004). The tools of encouragement. *Cyc-Online, 65.* Retrieved from http://www.cyc-net.org/cyc-online/cycol-0604-evans.html

Flett, G. L., & Hewitt, P. L. (2013). Disguised distress in children and adolescents "flying under the radar": Why psychological problems are underestimated and how schools must respond. *Canadian Journal of School Psychology, 28*(1), 12–27.

Gardner, H. (1983). *Frames of mind: The theory of multiple intelligences.* New York, NY: Basic Books.

Goleman, D. (1995). *Emotional intelligence.* New York, NY: Random House.

Goleman, D. (1998). *Working with emotional intelligence.* London, UK: Bloomsbury.

Goleman, D. (2006). *Social intelligence: The new science of human relationships.* New York, NY: Bantam.

Greene, R. W. (2010). *Kids do well if they can* [Video]. Retrieved from http://www.youtube.com/watch?v=jvzQQDfAL-Q

Greene, R. W. (2013). *The explosive child: A new approach for understanding and parenting easily frustrated, chronically inflexible children* (5th ed.). New York, NY: HarperCollins.

Greenland, S. K. (2011). *A whole new world.* Retrieved from http://www.susankaisergreenland.com/blog/a-whole-new-world.html

Hammill, D., & Elementary Teachers' Federation of Ontario. (2000). Be well, beware [Excerpt]. *After the chalk dust settles.* Toronto, ON: Elementary Teachers' Federation of Ontario. Retrieved from www.survivethrive.on.ca/files/upload/resource/11/81_bewell.pdf

Hincks-Dellcrest Centre. (2014). *The ABCs of mental health.* Toronto, ON: Author. Retrieved from www.hincksdellcrest.org/ABC/Teacher-Resource/Mental-Health-for-All-Children-and-Youth.aspx

Hockenbury, D. H., & Hockenbury, S. E. (2007). *Discovering psychology.* New York, NY: Worth. Retrieved from http://psychology.about.com/od/emotion/f/what-are-emotions.htm

Hoffman, J. (n.d.). *Kids can cope: Parenting resilient children at home and at school* [Parenting for Life booklet]. Toronto: ON: Psychology Foundation of Canada. Retrieved from http://www.psychologyfoundation.org/pdf/publications/ResilienceChildrenBooklet.pdf

Institute of Medicine and National Research Council. (2009). *Preventing mental, emotional, and behavioral disorders among young people: Progress and possibilities.* Washington, DC: The National Academies Press.

Institute of Positive Education. (2014). *Geelong Grammar School, exceptional education.* Victoria, Australia. Retrieved from http://www.ggs.vic.edu.au/School/Positive-Education/About-Positive-Education

International Institute for Restorative Practices Canada [IIRP Canada] [List of articles]. http://canada.iirp.edu/featured-articles.html

International Institute for Restorative Practices Graduate School. (2009). *Improving school climate: Findings from schools implementing restorative practices.* Bethlehem, PA: IIRP Graduate School.

Johnson, W., & Krueger, R. (2007). The psychological benefits of vigorous exercise: A study of discordant MZ twin pairs. *Twin Res Hum Genet, 10*(2), 275–283.

Joint Consortium for School Health [JCSH]. (2009). *What is comprehensive school health?* Retrieved from http://www.jcsh-cces.ca/upload/JCSH%20CSH%20Framework%20FINAL%20Nov%2008.pdf

Joint Consortium for School Health [JCSH]. (2010). *Schools as a setting for promoting positive mental health: Better practices and perspectives.* Retrieved from http://www.jcsh-cces.ca/upload/PMH%20July10%202011%20WebReady.pdf

Jones, S. M., Bouffard, S. M., & Weissbourd, R. (2013, May). Educators' social and emotional skills vital to learning. *Phi Delta Kappan, 94*(8), 62–65. Retrieved from kappanmagazine.org

Kahnweiler, J.B. (2014). Advice for introverts: How to thrive in the business world. In *American Management Association.* Retrieved from http://www.amanet.org/training/articles/Advice-for-Introverts-How-to-Thrive-in-the-Business-World.aspx

Keyes, C. L. M. (2002). The mental health continuum: From languishing to flourishing. *Journal of Health and Behavior Research, 43,* 207–222.

Kilpatrick, M. W. (2008). Exercise, mood, and psychological well-being: A practitioner's guide to theory, research, and application. *ACSM'S Health & Fitness Journal, 12*(5), 14–19.

Kirmayer, L., et al. (2007). *Suicide among Aboriginal people in Canada.* Ottawa, ON: Aboriginal Healing Foundation.

Kobus-Matthews, M., Agic, B., & Tate, M. (2012). *Culture counts: A roadmap to health promotion—A guide to best practices for developing health promotion initiatives in mental health and substance abuse with ethnocultural communities.* Toronto, ON: Centre for Addiction and Mental Health [CAMH].

Koenig, K. (2005). *The rules of "normal" eating: A commonsense approach for dieters, overeaters, undereaters, emotional eaters, and everyone in between.* Carlsbad, CA: Gürze Books.

Kuypers, L. (2011). *The zones of regulation.* San Jose, CA: Social Thinking.

Lantieri, L. (2008). *Building emotional intelligence: Techniques to cultivate inner strength in children.* Boulder, CO: Sounds True.

Leach, Mark M. (2006). *Cultural diversity and suicide: Ethnic, religious, gender and sexual orientation perspectives.* New York, NY: Hawthorn Press.

Leithwood, K. (2006). *Teacher working conditions that matter: Evidence for change.* Toronto, ON: Elementary Teachers' Federation of Ontario.

Lockhart, A., & Zammit, L. (2005). *Restorative justice: Transforming society.* Toronto, ON: Inclusion Press.

March J. S., & Vitiello, B. (2009). Clinical messages from the Treatment for Adolescents with Depression Study [TADS]. *American Journal of Psychiatry, 166*(10), 1118–1123.

Martin, A. (2008). *Motivation and engagement scale: Test user manual.* Lifelong Achievement Group. Retrieved from http://www.lifelongachievement.com

McCague, E., & Carney, P. J. (2011). The "magic" drug: A research base and how-to-approach in implementing physical activity in clinical and non-clinical populations. Poster session presented at the annual convention of the Canadian Psychological Association, Toronto, ON.

Mental Health Commission of Canada. (n.d.). *Initiatives: Opening minds.* Retrieved from www.mentalhealthcommission.ca/English/initiatives-and-projects/opening-minds

Mental Health Commission of Canada. (n.d.). *The facts.* Retrieved from http://strategy.mentalhealthcommission.ca/the-facts/

Mental Health Commission of Canada. (2008). *Mental Health Commission of Canada Anti-Stigma/Anti-Discrimination Planning Session Summary of Discussions, December 1, 2008.* Retrieved from http://www.mentalhealthcommission.ca/sites/default/files/filefield_private_download/Stigma_Anti_Stigma_Planning_Session_ENG_0.pdf

Mental Health Commission of Canada. (2012a). *Changing directions, changing lives: The mental health strategy for Canada.* Retrieved from http://strategy.mentalhealthcommission.ca/pdf/strategy-text-en.pdf

Mental Health Commission of Canada. (2012b). *Together against stigma: Changing how we see mental illness. A report on the 5th International Stigma Conference.* Retrieved from www.mentalhealthcommission.ca/English/system/files/private/document/Stigma_Opening_Minds_Together_Against_Stigma_ENG.pdf

MHealthy—University of Michigan Health & Well-Being Services. (2012). *Understanding U: Managing the ups and downs of life—What is mental health?*

Retrieved from http://hr.umich.edu/mhealthy/programs/mental_emotional/understandingu/learn/mental_health.html

National Association of School Psychologists. (2009). *Appropriate behavioral, social, and emotional supports to meet the needs of all students* [Position statement]. Bethesda, MD: Author.

Nummenmaa, L., Glerean, E., Hari, R., & Hietanen, J. (2013). Bodily maps of emotions. *Proceedings of the National Academy of Sciences of the United States of America [PNAS]*. Retrieved from www.pnas.org/cgi/doi/10.1073/pnas.1321664111

Oeland, A., Laessoe, U., Olesen, A., & Munk-Jorgensen, P. (2009). Impact of exercise on patients with depression and anxiety. *Nordic Journal of Psychiatry, 64*(3), 210–217.

Ontario Centre of Excellence for Child and Youth Mental Health. (n.d.). Mental health literacy by I. Manion, D. Papdopoulos, & K. Short [Presentation slides]. Retrieved from kidsmentalhealth.ca

Ontario Ministry of Education. (2002). *The Ontario curriculum unit planner: Special education companion.* Toronto ON: Queen's Printer for Ontario.

Ontario Ministry of Education. (2013). *Supporting minds: An educator's guide to promoting students' mental health and well-being* [Draft version 2013]. Toronto: Queen's Printer for Ontario. Retrieved from www.ontario.ca/edu

Ontario Ministry of Education, Student Achievement Division. (2011). Professional Learning Cycle DVD. SS/L-18ITEB.

Ontario Secondary School Teachers' Federation. (2012). *Full circle: First Nations, Métis, Inuit ways of knowing. A common threads resource.* Toronto, ON: Author.

Otto, M., & Smits, J. (2011). *Exercise for mood and anxiety: Proven strategies for overcoming depression and enhancing well-being.* New York, NY: Oxford University Press.

Paglia-Boak, A., Adlaf, E. M., & Mann, R. E. (2011). Drug use among Ontario students, 1977–2011: OSDUHS highlights [CAMH Research Document Series No. 33]. Toronto, ON: Centre for Addiction and Mental Health. Retrieved from www.camh.ca/en/research/news_and_publications/ontario-student-drug-use-and-health-survey/Documents/2011%20OSDUHS%20Docs/2011OSDUHS_Highlights_DrugUseReport.pdf

Pan-Canadian Joint Consortium for School Health [JCSH]. (2013). *Schools as a setting for promoting positive mental health: better practices and perspectives.* Second edition. Retrieved at http://www.jcsh-cces.ca/upload/JCSH%20Best%20Practice_Eng_Jan21.pdf

Parfitt, G., Pavey, T., & Rowlands, A. V. (2009). Children's physical activity and psychological health: The relevance of intensity. *Acta Pædiatrica, 98*(6), 1037–1043.

Payton, J. et al. M. (2008). *The positive impact of social and emotional learning for kindergarten to eighth-grade students.* Chicago, IL: Collaborative for Academic, Social, and Emotional Learning (CASEL).

Pearson, J., & Hall, D. K. (2006). *Reaching in…reaching out resiliency guidebook*. Toronto, ON: Child & Family Partnership [YMCA of Greater Toronto, The Child Development Institute, University of Guelph, George Brown College]. Retrieved from http://www.reachinginreachingout.com

Pike, D. (2014). *The gift of positive space groups: A transformation for LGBTQ students*. Toronto, ON: Canadian Education Association.

Public Health Agency of Canada [PHAC]. (2006). *The human face of mental health and mental illness in Canada*. Ottawa, ON: Author.

Raphael, R. (1998). Physical activity can relieve symptoms of depression and anxiety, improve mood, and may even reduce the risk of developing depression. *ACSM'S Health & Fitness Journal, 2*(2), 18–20.

Rashid, T. (2014, July). *Positive psychotherapy [PPT]*. Pre-conference workshop presented at the 2nd Canadian Conference on Positive Psychology, Ottawa, ON.

Ratey, J. J., with E. Hagerman. (2008). *Spark: The revolutionary new science of exercise and the brain*. New York, NY: Little, Brown.

Rawana, E., Latimer, K., Whitley, J., & Probizanski, M. (2009, November). Strength-based classroom strategies for teachers. *Canadian Teacher Magazine*.

Resiliency Initiatives. (2012). *Embracing a strengths-based perspective and practice in education*. Retrieved from the Resiliency Initiatives website: http://www.resil.ca

Richardson, C., Faulkner, G., McDevitt, J., Skrinar, G., Hutchinson, D., & Piette, J. (2005). Integrating physical activity mental health services for persons with serious mental illness. *Psychiatric Services, 56*(3), 324–331.

Roberts, K., Shields, M., de Groh, M., Aziz, A., & Gilbert, J. (2012, September). Overweight and obesity in children and adolescents: Results from the 2009 to 2011 Canadian Health Measures Survey. *Health Reports, 23*(3). Statistics Canada, Catalogue no. 82-003-X.

Roffey, S. (2012). Pupil well-being—Teacher well-being: Two sides of the same coin? *Educational & Child Psychology, 29*(4), 8–17.

Roffey, S. (2014). *Teacher wellbeing: What does the research say?* Retrieved from http://www.sueroffey.com/wp-content/uploads/2014/04/CDU-Teacher-Wellbeing-Relationships-Roffey.pdf

Saleebey, D. (2006). Power in the people. In D. Saleebey (Ed.), *The strengths perspective in social work practice* (4th ed.). Toronto, ON: Pearson Education.

Salovey, P., & Mayer, J. D. (1990). Emotional intelligence. *Imagination, Cognition, and Personality, 9*, 195–211.

Santos, R. G., Chartier, J. C., Whalen, J. C., Chateau, D., & Boyd, L. (2011). Effectiveness of school-based violence prevention for children and youth [Special issue]. *Healthcare Quarterly, 14*.

SBMHSA Consortium. (2013). *School-based mental health in Canada: A final report*. Retrieved from the Mental Health Commission of Canada:

http://www.mentalhealthcommission.ca/English/system/files/private/document/ChildYouth_School_Based_Mental_Health_Canada_Final_Report_ENG.pdf

Schenk, B. (2008). Restorative practice and our schools: A visionary journey [A report to the Kawartha Pine Ridge District School Board]. In *Improving School Climate: Findings from Schools Implementing Restorative Practices*. Retrieved from the International Institute for Restorative Practices Graduate School website: http://www.iirp.edu/pdf/IIRP-Improving-School-Climate.pdf

School Mental Health ASSIST. (2013). *Leading mentally healthy schools. A vision for student health and well-being in Ontario schools*. Toronto, ON: Author.

School-Based Mental Health and Substance Abuse [SBMHSA] Consortium. (2012). *School board decision support tool for mental health capacity building*. Educator Mental Health Literacy Roundtable.

Seligman, M. E. P. (1991). *Learned optimism: How to change your mind and your life*. New York, NY: Pocket Books.

Seligman, M. E. P. (2002). *Authentic happiness: using the new positive psychology to realize your potential for lasting fulfillment*. New York, NY: Free Press.

Seligman, M. E. P. (2004). *The new era of positive psychology* [Video]. Retrieved from http://www.ted.com/talks/martin_seligman_on_the_state_of_psychology.html

Seligman, M. E. P. (2011). *Flourish: a visionary new understanding of happiness and well-being*. New York, NY: Free Press.

Shanker, S. (n.d.). *Self-Regulation*. Retrieved from www.self-regulation.ca/download/pdf_documents/magforbooklet.pdf

Shanker, S. (2013). *Calm, alert, and learning: Classroom strategies for self-regulation*. Toronto, ON: Pearson Canada.

Sharkey B. J., & Gaskill, S. E. (2007). *Fitness and health* (6th ed.). Champaign, IL: Human Kinetics.

Smith, M., Segal, R., & Segal, J. (2014, October). *Stress symptoms, signs, and causes*. Retrieved from http://www.helpguide.org/articles/stress/stress-symptoms-causes-and-effects.htm#signs

Smith-Fowler, H. & Lebel, M. (2013). *Promoting youth mental health through the transition from high school - Literature review and environmental scan*. Ottawa, ON: Social Research and Demonstration Corporation [SRDC].

Smits, J., & Otto, M. (2009). *Exercise for mood and anxiety disorders*. Oxford, UK: Oxford University Press.

Stewart, S. L. (2008). Promoting indigenous mental health: Cultural perspectives on healing from Native counselors in Canada. *International Journal of Health Promotion and Education, 46*(2), 49–56. Retrieved from http://www.tandfonline.com/doi/abs/10.1080/14635240.2008.10708129#.U-jpg51zbcs

Stubbe, J. H., de Moor, M. H. M., Boomsma, D. I., & de Geus, E. J. C. (2007). The association between exercise participation and well-being: A co-twin study. *Preventative Medicine, 44,* 148–152.

Student Support Leadership Initiative (Oxford, Elgin, London/Middlesex). (2014). *Bounce back…again* (2nd ed.). Retrieved from http://www.mentalhealth4kids.ca

Student Support Leadership Initiative, Hamilton District Team. (2011). *Making a difference: An educators' guide to child and youth mental health problems* (4th ed.). [Developed for the Child and Youth Mental Health Information Network.]

Taylor, C., & Peter, T. (2011). *Every class in every school: Final report on the first national climate survey on homophobia, biphobia, and transphobia in Canadian schools.* Toronto, ON: Egale Canada Human Rights Trust.

Timperley, H., Wilson, A., Barrar, H., & Fung, I. (2007). *Teacher professional learning and development: Best evidence synthesis iteration* [Report to the Ministry of Education]. Wellington, New Zealand: Ministry of Education.

Ungar, M. (2008). Resilience across cultures. *British Journal of Social Work, 38,* 218–235.

Ungar, M. (2012). *Understanding resilience in schools and school systems* [Video produced as part of the Learning Partnership for building capacity for resilience]. Retrieved from http://www.youtube.com/watch?v=XJ482GgfZTs

Ungar, M. (2013). The impact of youth–adult relationships on resilience. *International Journal of Child, Youth and Family Studies, 4*(3), 328–336.

Ungar, M., Brown, M., Liebenberg, L., Cheung, M., & Levine, K. (2008). Distinguishing differences in pathways to resilience among Canadian youth. *Canadian Journal of Community Mental Health, 27*(1), 1–13.

United Nations Human Rights, Office of the High Commissioner for Human Rights. (1990). *Convention on the Rights of the Child* (Overview). Retrieved from http://www.unicef.org/crc/files/Rights_overview.pdf

Vesely, A. K., Saklofske, D. H., & Leschied, A. D. W. (2013). Teachers—The vital resource: The contribution of emotional intelligence to teacher efficacy and well-being. *Canadian Journal of School Psychology, 28*(1), 71–89.

Weisz, J. R., Sandler, I. N., Durlak, J. A., & Anton, B. S. (2005). Promoting and protecting youth mental health through evidence-based prevention and treatment. [Review, 175 refs]. *American Psychologist, 60*(6), 628–648.

Wellington Catholic District School Board. Strengths in Education project. Retrieved from www.strengthsineducation.ca

World Health Organization. (1996). Equity in health and health care: A WHO/SIDA initiative.

Yang, Y., & Raine, A. (2009, November). Prefrontal structural and functional brain imaging findings in antisocial, violent, and psychopathic individuals: A meta-analysis. *Psychiatry Research, 174*(2), 81–88.

Yerkes, R. M., & Dodson, J. D. (1908). The relation of strength of stimulus to rapidity of habit formation. *Journal of Comparative Neurology and Psychology 18,* 459–482.

Zeff, T. (2010). *The strong, sensitive boy.* San Ramon, CA: Prana.

Zelazo, P. D. (2014, May). Executive function, reflection, and neuroplasticity: Implications for promoting empathy in childhood. Keynote address presented at the *Roots of Empathy Research Symposium 2014,* Toronto, ON.

Chapter 1

1: Pan-Canadian Joint Consortium for School Health website
http://www.jcsh-cces.ca/index.php/about/comprehensive-school-health;
2–3: Source: Health and Welfare Canada. Mental health for Canadians: striking
a balance. Ottawa: Ministry of Supply and Services Canada; 1988.; http://
www.phac-aspc.gc.ca/publicat/human-humain06/pdf/human_face_e.pdf;
8: http://www.hincksdellcrest.org/ABC/Teacher-Resource/Mental-Health-
for-All-Children-and-Youth.aspx; **10:** Source: Shanker, S. (2013). Self-regulation.
Canadian Self-Regulation Initiative, http://www.self-regulation.ca/download/
pdf_documents/magforbooklet.pdf; **14:** Source: Martin E P Seligman,
"Flourish: a visionary new understanding of happiness and well-being", New
York: Free Press, 2011. p. 2.

Chapter 2

18: http://www.mentalhealthcommission.ca/English/system/files/private/
document/ChildYouth_School_Based_Mental_Health_Canada_Final_Report_
ENG.pdf; **20:** Source: Joint Consortium for School Health, 2010. P. 08.
http://www.jcsh-cces.ca/upload/JCSH%20Positive%20Mental%20Health%20
Perspectives%20Better%20Practices.PDF; **22:** Source: Canada. (2006). The
human face of mental health and mental illness in Canada. Retrieved from
http://www.phac-aspc.gc.ca/publicat/human-humain06/pdf/human_face_e.
pdf; **22:** Source: School Based Mental Health and Substance Abuse Consortium
(SBMHSA). (2012). School board decision support tool for mental health
capacity building. Educator Mental Health Literacy Roundtable.; https://
dl.dropboxusercontent.com/u/6199808/LeadingMentallyHealthSchools.pdf;
24: Source: Mental Health Commission of Canada, 2008, p. 9, http://
www.mentalhealthcommission.ca/English/system/files/private/Stigma_
Anti_Stigma_Initiative_Consensus_Meeting_Report_ENG_0.pdf; **24:** Source:
Copyright © 2014 Canadian Mental Health Association, http://ontario.cmha.
ca/mental-health/mental-health-conditions/stigma-and-discrimination/;
25–26: Sources: The Bell Let's Talk Initiative, http://letstalk.bell.ca/en/
end-the-stigma/facts/; Centre for Addiction and Mental Health (CAMH),
http://www.camh.ca/; Mental Health Commission of Canada, http://
www.mentalhealthcommission.ca/; The Stigma Associated with Mental
Illness, http://www.cmhanl.ca/pdf/Stigma.pdf; **27:** Source: Mental Health
Commission of Canada, ©2012 Mental Health Commission of Canada. p. 12.
http://strategy.mentalhealthcommission.ca/pdf/strategy-text-en.pdf;
27: Source: MHealthy–University of Michigan Health & Well-Being Services,
"Understanding U: Managing the Ups and Downs of Life–What Is Mental

Health?", 2012. http://hr.umich.edu/mhealthy/programs/mental_emotional/ understandingu/learn/mental_health.html; **28:** Sourced from Leading Mentally Healthy Schools, pp. 40–41, School Mental Health ASSIST, 2013; **29–30:** Source: Child and Youth Mental Health Information |Network, 2012, p. 7; http://cymhin.offordcentre.com/downloads/Making%20a%20 Difference%204-0.pdf; **29–30:** Source: http://www.kidsmentalhealth.ca/ documents/Res_TA1_MH_Literacy_Overview_Advisory_Council.pdf; **30–32:** Steve Charbonneau, Simcoe Muskoka Catholic District School Board; **37:** Source: Brown, Brené.(2012). Daring greatly: How the courage to be vulnerable transforms the way we live, love, parent, and lead. New York: Gotham.; **37:** Schools as a Setting for Promoting Positive Mental Health: Better Practices and Perspectives, January 2010 http://www.jcsh-cces.ca/upload/ JCSH%20Positive%20Mental%20Health%20Perspectives%20Better%20 Practices.PDF; **39:** Equity in health and health care: a WHO/SIDA initiative. (1996) http://apps.who.int/iris/handle/10665/63119; **40:** Supporting minds: an educator's guide to promoting students' mental health and well-being. Draft version 2013. http://www.edu.gov.on.ca/eng/document/reports/ SupportingMinds.pdf; **40:** Promoting indigenous mental health: cultural perspectives on healing from Native counselors in Canada. International Journal of Health Promotion and Education, 46:2, 49–56. Published online 17 May 2013. Retrieved from http://www.tandfonline.com/doi/abs/10.1080/146352 40.2008.10708129#.U-jpg51zbcs.; **43–44:** Carlson, J., Sperry, L., & Dinkmeyer, D. (1992). Marriage maintenance: How to stay healthy. Topics in Family counseling & Psychology, 1, 84–90.; **45–46:** Source: Gabriella Bator. **47–48:** Source: Ashley Oliver.

Chapter 3

53: Source: Lantieri, L., Building emotional intelligence: techniques to cultivate inner strength in children, 2008. P. 16; **53:** Source: Joint Consortium for School Health, 2010.; http://www.jcsh-cces.ca/upload/JCSH%20Positive%20 Mental%20Health%20Perspectives%20Better%20Practices.PDF; **54:** Source: Lantieri, L., Building emotional intelligence : techniques to cultivate inner strength in children, 2008. P. 16.; **54:** Erin Carney © Pearson Canada Inc.; **55:** Source: Salovey, P. & Mayer, J. Emotional Intelligence.(1990) Baywood Publishing Co. http://www.unh.edu/emotional_intelligence/EIAssets/ EmotionalIntelligenceProper/EI1990%20Emotional%20Intelligence.pdf; **55:** Source: Goleman, D. (1998). Working with emotional intelligence. Bantam Dell, a Division of Random House, Inc.; **55:** Source: Goleman, D. (2006). Social intelligence: the new science of human relationships. New York, NY: Bantam Dell, a Division of Random House Inc.; **57:** 2013 CASEL Guide: Effective social and emotional learning programs: Preschool and elementary school edition, Collaborative for Adademic, Social, and Emotional, 2012 Learning http://static.squarespace.com/static/513f79f9e4b05ce7b70e9673/ t/526a220de4b00a92c90436ba/138; **61:** Source: Hockenbury, D. H. & Hockenbury, S. E. (2007). Discovering psychology. New York: Worth Publishers.; **63:** Source: Nummenmaa, L., Glerean, E., Hari, R., &Hietanen, J. (2013) Bodily maps of emotions. Proceedings of the National Academy of Sciences of the United States of America (PNAS), January 14, 2014, vol. 111, no. 2. www.pnas.org/cgi/doi/10.1073/pnas.1321664111; **66:** Source: Shanker, S. (2013). Self-regulation. Canadian Self-Regulation Initiative, http:// www.self-regulation.ca/download/pdf_documents/magforbooklet.pdf; **67:** Source: Shanker, S. (2013).Calm, alert, and learning: classroom strategies for self-regulation. Toronto, Pearson Canada Inc.; **67:** Source: Shanker, S. (2013). Executive Functions: Self-Regulation and Emotion, http://www.naylornetwork. com/bco-nwl/pdf/Shanker_Interview.pdf; **71:** Erin Carney © Pearson Canada Inc.; **81:** Sourced from: Lantieri Building Emotional Intelligence (2008); **88:** Source: Bruce Schenk, "Restorative Practice and Our Schools: A Visionary Journey," Background Report to the Kawartha Pine Ridge District School Board, August 28, 2008, pp. 8, 10.

Chapter 4

93: Schools as a Setting for Promoting Positive Mental Health: Better Practices and Perspectives, January 2010 http://www.jcsh-cces.ca/upload/JCSH%20 Positive%20Mental%20Health%20Perspectives%20Better%20Practices.PDF; **96:** Source: "Embracing a Strength based Perspective and Practice in Education," Resiliency Initiative, p. 18 (2012); http://www.resiliencyinitiatives.ca/cms/ wp content/uploads/2013/05/Embracing a Strengths Based Perspective and Practice in Education.pdf; **96:** Source: "Embracing a Strength-based Perspective and Practice in Education," Resiliency Initiative, p. 3 (2012); **97:** Source: Excerpted from Embracing a Strengths-Based Perspective and Practice in the Classroom, Resiliency Initiative, 2012, p. 16.; **98–99:** Source: Embracing a Strengths-based Perspective and Practice in Education" Resiliency Initiative (2012), p. 4.; http:// www.resiliencyinitiatives.ca/cms/wp-content/uploads/2013/05/Embracing-a- Strengths-Based-Perspective-and-Practice-in-Education.pdf; **100:** Source: Keith Brownlee, Edward P. Rawana, Julia MacArthur "Implementation of a Strengths- Based Approach to Teaching in an Elementary School" Journal of Teaching And Learning, 2012, Vol. 8 No. 1, http://ojs.uwindsor.ca/ojs/leddy/index.php/ JTL/article/download/3069/pdf; **101:** Source: "Embracing a Strength-based Perspective and Practice in Education," Resiliency Initiative (2012). p. 10.; http:// www.resiliencyinitiatives.ca/cms/wp-content/uploads/2013/05/Embracing-a- Strengths-Based-Perspective-and-Practice-in-Education.pdf; **102–103:** Source: Edward Rawana, Kim Latimer, Jessica Whitley, Michelle Probizanski, Strength-based Classroom Strategies for Teachers, Canadian Teacher Magazine, Nov. 2009., http://www.canadianteachermagazine.com/archives/ctm_teaching_ideas/nov09_strength-based_classroom_strategies.shtml; **104:** Source: Keith Brownlee, Edward P. Rawana, Julia MacArthur "Implementation of a Strengths-Based Approach to Teaching in an Elementary School" Journal of Teaching And Learning, 2012, Vol. 8 No. 1, http://ojs.uwindsor.ca/ojs/leddy/index.php/JTL/article/download/3069/pdf; **105:** Embracing a Strengths-Based Perspective and Practice in Education, 2012 http://www.resiliencyinitiatives.ca/cms/wp-content/uploads/2013/05/Embracing-a-Strengths-Based-Perspective-and-Practice-in-Education.pdf; **109:** Gardner, H. (1983) Frames of Mind: The Theory of Multiple Intelligences. Basic Books, New York.; **115–116:** Sources: Susan Cain Quiet: The Power of Introverts in a World That Can't Stop Talking (2012). pp. 6, 7; Cherry, K. (2014). 5 signs you are an introvert. In About.com, http://psychology.about.com/od/personalitydevelopment/fl/5-Signs-You-Are-an-Introvert.htm; Diamond, S.A. (2012, May 26). Essential secrets of psychotherapy: Jung's typology, eudaemonology, and the elusive art of happiness. In Evil Deeds, http://www.psychologytoday.com/blog/evil-deeds/201205/essential-secrets-psychotherapy-jungs-typologyeudaemonology-and-the-elusive-; Kahnweiler, J.B. (2014). Advice for introverts: How to thrive in the business world. In American Management Association, http://www.amanet.org/training/articles/Advice-for-Introverts-How-to-Thrive-in-the-Business-World.aspx; **116:** Source: Susan Cain Quiet: The Power of Introverts in a World That Can't Stop Talking (2012). pp. 6, 7; **117:** Source: Susan Cain Quiet: The Power of Introverts in a World That Can't Stop Talking (2012). p. 12.

Chapter 5

130: Source: Martin E P Seligman, "Flourish : a visionary new understanding of happiness and well-being", New York : Free Press, 2011. p. 2; **136:** Full Circle: First Nations, Metis, and Inuit Ways of Knowing, A Common Threads Resource, 2012, Ontario Secondary School Teachers' Federation, http://www.osstf.on.ca/full-circle-first-nations-metis-inuit-ways-of-knowing; **137:** Source: Psychology Foundation of Canada; http://calgary.cmha.ca/files/2012/07/ResiliencyFactSheet.pdf; **137:** Source: Pearson, J., Hall, D.K., 2006 Reaching In Reaching Out Resiliency Guidebook, p. 1; **139:** "Bounce Back … Again", 2nd edition, Student Support Leadership Initiative. Oxford Elgin, London/Middlesex http://www.mentalhealth4kids.ca/healthlibrary_docs/BounceBackBooklet2014.pdf; **140:** Source: Pearson, J., Hall, D.K., 2006 Reaching In Reaching Out Resiliency Guidebook, p. 1.; http://www.reachinginreachingout.com/documents/Guidebook-06.pdf; **142:** Source: Dr. Ron Breazeale, Duct Tape Isn't Enough Survival Skills For

The 21st Century, 2009, p. 3.; http://www.buildingresilience.com/downloads/REACHING_HOME_DUCT_TAPE_total-book.pdf; **143:** Source: Pearson, J., Hall, D.K., 2006 Reaching In Reaching Out Resiliency Guidebook, p. 1.; http://www.reachinginreachingout.com/documents/Guidebook-06.pdf; **143:** Source: Pearson, J., Hall, D.K., 2006 Reaching In Reaching Out Resiliency Guidebook, p. 1; **145–146:** Source: Pearson, J., Hall, D.K., 2006 Reaching In Reaching Out Resiliency Guidebook, pp. 12–28.; http://www.reachinginreachingout.com/documents/Guidebook-06.pdf; **147:** Source: Developing and Using Cognitive Coping Cards, Anxiety BC; http://anxietybc.com/parenting/developing-and-using-cognitive-coping-cards; **148:** Source: http://www.susankaisergreenland.com/blog/a-whole-new-world.html; **150–151:** Sourced from: Building Resilience in Young Children: Booklet for parents of children from birth to six years, 2012, Best Start: Ontario's Maternal, Newborn and Early Child Development Resource Centre. http://www.beststart.org/resources/hlthy_chld_dev/pdf/BSRC_Resilience_English_fnl.pdf; **153–154:** Sourced from: Ungar,. Brown, Liebenberg, Cheung, & Levine., 2008, p. 6. **155:** Source: The Child and Youth Resilience Measure - 28, Resilience Research Centre. 2009. http://calmhsa.org/wp-content/uploads/2013/06/CYRM-28-Manual_20112.pdf; **160:** Source: © Canadian Society for Exercise Physiology, 2011. P. 1. http://www.csep.ca/CMFiles/Guidelines/CanadianPhysicalActivityGuidelinesStatements_E.pdf; **160–161:** Source: CSEP, Canadian Physical Activity and Sedentary Behaviour Guidelines Handbook, p. 5; http://www.csep.ca/english/view.asp?x=804; 168–169; **163–164:** Sourced from: Exercise, Mood, and Psychological Well-Being: A Practitioner's Guide to Theory, Research, and Application, American College of Sports and Medicine Health and Fitness Journal, Vol 12, No 5, Copyright © 2008 Lippincott Williams & Wilkins, http://journals.lww.com/acsm-healthfitness/pages/default.aspx; **166:** Source: Martin E P Seligman, Flourish : a visionary new understanding of happiness and well-being, Free Press, 2011. P. 28.; **172:** Source: Smith-Fowler, H. & Lebel, M. (2013), p. 6. Adapted from CMHA Ontario (nd); Health and Welfare Canada, 1988, Tudor, 1996, and Keyes, 2007.; http://www.srdc.org/media/199639/student_mental_health.pdf; **173:** Promoting youth mental health through the transition from high school – Literature review and environmental scan, April 2013, Social Research and Demonstration Corporation http://www.srdc.org/media/199639/student_mental_health.pdf.

Chapter 6

178: Source: Roffey. S., (2012) Pupil Well-being – Teacher Well-being: Two sides of the same coin? Educational & Child Psychology Vol. 29 No. 4 c The British Psychological Society.; http://www.academia.edu/2404110/Teacher_wellbeing_-_pupil_wellbeing_Two_sides_of_the_same_coin_2012_

Educational_and_Child_Psychology_29_4_8-17; **180:** Source: Goleman, D. (1998) Working with emotional intelligence. Bloomsbury Publishing, London.; **180, 181, 182–183, 192:** Source: Jones, S.M., Bouffard, S.M., Weissbourd, R., (2013) Educators' social and emotional skills vital to learning, Kappan Magazine, Vol 94, No. 8. kappanmagazine.org; http://www.casel.org/library/2014/2/26/educators-social-and-emotional-skills-vital-to-learning; **181:** Source: Vesely, Saklofske, & Leschied, Teachers–The Vital Resource: The Contribution of Emotional Intelligence to Teacher Efficacy and Well-Being, Canadian Association of School Psychologists. Sage Publications, 2013. P. 76.; http://cjs.sagepub.com/content/28/1/71.full.pdf+html; **189:** Source: Be Well, Beware. Elementary Teachers' Federation. Excerpt from "After the Chalkdust Settles," p. 9.; www.survivethrive.on.ca/files/upload/resource/11/81_bewell.pdf; **190–192:** Source: Kate Przybylski; **193:** Source: Roffey. S., (2012) Pupil Well being – Teacher Well being: Two sides of the same coin? Educational & Child Psychology Vol. 29 No. 4 © The British Psychological Society.; http://www.academia.edu/2404110/Teacher_wellbeing__pupil_wellbeing_Two_sides_of_the_same_coin_2012_Educational_and_Child_Psychology_29_4_8 17; **194–196:** Sourced from: "Healthy Tips for Teachers," Counselling and Member Services Department of the Ontario English Catholic Teachers' Association, p. 4.; www.survivethrive.on.ca/files/upload/resource/11/83_stress.rtf.

Inside Back Cover

Source: Nummenmaa, L., Glerean, E., Hari, R., & Hietanen, J. (2013). Bodily maps of emotions. Proceedings of the National Academy of Sciences of the United States of America (PNAS), January 14, 2014, vol. 111, no. 2. www.pnas.org/cgi/doi/10.1073/pnas.1321664111

Outside Front Cover

altanaka/Fotolia